HOME
ON THE
ROAD

ROGER B. WHITE

HOME

ON THE ROAD

THE MOTOR HOME
IN AMERICA

SMITHSONIAN INSTITUTION PRESS · WASHINGTON AND LONDON

FOR MY PARENTS,
F. JOSEPH WHITE AND
ESTELLE B. WHITE

© 2000 by the Smithsonian Institution

Editor: Robert A. Poarch
Designer: Janice Wheeler

Library of Congress Cataloging-in-Publication Data
White, Roger B. (Roger Byron), 1954–
    Home on the road : the motor home in America / Roger B. White.
        p.   cm.
    Includes bibliographical references and index.
    ISBN 1-56098-892-4 (alk. paper)
    1. Motor homes—United States—History.   I. Title.
TL298.W45 2000
629.226'0973—dc21   99-41425

British Library Cataloguing-in-Publication Data available

Manufactured in the United States of America
06 05 04 03 02 01 00   5 4 3 2 1

∞ The paper used in this publication meets the minimum requirements
of the American National Standard for Information Sciences—
Permanence of Paper for Printed Library Materials ANSI Z39.48-1984.

pages ii and iii: A tourist autocamp in Florida, 1925. Members of the
Isaacson family (left) of Minnesota owned three house cars and took
numerous vacation trips to Florida, Texas, and California. (Courtesy
Budd and Marguerite Andrews)

CONTENTS

ACKNOWLEDGMENTS

This book grew out of *At Home on the Road: Autocamping, Motels, and the Rediscovery of America,* an exhibition that opened at the Smithsonian Institution's National Museum of American History in 1985. As exhibition curator and a museum staff member, I assembled a permanent archive of motor home and trailer literature and expanded it as work on the book progressed. Much of the information for the exhibition and the book was gathered at the Library of Congress, the RV/MH Heritage Foundation in Elkhart, Indiana, and the Lost Highways Archives and Research Library in Philadelphia. This archive is housed in the museum's Division of the History of Technology and is available to researchers by appointment.

The study of motor homes is a revealing journey into the core of America's famous love affair with the automobile. The motor home was invented and reinvented many times by motorists who were attracted to its virtues, and its widespread appeal eventually led to the growth of a major manufacturing industry. I am grateful for the opportunity to obtain information from early motor-home owners or their descendants, builders of one-off recreation vehicles, dealers, and manufacturers, all of whom made important contributions to the invention, dissemination, and enjoyment of motor homes. The owners and builders of house cars, converted buses, pickup campers, van campers, and motor homes contributed many significant changes and refinements to the design and function of these vehicles and influenced their acceptance by the motoring public. Their combined story is a slice of Americana that has been hidden too long in the pages of magazines and diaries and in the memories of those who began the motor-home phenomenon many decades ago. It has been my privilege to tell their individual stories and to describe more generally the development of self-propelled camping vehicles.

Much of this book is based on the Smithsonian Institution's file of 125 interviews with motor-home owners, manufacturers, and dealers who were active between the 1920s and the 1990s. These interviews were arranged by the author and conducted by Peter Koltnow, former president of the Highway Users Federation and a member of the Committee on Transportation History of the Transportation Research Board at the National Research Council. Koltnow generously donated his time to the Smithsonian and pursued countless leads regarding motor-home pioneers and their descendants. His uncanny ability to locate these individuals, his tactful, probing way of questioning, his understanding of road transportation history, and his full, articulate notes added immeasurably to the substance and completeness of this book. Koltnow also telephoned research libraries on the author's behalf and obtained copies of motor-home literature for the Smithsonian's file.

Other Smithsonian Institution personnel who supported the research and documentation effort or offered wise counsel include Transportation Collections staff members Paula Johnson, Paul Johnston, Shirley Stanton, Susan Tolbert, and William Withuhn; John White, Curator Emeritus; Steven Lubar, supervisor of the Division of the History of Technology; Transportation Collections volunteers Roy Canfield, Jean Davies, Charles Johnson, Paul McCracken, William Peugh, and Robert Slusser; curatorial staff members Shannon Thomas Perich and William Yeingst; Archives Center staff member David Haberstich; Smithsonian Institution Libraries staff members Amy DeGroff, Lindsey Ealy, Rhoda Ratner, James Roan, and Stephanie Thomas; and Photographic Services staff members David Burgevin, Alan Hart, Dane Penland, Hugh Talman, and Jeff Tinsley.

Motor-home owners, makers, users, and relatives or associates of motor-home pioneers who contributed information include Elvin and Marguerite Andrews, Dorothea Baker, Stanford Bardwell Jr., Jordan and Betsy Bausher, Donald Bekins, Marcel Doss Berman, Clyde Beverung Jr., Isadore Bleckman, Kim Brower, Peter Brower, Burton and Evelyn Buther, Jeanne Caldwell, Richard Candee, Arthur Cieslak, Robert Crise, Roland Clermont, Betty Crow, D. Merlan DeBolt, Elaine Dodge, George Dorris III, Joyce Long Darby, Thomas Dorsey III, Howard Doss II, Thomas Duck, Richard Fithian, Robert French, Philip Geraci, Mrs. Walter Glascoff Jr., Walter Glascoff III, Clifford Handy, Helen Hardin, Blanche Hyde Heston, William Hobbins, Jean Holloway-Burkhardt, Delbert Hooper, Marshall Hyde, Kathleen Mudge Johnson, Eunice Kearney, Eric Krause, Steven Krause, Lisa Law, Jack and Maralyn Loos, Genny Luckey, George Mason, Louie Mattar, Helen McKay, Kent Mulholland, Barbara Neel, Donald Norquist, Richard and Bess Pierce, Harold Putzke, Richard and Jimmie Renner, Hugh Romney (Wavy Gravy), Jahanara Romney, Tommy Scott, Ernest Scrivener Jr., Wil Shriner, Otto L. Spaeth Jr., Howard and Audrey Stone, James Talmadge, Larry Vita, George Volk, Charles Way, Ramona Willis, and Cynthia Woolery.

Manufacturers, body makers, designers, and dealers who shared stories of their beginnings include John Allerding, Flxible Company; Robert Ausra, Cree Coaches; Sophia Backus, Sani-Cruiser Company; Bettye Baker, Life-Time Industries; George Barris, Barris Kustom; Freeland and Dorotha Bent, Cree Coaches; Charles Borskey, Sportsmobile; Phillip Buckminster, Dodge Division, Chrysler Corporation; Jean Case, Case Liv-N-Roam Cruiser; Walter Corey, Pickwick Company; Sheila Davis, Winnebago Industries; James Dudte, Flxible Company; Kirwan Elmers, Custom Coach Corporation; Ted Franco Jr., Lone Star Motor Company; Raymond Frank, Frank Industries; Ronald Frank, Frank Industries; William R. Graham, Coachette Company; Roland Gray, Blue Bird; Virginia Guerrant, Camp'otel Corporation; F. O. Haas, Kelson Engineering Company; Ruth Haas; Paul Hafer, Boyertown Body Company; Irene Hall, Alaskan Camper; John V. Hanson, Winnebago Industries; Joel W. Hemphill Jr., Hemphill Brothers Coach Company; Kristi Hovenga, Winnebago Industries; George Isaac, Meade Manufacturing Company; Michael and Elizabeth Keech; Walter Kiefer, Kelson Engineering Company; Angie King, Sport King Coaches; Sandra King, Sport King Coaches; John and Murdale Korleski, Victor Coach Industries; Eugene Krager, Krager Koach; Rose-marie Leloia, Meco Distributors; J. R. Leonard, Condor Sales Service; Paul and Pixie Lowry, Roaminghome Company; Ronald McNamee; Merle McNamee, Kamp King Koach; Elwyn McNaughton, Sani-Cruiser Company; David Mitchell, Mitchell and Sons; Harry Mitchell Jr., Mitchell and Sons; Thomas Moroney, Moroney Body Works; Thomas Murray, General Motors Corporation; Nancy Nix, Sportsmobile; Russell Noble, Dodge Division, Chrysler Corporation; Patty Baker Perreira, Life-Time Industries; Dorothy Powell, Powell Manufacturing Company; Mabel Maidl Privateer, Pullman campers; William Purser, Blue Bird; George Reimlinger, Streamline Trailer Company; Marcus Simon, Lone Star Motor Company; Howard Smith, Wolverine Camper Company; Leonard Stam, Stam Auto Body; Brooks Stevens; Kipp Stevens, Brooks Stevens Design Associates; John E. Tillotson II, Ultra Van; Kenneth Utterback, Flxible Company; Herbert von Rusten, Dodge Division, Chrysler Corporation; Lois Walterhouse, Cree Coaches; Karla Waterhouse, Volkswagen of America; Linda Watren, Airstream; Paul Wolfewas, Streamline Trailer Company; and Scott and Barbara Zink, Ryder Homes.

Staff members and volunteers at libraries, historical societies, museums, and recreation vehicle organizations contributed copies of pertinent and often invaluable newspaper and magazine articles, diaries, and other pieces of information. Of greatest help in this regard were Maxye Henry, T/L Enterprises; Al Hesselbart, RV/MH Heritage Foundation; David Humphreys, Recreation Vehicle Industry Association; Pamela Kay, Family Motor Coaching Association; Todd and Kristin Kimmell, Lost Highways Archives and Research Library; Gary LaBella, Recreation Vehicle Industry Association; Christine Morrison, Recreation Vehicle Industry Association; Art Rouse, T/L Enterprises and Good Sam Club; Jean Richter, Family Motor Coach Association; Larry Scheef, American Truck Historical Society; and Kenneth Scott, Family Motor Coach Association. Others who contributed include Patsy Anderson, Graceland, Memphis, Tennessee; Naomi Baker, Yorkshire Historical Society, Delevan, New York; Marianna Bartholomew, Catholic Church Extension Society; Thomas Behring, Behring Auto Museum, Danville, California; Mitzi Caputo, Huntington Historical Society, Huntington, New York; Robert Casey, Henry Ford Museum, Dearborn, Michigan; Bradley Collins, Catholic Church Extension Society;

Donna Crippen, El Monte Museum of History, El Monte, California; Riva Deans, Arizona Historical Society; Thomas DuRant, National Park Service; James Evirs, Massachusetts Beach Buggy Association; Robert Fuhrman, Mercer County Historical Society, Mercer, Pennsylvania; Mary Jean Gamble, Steinbeck Center Foundation, Salinas, California; David Geisler, Pioneer Auto and Antique Town, Murdo, South Dakota; Ronald Glass, LeTourneau University; William Golden, Steinbeck Center Foundation, Salinas, California; Willis Goldschmidt, Museum of Transportation, St. Louis; John Gonzales, California State Library; Ronald Grantz, Detroit Public Library; Terry Harrison, Mason City Historical Collection, Mason City, Iowa; Ernest Hartley, Towe Ford Museum; Ronald Hebb, Massachusetts Beach Buggy Association; Shirley Heise, Family Camping Museum, Richmond, New Hampshire; Melissa Hollister, Chemung County Historical Society, Elmira, New York; Eva Johansen, Meade County Historical Society, Meade, Kansas; Robert Johnson, San Jose Public Library, San Jose, California; Erwin and Dorothy Klein, Cortland-Bizetta Historical Society, Cortland, Ohio; Elizabeth Krehbiel, Elkhart County Historical Society, Bristol, Indiana; Wendell Lauth, Cortland-Bizetta Historical Society, Cortland, Ohio; Mark Lawson, Milwaukee Institute of Art and Design, Milwaukee, Wisconsin; Anna Maday, Public Libraries of Saginaw, Michigan; Karen Martin, Huntington Historical Society, Huntington, New York; Randy Mason, Henry Ford Museum, Dearborn, Michigan; James May, S. C. Johnson and Son; Bernard McTigue, Special Collections, University of Oregon; Albert E. Meier, Motor Bus Society; Alice Preston, Brooks Stevens Automotive Museum, Mequon, Wisconsin; Cynthia Read-Miller, Henry Ford Museum, Dearborn, Michigan; David Nathanson, National Park Service; Karen Niemeyer, Thorntown Public Library, Thorntown, Indiana; Joyce Rupp, Kellogg Company; Barbara Saunders, Sanilac Historical Museum, Port Sanilac, Michigan; Sandy Saunders, National Automobile Museum and Harrah Collection, Reno, Nevada; Judy Simonsen, Milwaukee County Historical Society, Milwaukee, Wisconsin; Ann Sindelar, Western Reserve Historical Society, Cleveland, Ohio; Irene Sniffin, Huntington Historical Society, Huntington, New York; Nancy Solomon, Huntington Historical Society, Huntington, New York; James Waechter, Wayne County Historical Museum, Richmond, Indiana; Kenneth and Helen Waite, Massachusetts Beach Buggy Association; Kenneth Wells, Boyertown Museum of Historic Vehicles, Boyertown, Pennsylvania; Jon Williams, Hagley Museum and Library, Wilmington, Delaware; and June Yoder, Holmes County Public Library, Millersburg, Ohio.

Finally, my colleagues in the small but growing field of recreational travel history contributed many valuable insights and copies of significant primary and secondary literature. Chief among these individuals are Warren Belasco, Timothy Davis, Carlton Edwards, David Harmon, John Margolies, Curt McConnell, Taylor Vinson, Terry Young, Donald Wood, and David Woodworth. Others who contributed include Brooks Brierley (Pierce-Arrow house cars), Thomas Brouillette (Volkswagen campers), Fred Buffington (Helomido house car), Gilbert Burmester (Fred Kohlmeyer's house car), Richard Cassutt (Nash bed), Larry Claypool (Corvair van campers), James Craig (Ultra Van), Jerry and Kirsten Deal (Raise the Roof house cars), Richard Decker (Ultra Van), James Dworschack (Nash bed), Rene Elliott (Linn Haven house car), Walter Gosden (Franklin camping car), Norman Helmkay (Ultra Van), Jay Hunt (Roy Hunt's house cars), John Katz (Roy Hunt's house cars), Roy Neal (Ultra Van), David Newell (Corvair van campers), Merle Norris (Tom Mix's house car), Tony and Jan Noto (Cortez motor homes), Larry Plachno (bus conversions), Kenneth Poynter (Hudson automobiles), Stephen Raiche (license plates), Ronald Szustakowski (Persons house car), Ray Ter Veer (Krause house car), Robert Trousil (Ford house cars), J. H. Valentine (Tourist automobiles), Richard Wager (E. J. Pennington's house car design), Bernard Weis (Pierce-Arrow house cars), James Weller (Linn Haven house car), and Kenneth Wheeling (horse-drawn camping wagons).

To all of these individuals, I offer my sincere thanks for rare glimpses into the history of machines for living and the varied experiences of their owners and makers.

INTRODUCTION

In 1901 naturalist John Muir observed, "Thousands of tired, nerve-shaken, over-civilized people [have found] that going to the mountains is going home; that wildness is a necessity."[1] Within a few years of Muir's insightful comment, thousands of urban motorists returned to nature for pleasure trips, but some kept nature within the sphere of their domestic activities by combining the virtues of automobiles and houses. Road vehicles long had served as homes for the itinerant, either by choice or of necessity, but living in a vehicle was not common or widely accepted among homeowners until the beginning of recreational motoring. As middle- and upper-class Americans learned to use the automobile for a multitude of errands and social activities, it became virtually an extension of the home because of its shelterlike qualities, speed, and readiness. When couples and families began to explore rural and wilderness areas as a pleasure activity, they used the automobile as a buffer, transferring the sophisticated furnishings, technological systems, and daily routines of home to the healthful attractions, scenic splendors, and deprivations of the outdoors. More than consumers of the latest products from Detroit and other centers of motor vehicle manufacturing, some motorists proactively shaped the future of recreational travel by converting their automobiles into simplified homes on wheels.

Motorists further combined the home motif with rapidly evolving truck and bus bodies to create the house car, a new type of portable accommodation that was more efficient and comfortable than an automobile but more flexible and less formal than hotels. In many instances house-car owners' explorations into wilderness areas preceded the establishment of overnight lodgings and brought the first domestic comforts to those areas. House-car owners combined the security and acceptability of circular mobility—travel that began and ended safely at home—with the escapist pleasures and exciting risks of itinerant living. Their enthusiasm for adapting motor vehicles to their recreational needs ultimately led to the establishment of a manufacturing industry for motor homes and other recreation vehicles, an industry that has grown dramatically as each generation discovered the pleasures of living on the American roadside.

In the colonial and early national periods roads were arteries of communication, commerce, and settlement, and in the minds of most Americans they merely bridged the vast expanses of wilderness between their homes and specific destinations. The only domestic comforts available to land travelers were roadside taverns. Few and far between, taverns became important nodes of socializing and exchanging information for stagecoach riders, wagoners, herdsmen, peddlers, and others who plied the roads. The land itself was not an accepted place to spend the night, although settlers seeking homesteads, emigrants in wagon trains, merchant traders, hunters, trappers, and other exploratory travelers often were compelled to live beyond civilization's edge for extended periods. This was seldom a pleasure. Seymour Dunbar, an early transportation historian, wrote, "If the traveler in any part of the country left the beaten track, even but for a few miles, he found himself amid that 'most howling wilderness' which appalled the earliest immigrants and presented such formidable obstacles to any advance through it."[2]

As the population grew and spread westward, rural land became private homesteads, and the barrier between travelers and roadside land took on legal and cultural aspects. In the nineteenth century growing numbers of Gypsy peddlers, horse traders, and fortune-tellers, wandering musicians, singers, jugglers, circus performers, hoboes, tramps, and other itinerant Americans traveled on rural roads, many making the roadside their home. Their rootless, unorthodox lifestyles and unauthorized use of private land often evoked strong disapproval and distrust among property owners. In the 1890s an advocate of good roads wrote,

"It is not one of the legitimate uses of the highway for a traveler or a loafer to stop in front of your house to abuse you with blackguardism [ruffian-like behavior associated with a lower-class entourage], or to play a tune or sing a song which is objectionable to you; and if you request him to pass on and he refuses to go, you may treat him as a trespasser and make him pay damages and costs, if he is financially responsible."[3] Farm families and ranchers sometimes boarded legitimate travelers overnight, but many groups of itinerant people were regarded as illegitimate intruders in an orderly world of property ownership and sheltered home life.

In the second half of the nineteenth century a new class of itinerant people appeared on the roadside as thousands of urban residents found recreational uses for rural roads. Artists and writers absorbed the majesty and beauty of nature and found inspiration for paintings and literary works. Naturalists studied and made images of birds and other wildlife. The concept of an annual vacation spread among professionals and other middle-class Americans as work schedules became rigid and work routines became mentally taxing. Urban congestion, heat, epidemics, and pollution sent vacationers into the countryside in search of healthful and natural settings that were physically beneficial and reconnected them with America's agrarian past and the grand "manifest destiny" of exploring and domesticating its open spaces. Railroads provided inexpensive transportation to scenic areas and resort hotels, but many recreation seekers preferred independent pursuits: cycling on country roads, hunting, fishing, or tent camping in forests. The cycling fad of the 1880s and 1890s was America's first love affair with road travel as a recreational activity; however, as with wandering or homeless people, roving cyclists often irritated rural landowners. Historian Michael L. Berger noted that "city folk, limited only by roads and their own energy, had swarmed into the country [on bicycles] and picnicked where they wanted on what they wanted—frequently including the farmer's animals, vegetables, and fruit."[4]

By the turn of the century the lure of the open road even inspired some urban vacationers to imitate Gypsies. A rambling trip in a horse-drawn, replica Gypsy wagon was a favorite form of vacation in England from the 1880s to the 1910s; horse-drawn camping vehicles were less common in the United States, but they were no less colorful. One affluent family in Hartford, Connecticut, owned a converted delivery wagon with paintings of President William McKinley and the USS *Maine* on its sides. On several occasions they drove it to a riverside glen near West Lebanon, New Hampshire, "a favorite camping ground for nomadic horse dealers, lace makers, and the less reliable fortune tellers, all commonly classed as 'Gypsies.'"[5] Another Gypsy-like camping wagon belonged to Stephen F. Hart and John A. Leighton of New York, who took guests on trips to nearby mountains. Their inn on wheels was furnished with bunks for nine people and could carry provisions for three weeks.[6]

Americans did not own camping vehicles in large numbers until automobiles were mass produced in the early twentieth century. With the power and range of internal-combustion touring cars, motorists roamed dirt roads all across the nation during pleasure outings, and they used their automobiles to domesticate the roadside and the open spaces that lay beyond it. As an alternative to inns, hotels, and farmhouses, many motorists spent the night beside the road in tents or in cars that they modified for sleeping and dining. Tinkering with the seats in an automobile was a pleasure for motorists, but living beside the road did not come easily at first. Some motorists were hesitant to stay in places were they were unprotected and sometimes unwelcome. But their contagious enthusiasm for motoring, their intense desire to integrate nature with their home routines, and the automobile's rapidly developing function as an extension of the home spurred more motorists to adapt their cars to a more homelike environment with privacy, intimacy, and security.

Eventually these autocampers felt comfortable in their homemade car-homes. They relished the revival of flexible, individualistic turnpike travel, now with homestyle family lodgings instead of taverns. By the late 1910s some motorists even built enclosed house cars or "motor bungalows"—small versions of suburban houses—complete with furniture, plumbing, and cooking facilities. Many others towed simpler tent trailers purchased from manufacturers. In many places, house cars and trailers were the only homelike accommodations for the road, and their owners brought a new level of domesticity and sophistication to remote parts of the country.

Living in vehicles became a fad among adventurous vacationers in the 1920s. With ten to twenty million motorists on the road, the road-

Grace and Edward Renner and their house car, 1919. (Courtesy Richard and Jimmie Renner)

side became a busy corridor checkered with campgrounds, gasoline stations, restaurants, stores, billboards, and tourist attractions. Americans now felt at home on the road because it had become an elongated, motorist-oriented community with commercial clusters scattered along its length. Designated autocamps beside the road or within government-owned parks and forests provided convenient, friendly places to spend the night. Millions of autocampers slept in cars, tents, or cots attached to their cars, and hundreds purchased trailers with built-in folding tents. Hundreds more built wooden house-car bodies and placed them on automobile chassis. A small manufacturing industry sprang up to satisfy those who lacked the necessary carpentry skills to convert their own cars. More than a tent, touring car, or tent trailer, a house car's living space was a portable parlor and bedroom, its windshield a picture window on America.

Even though a house car, tent trailer, or touring car outfit saved autocampers time while setting up and breaking camp, road travel in the 1920s was still painfully slow. A trip from New York to Florida, for example, took five days versus one day by train. Motorists reveled in sightseeing and mingling with travelers from other parts of the nation. They combined the familiar comforts of home with the conveniences of roadside autocamps and fashioned a new system of lodging that was

The Renners' house car in the West, 1919. (Courtesy Richard and Jimmie Renner)

personal, flexible, intimate, and informal. A motor bungalow extended the duration of a road trip from weeks to months or even years, and for some tourists this type of vehicle became genuinely a home away from home.

A trip in a house car was always a mixture of challenges, difficulties, and pleasures. Every house car was an experiment in terms of its design and construction. Emergency adjustments and repairs were often needed. A dirt or gravel road was an adversary to be reckoned with. The roadside, however, had become a friendly place filled with interesting, helpful people, both local and transient, and unusual occurrences that made the trip a joy and a memorable chapter in motorists' lives.

The problems and pleasures of house-car travel were recorded in notes and diaries kept by a small number of motorists, including the Renners of Des Moines, Iowa. In 1919 Edward and Grace Renner hired the Lagerquist Carriage and Auto Company, a body maker in Des Moines, to build a house-car body, which they placed on a Ford Model T truck chassis. The Renners and their children, Ralph and Mildred, toured the Pacific coast from northern Washington to southern California. Ralph Renner later recalled some of their tribulations:

In Colorado and Wyoming we found the truck not able to go up mountains, so in Worland, Wyoming, we had special gears and axle installed. Had five or six gears. No trouble going up but if the gear was in neutral, you had no brakes. In Yellowstone going down from the highest peak, Dad got the gear in neutral and with no brakes ran into the mountain on the right side to stop. Turned upside down, bent front axle. Dad hitchhiked to Billings, Montana, for repairs. . . . [He] said we would have to remove the front end—axle and spindle—and take bent parts to a blacksmith working on a road gang. We had very few tools but made do—got it to the blacksmith, straightened it, and put it back together in three days. It worked fine the rest of the trip. My mother, sister, and I had to carry snow from the shady part of the mountain for drinking water and all our needs. Roads were so rocky—tires lasted only 1,000 to 2,000 miles. Everyone stopped on the mountain to give us a hand, and it took very few strong backs to roll the motor home over and get the wheels on the road.[7]

After the nation's first taste of long-distance motoring in the 1920s, the roadside environment changed frequently and dramatically, as did motorists' preferences for recreational travel. The dismal conditions of autocamps during the Depression all but ended the first autocamping boom; middle-class vacationers in the 1930s preferred attractive, cottage-like house trailers, exclusive trailer parks, or tourist courts instead of car-tents and house cars. In the prosperity of the 1940s and 1950s highways were paved and multilaned, and new, modern turnpikes skirted the most congested cities and towns. Motor homes, essentially motorized house trailers, emerged from the booming vacation market of the 1950s, as did manufactured pickup campers and van campers. The striking advantages of self-propelled recreation vehicles—maneuverability and all-enclosed comfort—rekindled interest in traveling by house car. It was illegal to ride in a house trailer, but postwar families who made or purchased streamlined house cars, pickup campers, or van campers enjoyed the intimate experience of riding together in an easy-to-drive home away from home.

By the 1960s fast, straight interstate highways made long trips smooth and unimpeded. Thousands of Americans fell in love with modern, factory-built motor homes. Unlike trailers, motor homes were not subject to reduced speed limits on highways, and drivers could take advantage of speeds of 70 miles per hour or more. In the early 1960s hundreds of affluent suburbanites became enchanted with the handsome, efficient Dodge motor home and several other makes, and they easily transferred their rancher or Cape Cod style of living to these portable vacation homes equipped with everything from automatic transmissions to forced-air furnaces. In the late 1960s Winnebago became America's best-selling motor home and the most conspicuous symbol of the surging popularity of homes that one could drive. Vacationers in the space age had discovered the fun of these space capsules on wheels; between 1961 and 1973 output soared from 200 to 65,300 motor homes per year.

The gasoline shortages and gasoline price increases of the 1970s curbed the growth of motor-home sales, but the motor home has remained a staple of recreational travel and one of the most prominent symbols of Americans' determination to see their country and enjoy their expanded leisure time to the fullest. More than 130,000 motor-home owners had joined the Family Motor Coach Association by 1990, when Richard Renner, grandson of Edward and Grace Renner, and his wife, Jimmie, became members. In their 1984 Revcon motor home, the Renners visited some of the places that Richard's grandparents had visited in their house car in the 1920s. Even on smooth, modern highways, tire blowouts were a problem; but the Renners, like most motor-home owners, enjoyed a heightened sense of comfort and freedom as they cruised along in their self-contained, streamlined house on wheels.

The development of motor homes and trailers followed separate paths. For the sake of thoroughness and cohesiveness, only self-propelled recreation vehicles are examined in this book. Two threads link the house-car fad of the 1920s, the popularity of pickup campers in the 1950s, and the motor-home mania of the 1960s and beyond: the intense enthusiasm of their owners and the intimate pleasure of traveling in a vehicle that was both an oversized car and an undersized house. Fifty years passed between the 1910s, when the earliest house-car and pickup-camper prototypes were created, and large-scale factory production of those vehicles. This delay reflects motorists' incremental contributions to the conversion of motor vehicles into homelike environments and the changing demand for self-propelled recreation vehicles. Please enjoy the ride as you read this story, at times personal, of the design of motor vehicles for living.

1 EARLY HOMES ON WHEELS

During the cycling craze of the 1880s and 1890s, thousands of men and women fled America's cities in their leisure time and explored rural roads on bicycles. They discovered the novelty and thrill of controlling their transportation and seeing the countryside without depending on the fixed routes or staccato rhythms of passenger trains and trolleys. Along the way they carefully noted interesting sights and the condition of old wagon roads and turnpikes that had never before served as conduits for hordes of tourists. Cyclists absorbed rural scenery, visited historic houses, dined at ancient roadside inns, and learned the addictive pleasure of exploring a new sight around every bend in the road. They did not yet think of the roadside as a home away from home, but often they packed clothing, toilet articles, and sundries in a valise, tied it to the handlebars, and spent the night in small-town hotels.

When automobiles came on the market in the late 1890s, Americans who could afford them discovered motor trips as a novel alternative to cycling, trolleys, and passenger trains. By the first decade of the twentieth century, the speed, range, and excitement of driving had attracted thousands of automobile owners to a pastime that became known simply as "touring." Motor touring was much more challenging than cycling because of the greater size and weight of an automobile. Unlike cyclists, who could push or carry their light machines over difficult spots, motorists learned to accept and even enjoy arduous experiences that summoned their "pioneer spirit" and tested their mechanical and driving skills. In the early days of touring, most roads were so primitive that it took courage and patience just to drive on them. Intercity roads had atrophied in the late nineteenth century as Americans grew increasingly dependent on passenger trains. Like cyclists, early motorists rediscovered grass-covered wagon trails—dirt roads traversed by horse-drawn wagons, buggies, and stagecoaches—and turnpikes that had not seen heavy traffic in decades. So prevalent were these types of roads that early automobiles followed the twin ruts made by wagon wheels, mounds of stones, dirt, or tall grass between the ruts often obstructing their low-slung chassis. In many areas, particularly the West, motorists had to contend with an active, ever-changing landscape; heavy rains turned roads into thick mud, washed out whole sections of roads and bridges, and widened streams and gullies. Motorists often found themselves fording streams and making their way around obstacles much the way travelers did with horses and wagons.

The minimal engineering standards of American roads were barely adequate for horse-drawn vehicles and were totally incompatible with motor vehicles. At the turn of the century only about 150,000 miles of roads were paved. Where the terrain was steep and rugged, there was no grading or leveling to smooth the way for automobiles. At wide streams motor vehicles crashed through flimsy wooden bridges built for buggies and farm wagons. Road bridges across major rivers were few and far between, and motorists were forced to choose between a long detour or a bumpy crossing on a railroad trestle, a dangerous practice at best. Despite some efforts to provide directional signs, there were vast expanses of land, particularly in the West, where there was nothing at all, and motorists had to follow railroad tracks or telegraph lines that ran toward their destinations.

Before the 1910s there were no specialized services or lodging places for motorists. Hotels, restaurants, general stores, hardware stores, and blacksmiths adapted as best they could, dispensing lodging, food, gasoline, supplies, and repairs. Like their cyclist counterparts, most motorists relied on the limited comfort of commercial hostelries, which ranged from drummers' hotels (for traveling salesmen) to historic inns to meager huts with pretentious signs reading HOTEL. Most motorists preferred the comfort and amenities of commercial lodgings, but some found them to be too formal, incompatible with their dusty appearance, and inconsistent with their desire for contact with the outdoors.

Some motorists tried camping out. Men and women who drove long distances often camped beside their automobiles because it was more convenient or because they enjoyed being outdoors. H. Nelson Jackson and Sewall Crocker, who made the first transcontinental automobile trip in the spring and summer of 1903, carried sleeping bags and slept on the ground beside their Winton touring car or under the car when it rained.[1] In the same year Hugh L. Willoughby drove from Saratoga Springs, New York, to Newport, Rhode Island, in his Autocar and carried "a full camp outfit."[2] In 1906 Winfield ("Win") and Emma Gehr and the William E. Camfield family traveled in a Glide automobile from Washington State to New York City, often camping in picturesque settings. "We didn't dare go to a hotel, as we looked worse than tramps," wrote Win Gehr about a Sunday afternoon in Missoula, Montana, "and only had 35 cents all told. So we drove off about four miles and camped out."[3] Harriet White Fisher, a manufacturer of anvils, vises, and rail joints, who drove from California to New Jersey in 1910, usually stayed in hotels, ranch houses, cottages, or mountain houses, but on at least one occasion she camped beside a spring in Wyoming.[4]

Few motorists slept in their automobiles. The first factory-produced automobiles were not good shelters; until the late 1920s most just had folding tops and translucent, snap-on side curtains that offered minimal protection from wind and rain. The seats did not move or fold, and they were not wide enough for a person to lie down on. Occasionally rough weather prevented motorists from reaching their preferred accommodations, which prompted them to spend the night in their car as an alternative to sleeping on the ground. Nellie Camfield and her five-year-old son, William, slept in their Glide car one night after a cloudburst left them standing in water almost to their knees. Alice Huyler Ramsey, a young, mechanically inclined motorist who became the first woman to drive an automobile across the United States in 1909, almost always stayed in hotels, but heavy rains and a swollen creek forced her and her female companions to spend a night beside the road, much against their wishes. In her memoir of the trip, Ramsey wrote:

Dusk came on. The water still showed no sign of receding. So we gathered up our paraphernalia, mumbling that we guessed we'd have to sleep right here, and dolefully climbed back into our seats. . . . The top was raised and the [side] curtains attached; also the piece which acted as a windshield was down in front. The only relief from a sitting position for the driver was putting both booted feet up on the dashboard. With head leaning back against the upright rib of the top—and boy, was it hard!—I spent the hours of darkness.[5]

Although these early experiments with automobile "bedrooms" were awkward and unplanned, they introduced motorists to the possibility of sleeping beside the road in their vehicles. But if automobiles were not designed for overnight use and most motorists were unwilling to spend the night outdoors, how did the automobile become transformed into a "home" on wheels? How did roadside camping become so appealing that thousands of tourists turned their motor vehicles into portable bedrooms and dining rooms?

Some experiments with car sleeping were intentional and involved homemade modifications to automobile bodies. In 1905 Percy Megargel and David Fassett drove a Reo touring car from New York City to Portland, Oregon. They often slept in the car, "not that we were compelled to do so," Megargel said, "but we wished to test its sleeping qualities." The two young men altered the front seat so that it tilted forward, and they placed seat cushions in the rear to form a double bed. Sometimes they slept under a canvas cover that buttoned snugly over the seating area.[6]

As more motorists searched for pleasure in the outdoors, a growing number began to think of a touring car as an aid to camping. Sporting enthusiasts were among the earliest to use touring cars in this way. Camping while hunting or fishing had been a popular leisure activity since the nineteenth century, and many hunters and anglers carried manufactured camping equipment such as tents, ovens, blankets, and candle lanterns. When touring cars came on the market, sportsmen used cars instead of horses and wagons, pack animals, or human porters to carry their equipment. Montie C. Ramsey, a carpenter in Grand Junction, Colorado, regularly drove his 1904 Rambler on hunting and trapping excursions in the Rocky Mountains.[7] Judge James B. Dill of East Orange, New Jersey, took an annual fishing trip to Maine in his automobile, driving through fields and woods and camping at favorite fishing spots.[8] In 1908 Ira H. Morse, H. J. Tenney, two of their friends, and a guide left Lowell, Massachusetts, in a Pope-Hartford roadster and went hunting in the Maine woods, sleeping in a large folding tent.[9] And in about 1908 seven New York City men packed their guns and dogs and enjoyed motor hunting and camping in New Jersey with a chauffeur and special "automobile tents" made by Abercrombie and Fitch, the New York sporting-goods company.[10]

Inventive sportsmen found ways to turn their automobiles into tents on wheels. Roy A. Faye, a Boston electrician, and Freeman N. Young, an electrical engineer in Arlington, Massachusetts, built a special sleeping body and installed it on an automobile chassis in 1905. Every summer between 1905 and 1908 they traveled to the Maine woods in this vehicle with a party of sporting enthusiasts. The body frame was made of hardwood and iron and held four bunks, two above and two below. The bunks had pneumatic mattresses with army blankets, rubber blankets, and pillows, and, during the day, the bunks could be folded away. There was also a special place in the camping car for Faye's bird dogs. The car had electric incandescent lights, an icebox, and a radio with an elaborate folding antenna connected on top of the vehicle.[11]

The novelty, informality, and pseudonomadic qualities of "auto-camping" were irresistible and soon attracted many motorists who were not sports enthusiasts or making transcontinental journeys but merely were sightseeing and enjoying nature. As early as 1905 *Outing* magazine urged motorists to try camping and recommended that they carry a tent, sleeping bag or hammock (depending on the season), and other camping paraphernalia.[12] In the same year *Country Life in America* made a similar appeal to its readers:

> Touring is at best a rather ordinary performance because of its being over-done — everybody tours who has a month's car lease in his pocket. Automobile camping is an entirely new feature of the sport, strongly appealing to the genuine chauffeur, and has not as yet been taken up generally because few know how to do it — how to pitch camp and be comfortable. But such a thing is quite possible, and no expert knowledge is required, only a good deal of forethought.[13]

In his definitive history, *Americans on the Road: From Autocamp to Motel, 1910–1945,* Warren James Belasco explained that the appeal of autocamping was in its independence, romanticism, and simplicity.[14] Driving automobiles and sleeping in cots and tents allowed families and couples to enjoy nature close at hand and tour at their own pace, without the limitations of passenger trains and railroad timetables or the formalities, expenses, and impersonality of hotels. Autocamping was so slow and cumbersome that these practical advantages alone cannot explain its popularity. Early "autogypsies," as they romantically called themselves, temporarily abandoned their homes in favor of an unstructured, itinerant lifestyle. In its early form autogypsying stressed primitivism and family harmony, not domestic comfort. Most autocampers spent the night in pastures, schoolyards, and other roadside places that were not formally designated for their use. They explored hard-to-reach places, dressed and dined informally, and recreated their home life in rural settings without pressures and distractions. Autocamping families and couples were less interested in the challenges of setting up a home in the wilderness and more interested in increasing family harmony. They hoped that the isolation and simplicity of autocamping would erase the cares, pressures, and divisiveness that modern living, with its ever-increasing pace and complexity, had brought to the urban and suburban setting.

Despite the fundamental austerity, a growing number of autocampers tried to imitate not only the peripatetic Gypsy lifestyle but the homelike environment of the Gypsy wagon. These inventive individuals tried to create more substantial, efficient camping environments by turning their automobiles into simple, self-contained homes on wheels. Some autogypsies found pleasure in maintaining the formalities of home life in wilderness settings, and they tried to combine housekeeping with nomadism. On a practical level, they were simply reluctant to leave the comforts of home behind. Many autocampers quickly came to dislike tent camping because of its laborious, time-consuming set-up chores and closeness to animals, insects, and the cool, damp earth. Instead of "roughing it" they turned their touring cars into makeshift bedrooms and dining rooms by modifying certain areas for sleeping, dressing, and dining. The sleeping space in a modified touring car was high above the ground, and it was much easier to break camp and move to the next location with a touring car home than with a tent.

The earliest sleeping cars reflected both men's and women's needs

By the early 1910s some autocamping couples turned their touring cars into bedrooms and kitchens on wheels. A touring car bed was above insects, animals, and the damp earth, and it reminded autocampers of their comfortable homes. (Courtesy Library of Congress)

and expectations in a portable home environment. In about 1909 William J. Burt, superintendent of the Auto Vehicle Company in Los Angeles, designed and installed a special interior for a Tourist, a standard touring car manufactured by his company. In Burt's one-off version the front seat back was hinged and could be lowered to the level of the rear seat; a hinged footboard on the front seat could be raised, forming a double bed 6 feet long. The front seat back also could be detached and laid flat to form a table. Travelers could dine while seated in the rear seat. A one-burner acetylene gas stove, fueled by a Prest-O-Lite tank, was fitted into the compartment. Far from "roughing it," Burt installed the formal comforts of home: a set of dishes, table linen, silverware, glasses, bottles, aluminum cookware, and other utensils. A folding dresser in the rear had a dressing table, an oval mirror, and plush-lined leather pockets for purses, brushes, combs, and other toilet articles. Two hammocks strung from the folding top provided storage for clothing. The interior of the car was illuminated with four tungsten electric lights powered by a separate battery.[15]

Autogypsies turned car sleeping into a more or less domestic experience. In about 1911, for example, Herman C. Newton, a Chicago dentist, and his wife, Katherine, spent six weeks touring the Northeast in their modified Franklin touring car. The Newtons installed a hinged front seat so that the folded-down seat back and the rear seat formed a bed. A pneumatic mattress completed the improvised bed, and snap-on side curtains were fitted with mosquito nets. The Newtons cooked on an alcohol stove inside the car and folded the front seat forward so that they could use its wooden back as a dining table. Cooking and eating utensils and bedding were stored on the runningboard. Like other autogypsies, the Newtons were escaping their daily routines and urban environment and were enjoying an independent tour of the countryside. The Newtons felt that their "tent" on wheels, with its domestic features, was far superior to a tent on the ground. They were extending the reach of their home with a portable version of it and were taking some of its comforts and security with them. Instead of relishing the joys of camping and learning to tolerate life in the outdoors, they resisted the outdoor environment and perpetuated domestic rituals. Katherine Newton wore a house dress and wielded a feather duster, and at night the Newtons protected their mobile domain with a burglar alarm consisting of a trip cord tied to an alarm clock.[16]

Even more than ordinary autocamping, the refined, domestic environment of Burt's and Newton's special camping cars reflected the new symbiosis of house and car in the middle and upper classes. Visually and functionally, the automobile was becoming an extension of the house and the primary link between home, community, and the countryside. With its architectonic form, an automobile body bore a subtle resemblance to a house; it had a wooden frame, exterior sheathing, "roof," upholstered seats, rug, clock, front "window," and exterior lamps, and it was clad in paint that could be polished with household wax. The owner could purchase accessories that enhanced the automobile's comfort, convenience, or appearance; one woman wrote, "One should furnish a motor as they should a house, by degrees."[17] The automobile carried the family to church, community gatherings, and homes of friends

Only wealthy people could afford a stylish Pierce-Arrow camper, which had tooled leather upholstery and a telephone connection between the chauffeur and passengers. The Pierce-Arrow Motor Car Company made touring landaus from 1910 to 1913. (Courtesy National Museum of American History, Smithsonian Institution)

and relatives. It also took them on sightseeing excursions. The spacious, breezy touring car was designed to satisfy not only the practical transportation needs of families but also their desire to enjoy the countryside. With the right automobile, a home in the country became an appealing option for many city dwellers; ex-urbanites commuted to work in their touring cars instead of depending on railroads or trolleys. And for some excursionists, like the Newtons, the touring car itself became a miniature country home on wheels.

As touring became more popular, automobile manufacturers soon began producing cars that were specially equipped for sleeping and dining. But like production automobiles, the earliest commercially built campers on wheels were for wealthy motorists. In January 1910 the Pierce-Arrow Motor Car Company unveiled its 6-cylinder touring landau at an automobile show in New York City's Madison Square Garden. The elegant, chauffeur-driven automobile was made in limited quantities and was furnished with deluxe camping appointments: a folding washbasin in back of the front seat, a toilet, water tank, tooled Cordovan leather upholstery, and a roof rack and a rear boot for trunks. In place of the runningboards were storage boxes with space for tools, accessories, and supplies. A sliding drawer under the rear seat contained a luncheon kit. The initial selling price was $8,250, which did not include the trunks, priced at $200, or the luncheon kit, priced at $65.[18] By comparison, a 1910 Ford Model T touring car cost $950.

Several wealthy businessmen owned Pierce-Arrow touring landaus. One special version was built for Pierce-Arrow's president, George K. Birge. The interior, which was designed by Pierce-Arrow staff member Herbert M. Dawley, had hot and cold running water, a hinged washbasin, a cabinet containing linens, cutlery, and thermos vessels, and a toilet under part of the rear seat. The rear seat and its back cushion could be arranged to form a bed.[19] Another touring landau belonged to a Texas oil man who drove through several countries and reportedly crossed the Gobi Desert. Another owner was a San Francisco businessman who planned to tour the United States and Europe; painted "English coach yellow," his vehicle had an icebox in place of the washbasin.[20] Charles William Post, the breakfast cereal magnate, paid $8,250 for a touring landau with leather upholstery, hot and cold running water, a compartment for food storage, service hampers, a toilet, and two trunks on top and four on the rear. He and his wife, Ella, traveled extensively in this car, which was painted "old coach yellow and black."[21]

Pierce-Arrow soon renamed its touring landau the "George Washington coach," a change that exemplified the nostalgia for eighteenth-century road travel so evident in motor touring in the 1910s. Travelers thought of themselves as trailblazers as they rediscovered old wagon roads and turnpikes. Motorists' organizations surveyed and marked automobile "trails," often borrowing names of historic wagon roads or heroes of Revolutionary War land battles. Spending the night in roadside inns recalled the days when taverns were used as rest stops by passengers in carriages and stagecoaches. Like nineteenth-century carriages that bore family crests, the George Washington coach identified the owner's social status and conveyed his or her pride of ownership. On each door was the Washington family coat of arms, and on the upper door panels were paintings of Mount Vernon and Washington, D.C., by Ernest Fosbery, an artist in Buffalo, New York. The George Washington coach also sported a new exterior color scheme of green with brown striping.[22]

HIGHWAY PROMOTERS HIT THE ROAD IN MODIFIED TRUCKS AND BUSES

Wealthy Americans also introduced the earliest enclosed, fully furnished camping vehicles. The possibility of constructing such a vehicle had intrigued many tourists since the earliest days of motoring. In 1901 a western couple reportedly intended to explore the back roads of the United States in their "traveling van"—a converted street railway car. A gasoline engine and an enclosed observation and operating platform had been added to the front of this 4-ton vehicle, and a porch had been added to the rear.[23] In 1902 William W. Dake, president of the Dake Drug Company in Rochester, New York, was planning to build a vacation vehicle about 2 feet longer than a touring car and enclose it with detachable glass walls. Bunks would accommodate family members when nightfall found them on a remote country road.[24]

In 1903 the American automotive trade press published numerous descriptions of a large, lavishly equipped house on wheels owned by a wealthy gentleman in Bordeaux, France. Named Le Bourlinguette, this vehicle was patterned after private railroad cars but was referred to as a "motor caravan" or "automobile house car." The rectangular, enclosed body, which was built by Lafitte et Compagnie of Bordeaux, was approximately 20 feet long. A Panhard engine was installed in the front compartment of the vehicle; its average speed was 11 to 13 miles per hour, with a maximum of about 19 miles per hour. The forward compartment contained seats for four passengers and a folding bunk for the chauffeur/mechanic. The center compartment was furnished with convertible furniture: four folding beds, lockers that served as seats, and a dining table that concealed two lavatories with hot and cold running water. The rear compartment housed a kitchen and pantry with a gasoline stove, icebox, china closet, wire closet, and storage lockers. In the summer of 1904 this vehicle was driven on a tour of Touraine, Normandy, Brittany, and Lavoie. In the same year the owner traveled from

Bordeaux to Paris, a distance of 375 miles, living in the house car for three days.[25]

Public excitement over Le Bourlinguette may have inspired one of the earliest American house-car designs. In 1904 Louis D. Shoenberg, a long-time partner in the May Department Stores Company and president of its Cleveland branch, ordered a sleeping car from the Cleveland Motor Company and planned to take a party of friends to the Louisiana Purchase Exposition in St. Louis. Designed by E. J. Pennington, a pioneer automobile builder, the mammoth vehicle was said to have three different bodies: a touring body, a racing body, and an enclosed, limousine-style body with a kitchen, dining room, and sleeping accommodations for ten people. The engine was rated at an incredible 408 horsepower according to one source. It is not known whether this vehicle was actually built, but regardless of the outcome, Pennington's concept and the attendant publicity certainly reflected growing public interest in houses on wheels.[26]

Wealthy advocates of automobile travel and pleasure driving began to use the capacity and power of trucks and buses to create vacation vehicles that were more sophisticated than a Pierce-Arrow touring landau or a modified touring car. By the early 1910s many successful, prominent businessmen were devoting their time and energy to motor vehicle production or the construction of paved highways. Some of these executives had risen through the ranks of automobile manufacturing companies and had made their fortunes by supplying automobiles or automotive accessories to the burgeoning market. Others had shifted their attention from older, well-established industries to the new fields of automobile production and highway travel. These visionaries shared a belief that a system of highways and personal motor vehicles could provide a means of long-distance travel that was more flexible and enjoyable than passenger trains, and some eagerly participated in motor touring and camping trips. Living in novel camping cars and house cars patterned after trucks or buses, a few automotive executives and highway developers ushered in a new form of travel that combined the privacy of a Pullman car and the range of an automobile.

Several businessmen commissioned camping vehicles that were based on delivery trucks, which had open, framelike wooden bodies. Sparsely furnished delivery-truck campers were not very homelike, but

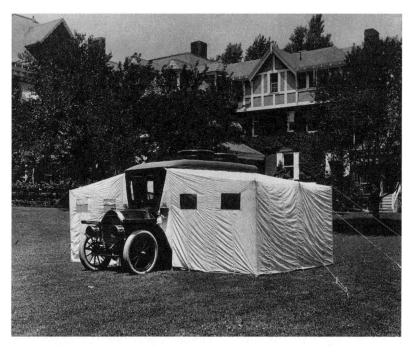

In about 1911 T. Coleman du Pont commissioned a camping truck to inspect a new highway in Delaware that he funded. Good-roads advocates like du Pont adapted trucks for roadside living by adding camp-style sleeping and cooking equipment. (Courtesy Hagley Museum and Library)

they were more spacious and powerful than automobiles. Owners of truck campers lived in their vehicles while vacationing, surveying routes for new highways, and inspecting highways that were under construction. These camping-car pioneers pushed back two frontiers—highways and camping vehicle design—both of which ultimately benefitted average and recreational motorists. However, the enthusiasm of highway developers far exceeded the reality of unimproved or minimally improved roads, pitifully slow travel, and countless hazards that required bravery and patience.

An early example of a delivery truck modified for camping was built in about 1911 for T. Coleman du Pont, president of E. I. du Pont de Nemours and Company. An enthusiastic supporter of good roads, du Pont undertook at his personal expense the construction of a paved express highway from northern Delaware to the southern part of the state.

Later numbered U.S. 13, the Coleman du Pont Road was revolutionary because it skirted towns instead of passing through them. Du Pont had a camping car built to his specifications for use in supervising the highway's construction. The camping car supplemented a fleet of Pierce-Arrow automobiles that were also used in the construction work.

Du Pont's camping car had a Stoddard-Dayton chassis and an express delivery body modified according to du Pont's ideas. The body had roll-down side curtains, a 6-foot mattress stuffed with hair, lockers containing a stove and cooking utensils, blankets, and a metal icebox. Some of the lockers were upholstered and served as seats. Other storage units on the exterior of the car held tools, tires, supplies, and two silk tents that attached to either side of the car to provide additional sleeping space. Underneath the vehicle's top were racks for storage boxes, drawings, and plans, and above the top was a railing containing four extra tires. A storage battery and dry cells powered interior electric lights.[27]

The Packard Motor Car Company built a camping car similar to du Pont's in about 1911 for its president, Henry B. Joy, an avid camper, automotive enthusiast, and good-roads advocate. Like Theodore Roosevelt, Joy as a young man had regained his health by moving to the West and living a vigorous, outdoor lifestyle. Joy remained a strong believer in the restorative powers of outdoor recreation. He commissioned his first trucklike camping car "as a suggestion to sportsmen who wish to go hunting and remain independent of hotels."[28] Joy planned to take an extended trip in the camping car, which had a Packard chassis rated at 30 horsepower, side curtains, and seats that converted into bunks. Storage lockers under the seats and floorboards held a tent, grate, canvas water buckets, self-cooling water bags, food bags, air-tight tin cans, a "fireless cooker," axes, lanterns, cooking utensils, and dishes.[29]

Joy's career symbolized the rising profile of automobile manufacturers and reflected America's changing transportation habits as automobiles began to rival railroads. The son of a railroad executive, Joy had become a railroad-terminal executive by the 1890s. In 1902 he purchased an interest in the Ohio Automobile Company, which had been organized to manufacture James Packard's automobile. Joy then became general manager of the reorganized Packard Motor Car Company and served as its president from 1909 to 1916. He guided the Packard firm to a prominent position in the luxury car field, and under his leadership the firm acquired its national reputation for excellence in engineering.[30]

Joy was cofounder of the Lincoln Highway Association and was its first president, serving from 1913 to 1917. In 1913 he and Frank H. Trego, a Packard engineer, undertook a survey of possible routes for the Lincoln Highway, which was planned as the nation's first transcontinental highway. They traveled from Omaha to San Francisco in a trucklike camping car with PACKARD GOOD ROADS lettered on one side and PACKARD TESTING CAR on the other. This vehicle, which had a Packard chassis rated at 48 horsepower and an express delivery body with roll-down side curtains, was fitted with sleeping bags, an alcohol stove, and electric lights. It was displayed at the New York Sportsman's Show in 1914.[31]

In the spring of 1916 Joy outfitted a similar camping body on a new Packard V-12 chassis and shipped this vehicle to El Paso, Texas. He and Packard engineer William R. McCulla drove it from El Paso into Mexico, where they inspected Packard trucks that were carrying supplies for General John Pershing during his pursuit of Mexican terrorist Pancho Villa. Later Joy, his wife, Helen, and their son, Henry B. Joy Jr., used this vehicle for family camping trips.[32]

Similar camping trucks featured rudimentary furniture and utilities that made more efficient use of space and converted the cargo area into a room. One such vehicle was built for John K. Deane, a wealthy businessman in Malden, Massachusetts. Completed by the Woonsocket Wagon Manufacturing Company of Woonsocket, Rhode Island, in 1914, this vehicle had a 10-foot wire screen delivery body mounted on a 6-cylinder chassis. The entrance was in the rear, and inside were four folding bunks, electric lights, and places for a stove and icebox.[33] Another furnished camping wagon was designed under the supervision of its owner, H. M. Butts, in about 1914. This vehicle had seats that folded into beds for three people, a clothes closet, electric lights, sleeping hammocks that were hung outside the vehicle in concealed sockets, and heavy planks that could be made into a table or bed. Seven passengers traveled approximately 1,600 miles in this vehicle from Denver to Los Angeles on a 15-day trip in late 1914 or early 1915.[34] Camping cars like those of Deane and Butts were incremental steps toward fully furnished homes on wheels.

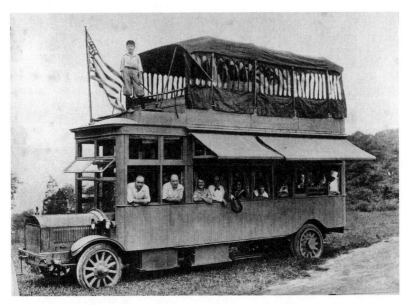

The Conklins of Huntington, New York, made house-car travel a family experience. Roland Conklin's bus factory built the Gypsy Van, and in the summer of 1915 the Conklin family set out to see America. (Courtesy Huntington Historical Society)

Despite the grand visions of E. J. Pennington and others who were fascinated by houses on wheels, the earliest American house cars with solid walls were sparsely furnished and were little more than enclosed versions of camping trucks. These trucks were spacious and weather-tight, but their plain bodies hardly evoked images of domestic comforts and touring pleasures. The circa 1911 Motor Bungalow of D. H. Lyon of New York had a specially designed, trucklike body on an Autocar truck chassis. The body had solid walls with glass windows on the sides and doors with glass windows on the rear. The interior of the vehicle was fitted with a divided cushion that folded to a width of 15 inches on either side. At night the 6-foot-long cushion unfolded to cover the entire width of the vehicle and form a bed. In the rear of the compartment was a small gasoline stove, an icebox, and a metal box containing cooking utensils and dishes. A silk tent fly, thrown over the vehicle, provided additional space at night.[35]

Eventually, the romantic appeal of autogypsying led one wealthy American couple to combine the notion of a Gypsy wagon with a motorized commercial vehicle and create an enclosed, fully furnished house on wheels. In 1915 motor-bus executive and good-roads advocate Roland R. Conklin and his wife, Mary, created the most elaborately furnished American house car of its day, the innovative Gypsy Van. The Conklins were emulating British tourists, who had traveled in imitation, horse-drawn Gypsy wagons since the 1880s; by 1913 Britain's Caravan Club had approximately 300 members.[36]

Like Henry Joy's metamorphosis from a railroad executive to an automobile manufacturer, Conklin's changing career interests reflected the growing economic and social importance of motor vehicles. Conklin formed a company that began selling farm mortgage loans in Kansas City in the 1880s. After the Panic of 1893 his firm became a receiver for failed farm mortgage companies, making Conklin a nationally prominent fiscal manager. During the Spanish-American War, his company was the U.S. government's fiscal agent in Cuba. Conklin developed Cuba's roads, railroads, telephone network, and sugar mills, and in 1901 or 1902 he imported six motor buses to the island nation. As motor buses developed, Conklin became interested in manufacturing and operating buses in American cities. In 1912 he organized the New York Motor Bus Company and applied for a franchise to operate buses in New York City. He received tentative approval for this service in October 1915, but two years later this decision was reversed and he lost the franchise to a rival bus company. Conklin's Gas-Electric Motor Bus Company built several buses in Manhattan, however, and one of them ran in Chicago in the summer of 1915 under the banner of Conklin's Chicago Motor Bus Company.[37]

Conklin took a vigorous interest in automobile travel and the improvement of roads in the United States. He was a member of the Automobile Club of America, and as president of the Huntington Association, he encouraged the development of good roads near his Long Island estate in Huntington, New York.[38] In 1915 Roland and Mary decided to visit the Panama-Pacific International Exposition in San Francisco, and, like many adventurous motorists, they chose to take the long journey on country roads in a motor vehicle.

The inspiration to build a buslike house on wheels seems to have been on Mary Conklin's mind as well as her husband's. In her memoir she wrote:

I don't know how the idea originated, nor with whom. Possibly it was a case
of spontaneous generation developing in all our minds at about the same
time. In any event, we found ourselves at various family gatherings discussing
the possibility of converting a second-hand motor bus into a Gypsy Van, with
beds and kitchen, and using it for camping expeditions. We had tried such
jaunts with touring cars and we realized what a great improvement it would
be if we never had to erect or fold tents but could eat, live and sleep in a specially designed car as we traveled along. Then came to mind the pictures of
gypsy wagons, and the carefree, independent life their occupants lived; and
to the older ones, remembered tales of pioneer prairie schooners crowded
with children's laughing faces as they trailed across the plains seeking an
Eldorado in the West.

  Possibly, it was these memories that inspired the ambitious idea of crossing
the continent. At first we thought of it as a joke, but the idea was too fascinat-
ing to be dropped. Would it be practicable? Not with a second-hand motor
bus. No, but with a new vehicle built especially for the purpose, it might be
done.[39]

Copying city buses, which had appeared in the early 1910s, Conklin's
Gas-Electric Motor Bus Company built a 25-foot, 8-ton Gypsy Van that
dwarfed everything else on the road. The body, which was clad in ash
varnished to a brownish gray, had forty-four windows with awnings,
screens, and shades. The upper deck was fitted with a folding top, side
curtains, seats, lockers, and a motorcycle for side trips and emergencies.
The 6-cylinder, 60-horsepower bus chassis, painted gray-green, was designed not for speed but for power and traction to negotiate the difficult
roads that the Conklins would encounter. The transmission had nine
forward speeds and three reverse speeds. The tires were solid rubber,
and the rear axle had four wheels. The Gypsy Van was also equipped
with a motor-driven winch, a knocked-down, steel-and-plank bridge
that could cover voids up to 15 feet, and canvas strips to tread over sand
patches.

  The Gypsy Van's homelike interior added a stylish touch to camping
vehicles and set a standard for virtually all American house cars that
would follow through the 1920s. From convertible sofas with throw pillows to silk curtains on brass rods and a fully equipped kitchen, the
Gypsy Van boasted most of the comforts of home. A parlorlike room
was furnished with a sofa and two armchairs that converted to beds, and

The interior of the Conklins' Gypsy Van was similar to their mansion, which was styled after English manor houses. The elaborately furnished Gypsy Van set a standard for virtually all house cars that followed. (Courtesy Huntington Historical Society)

four folding, Pullman-style upper berths that let down from the ceiling. There were 6.5 feet of standing room. There was a folding dining table that was stored in the ceiling when not in use, and there were homey touches such as a folding desk, concealed bookcase, and phonograph. The Gypsy Van's central room was trimmed with gray Spanish linen upholstery and valances with green, blue, and red designs. The interior woodwork was light neutral ash, and the floor covering was pressed cork. Carved wooden panels covered partitions between compartments.

The Gypsy Van also had elaborate utilities that earlier camping vehicles lacked. A separate generator and battery supplied electricity for interior lights, a range-oven-broiler, a water heater, small appliances ranging from a fan to two vacuum cleaners (one for upholstery and one for clothes), and tools, including a drill, emery wheel, and soldering iron. A water tank on the roof was connected to an auxiliary water pump driven by the vehicle's engine; this system fed a porcelain sink in the kitchen and a folding metal washbasin and shower in the bathroom. The cold tap water passed through a coil in the icebox and provided chilled drinking water.

The Gypsy Van reflected the Conklin home more than a Gypsy wagon. Rosemary Farm, the Conklin estate near Huntington, New York, provided a fertile environment for the conception of the Gypsy Van. The mansion, designed by architect Wilson Eyre in the style of an English manor house, had decorative woodwork and carved wooden panels similar to those in the Gypsy Van. The rooms of the house were filled with massive furniture pieces and antique paintings. Rosemary Farm combined the elegance of an estate with the self-sufficiency of a farm. The Conklins attempted to raise most of the food that they consumed, and they sold products from their farm at a local market. The mansion was flanked by a dairy, garden, chicken house, piggery, fish pond, and crops.[40] It is not surprising that the owners of this pastoral microcosm, so complete, well-equipped, and aesthetically pleasing, would create such a domestic microcosm on wheels. The design of the Gypsy Van grew out of the Conklins' love of romantic English motifs, their interest in domestic engineering and self-sufficiency, and their zeal for travel and adventure.

When setting out for California in the Gypsy Van, the Conklins pushed back the frontier of long-distance motor travel still further and made house-car travel a family activity. Although the risks and difficulties of transcontinental motor travel were still present, such journeys were becoming more inviting to adventurous motorists. Transcontinental motor journeys had been made by autocampers (Jackson and Crocker in 1903), a motorcyclist (George Wyman in 1903), a family (the Camfields in 1906), a woman driver (Ramsey in 1909), and truck drivers (A. C. Thompson and George McLean in 1911). There was widespread anticipation that coast-to-coast highway travel would become commonplace within a few years. The construction of the Lincoln Highway (U.S. 30), which began in 1913, greatly stimulated public interest in transcontinental automobile travel, as did the Panama-Pacific International Exposition of 1915, a major West Coast attraction. Now the Conklin family would attempt to cross the country in a house on wheels and, in doing so, domesticate the road through the West.

After test drives in the hills of New Jersey and Westchester County, New York, and the sands of eastern Long Island, the Gypsy Van, carrying the Conklins and their party, left Rosemary Farm on Saturday, August 21, 1915. The party included their children, Roland, Julia, and Rosemary, and Helen, a friend of Julia, Harry Conklin and Fred Conklin (nephews of Roland Conklin), a chauffeur, and a steward. The Conklins planned to follow completed portions of the Lincoln Highway much of the way, but they agreed to deviate from this route to see interesting sights.[41] On the second day of the trip the house on wheels waddled into a dilemma. The Conklins followed a detour on a state road north of Briarcliff, New York, to avoid a narrow bridge. Veering to let an approaching automobile pass, the Gypsy Van slid into a ditch and tilted precariously. The Conklin party spent the night in Briarcliff Lodge, and later the Briarcliff Fire Department pulled the Gypsy Van back onto the road through the efforts of dozens of men and several teams of horses.[42]

Traveling 50 to 60 miles per day, the Conklins stopped at Albany, Niagara Falls, Cleveland, and other places. On September 20 they reached Chicago, where they decided to ship the Gypsy Van by rail to Sacramento, California, to shorten the duration of the trip and avoid harsh fall weather and treacherous western roads.[43] Roland and Mary Conklin traveled by train from Chicago to San Francisco; the nephews accompanied the Gypsy Van on its rail journey to Sacramento and drove the vehicle to San Francisco on October 12, 1915.[44] Summing up the experience, Roland Conklin was philosophical about the practical value of the home on wheels. "If the trip of the Gypsy Van does no more than to call to the attention of a large number of people the desirability of good roads," he remarked to a newspaper reporter, "it will have served a most useful purpose."[45]

Conklin's modesty notwithstanding, the Gypsy Van influenced the design of camping vehicles for decades. The Conklins' journey was widely publicized in newspapers, popular magazines, and automotive trade journals and introduced many Americans to the concept of a vacation home on wheels.[46] Other wealthy Americans soon owned bus-like house cars, and by the 1920s Americans of average means were converting motor buses to house cars or were building their own buslike bodies. The homey, attractive interior of the Gypsy Van set the tone for almost all house cars of the 1920s, large or small. The concept of a converted bus would appeal to many vacationers throughout the century.

From rolling camps to make-believe homes on wheels to luxurious house cars, motor vehicles were evolving from basic transportation to portable shelters that insulated their occupants from their surroundings during recreational journeys. Whether they were backyard tinkerers or owners of elegant landaus, early sleeping-car owners were less interested in living in nature and more interested in looking at nature from the secure, convenient quarters inside their homelike vehicles. Increasingly, adapting and enjoying the vehicle itself became the focus of their pleasures. Instead of escaping their homes completely, they tried to combine the comfort, security, and familiarity of home with the range and flexibility of the automobile and the pleasures, simplicity, and rustic environment of rural America. In the late 1910s and 1920s they would seek the best of all three spheres.

2 HOUSE CARS AND THE AUTOCAMPING CRAZE

n the 1920s autocamping swelled as millions of Americans temporarily left their homes and fled their responsibilities to enjoy itinerant, Gypsy-style vacations in their automobiles. Despite the rapidly growing number of people sharing the road and roadside services, the appeal of nomadism, independence, and family cohesion remained strong. Autocampers believed that they could grow closer to each other by "living off the land" and escaping the dictatorial constraints of work and school schedules, home management, mass transit, mass media, and consumption of manufactured goods. But instead of "roughing it" in the woods, as hunters and anglers did, autocampers reconstructed the routines and furnishings of their homes in simplified forms. As Warren Belasco pointed out, autocamps were clusters of "cheap summer cottages" that spread like tiny resort villages on the outskirts of towns. Family members were assigned domestic responsibilities so that preparation of bedding, cooking equipment, menus, and meals would proceed efficiently at each campsite. Autocampers enjoyed making conversation with their "neighbors," examined each other's vehicles and camping outfits, and shared information about roads and destinations.

While autocamping remained a pseudorustic experience, it also became more systematic and materialistic. Families believed that they were "living like Gypsies," but in reality they depended on laundries and rest rooms at autocamps and set up portable facsimiles of their homes beside their vehicles. Demand for portable, manufactured sleeping and dining equipment grew dramatically; sporting-goods dealers, autocamping equipment specialists, and other companies issued catalogs with a wide range of equipment available at modest prices. Most of these accessories were miniature, lightweight versions of home furniture. A folding table with folding chairs substituted for a dining room suite, a gasoline stove substituted for a kitchen range, a portable food cabinet substituted for a pantry, and a tent substituted for a bedroom. With the proper equipment, autocampers could feel "at home" without the burdens of running a fully equipped household.

Several companies manufactured small, two-wheel camping trailers with collapsible tents attached. Tent trailers were lightweight and easy to tow, and they provided a sleeping area that was above the ground. They also reduced the amount of dismantling and packing at each campsite. Among the most popular makes of tent trailers in the 1920s were Auto-Kamp, Chenango, Lippman Kamprite, and Zagelmeyer. Most trailers were furnished only with beds, a gasoline cookstove, icebox, and storage drawers. Although these furnishings were rudimentary, they made the tent trailer more than just a tent on wheels; many trailers had full-height screen doors with steps, giving them a cottage-like ambience.

At the physical and emotional center of every autocamp setting was the family car. A symbol of family unity and security, the car at rest took on a houselike quality as a locus of sleeping and food preparation. In a typical camp setting the car served as a staging platform for a fly tent, a support for a cot attached to a runningboard, and a convenient surface for a portable pantry, cookstove, kitchen utensils, clothing, and other paraphernalia. Autocampers learned to use their automobiles as beds to provide more sleeping space and reduce the arduous chores involved in making and breaking camp. Like a trailer, a cot placed over an automobile's seat backs was high above the earth, and side curtains offered almost as much protection against wind and rain as did a tent or trailer.

Some autocampers purchased inexpensive in-car cots, such as a Jim-Harry Auto Camp Bed, Moto-Kamp Bed, Rambler Bed, Red Head Autobed, or Kumfort Kot. These and other cots were specially designed by manufacturers of camping equipment and aftermarket automobile accessories to be installed inside a touring car or sedan. A typical cot was constructed of heavy canvas and a wooden or tubular metal frame with hinged segments and accommodated two people side by side. A jointed cot could be folded easily and stored on the floor, tied to a runningboard, or strapped inside the automobile top during the day.[1] There were several ways to attach a cot to an automobile's interior. One type of cot lay on top of the seat backs, and some examples of this type had small rests on the bottom of the cot. Another type rested on the rear seat cushion and the folded-down front seat. A third type of cot was tied to the top posts of the automobile and stretched from front to back like a hammock. The canvas was drawn tight enough not to sag, and some cots had webbing or springs for extra support. In some cases, the front and rear automobile seat cushions were detached and placed on the cot to serve as a mattress. In other instances, children slept beneath the cot on the seat cushions.

Despite the availability of inexpensive cots, many autocampers preferred to make their own sleeping arrangements by modifying their automobiles. In 1915 J. W. Lawlor and his wife toured the East Coast in a Ford Model T touring car equipped with front seats that folded back. At night they fastened muslin curtains over the car's isinglass side curtains and slept in the car on felt pads laid over the seat-bed. An oil lantern provided a night light, and a tent served as a dressing room and kitchen.[2] Another Model T owner cut and hinged the front-seat back so that it tilted to the rear, aligning with the rear cushion to form a bed. The seat back was held in place by pin-type door hinges. The sleeping compartment was protected by mosquito netting and celluloid side curtains.[3]

Some individuals who modified automobiles for sleeping drew on their skills as mechanics or machinists. In 1916 A. G. Sharkey, mechanical superintendent for a Chandler automobile distributor in southern California, converted two 6-cylinder Chandlers into camping cars with sleeping berths. One car had folding front and rear seats with bed cushions stored beneath them. The other car had hinged front seats that tilted sideways over the runningboards, clearing enough floor space inside the car for a mattress, which was stored in the back of the car when not in use.[4] Harris T. Dunbar, vice president of the Buffalo Foundry and Machine Company in Buffalo, New York, hired a blacksmith, tent maker, and planing mill to replace the folding top on his 1920 Franklin touring car with a special top fitted with a bed in the rear. An additional canvas shelter unfolded from the rear of the car. During a four-month vacation in 1922, Dunbar and two other people drove from Buffalo to Cheyenne, Wyoming, and back in the modified vehicle, which was named the Locomotel.[5]

Several automobile manufacturers noticed motorists' efforts to equip their automobiles for sleeping and began selling moderately priced automobiles with seats that converted into beds. From 1914 to 1916 the Spaulding Manufacturing Company of Grinnell, Iowa, offered a touring car with a hinged front seat back that folded down so that the front and rear seat cushions formed a bed 6.5 feet long. The seat back was secured at the top by two knurled-head bolts that could be loosened or tightened. The 1914 model was also equipped with an inflatable mattress and an electric reading lamp. At $1,730, the 1915 model, which was variously called a sleeping car, Spaulding Sleeper, or Spaulding Home Car, cost $50 more than the Spaulding Model H five-passenger touring car on which it was based.[6] In 1915 the Jackson Automobile Company of Jackson, Michigan, was selling a sleeping car for $25 more than the price of a Jackson touring car. The back of the front seat was held in place by catches; when lowered, the seat back rested on folding steel legs, and the rear seat cushion was turned around to make a level bed surface.[7] The Pan, a sleeper touring car built between 1918 and 1922 by the Pan Motor Company in St. Cloud, Minnesota, had a lever that turned the seats into a double bed.[8] And in the early 1920s the Flapper camping body, which had fold-down seats that formed a bed for two, was advertised by a New York City company in sizes to fit common automobile chassis such as Ford, Gray, Star, Chevrolet, Essex, Maxwell, and Dort.[9]

The availability of closed cars to middle-income Americans brought a new level of comfort, sophistication, and self-containment to their personal transportation and camping trips. For a half century closed vehicles had been symbols of affluence; only the wealthy could afford handmade coaches, landaus, broughams, and other closed carriages with fine upholstery and luxurious appointments. Closed vehicles graced the driveways and porte cocheres of America's finest mansions. When automobiles appeared, only the well-to-do could afford the handsome, enclosed town cars, limousines, berlines, and sedans that replaced closed carriages. But by the 1920s Ford's price cuts, General Motors's graduated prices and models and their innovative installment purchase plan, and a flourishing used-car market put elegant closed cars within the reach of average motorists. Production of sedans and coupes rose from 22 percent of all U.S. and Canadian output in 1921 to 89 percent in 1929.[10] With attractive colors and plush upholstery, even inexpensive closed cars for the masses were comfortable "rooms on wheels."

Almost overnight, the sedan became an essential adjunct to the middle-class home. Housewives, who were expected to manage the household, take care of the children and the family's shopping needs, and drive their husbands to and from the commuter train station, preferred sedans because of the comforts they afforded and the secure environment they provided for children. The sedan proved to be so compatible with the home in other ways that it became virtually an extra room. Architectural historian Folke T. Kihlstedt pointed out that the relationship of house and closed car was so strong that the parlor atrophied as the automobile became the place of choice for intimate socializing and travel to places of diversion. In recognition of the family sedan's growing indispensability and roomlike environment, Kihlstedt noted, the garage was moved from the obscurity of the backyard to a prominent spot beside and attached to the house.[11]

The closed car's advantages for touring were not obvious at first. Its interior tended to be hotter than a touring car and not as well ventilated, and the greater weight of a closed car caused it to vibrate on rough roads or sink into mud. But motorists came to appreciate the privacy of a sedan and the protection it offered from wind, rain, and cool nighttime temperatures. As early as 1915 Samuel Sproat, an employee of the McCray Refrigerator Company, toured New York and Massachusetts with his wife in a Studebaker sedan specially equipped with seats that converted to a double bed.[12] In the 1920s many autocampers placed commercially made cots or auto beds inside their sedans, and many others altered the automobile's seats so that they could form beds. So many Ford Model T owners cut and hinged their seats for sleeping purposes that one make of automobile bed, the ABC Ford Car Bed, was designed to be placed on the folded-down seats inside a Ford sedan.[13]

At least one automobile manufacturer sold a moderately priced closed car with a built-in bed. In October 1923 Willys-Overland introduced the Overland Champion, a small sedan with an interior that could be converted to a sleeping compartment by removing the front-seat back and rearranging the seat cushions. The rear seat area, with the seat removed, also could be used to carry cargo. In June 1924 the Champion was renamed the Overland coupe-sedan but retained the special bed feature.[14]

Like owners of custom-body automobiles, some affluent owners of closed cars preferred to have their bedding arrangements custom made by professional body makers. In 1924 the J. B. Judkins Company, a closed-car body maker in Merrimac, Massachusetts, built a one-off sleeper body for a customer in Columbus, Ohio. This automobile, which had a landau-type body on a Lincoln chassis, had hinged front-seat backs that were held in place by locking plates until lowered for night use. The rear seat had two lower cushions; at the turn of a handle, the bottom cushion rolled forward to meet the lowered front-seat back. The other lower cushion on the rear seat tilted to form a pillow.[15] In 1925 a Pierce-Arrow owner in New Rochelle, New York, had his car modified by a local shop so that he could tour and sleep in it en route to Florida. The shop removed the glass partition and installed front seats with hinged backs that folded down until the robe rail rested on the floor. The seat back aligned with the rear seat to form a bed, and air mattresses were inflated and placed on the bed.[16]

HOUSE CARS

In the late 1910s and early 1920s motorists of average means began paying more attention to the "carriage" side of the horseless carriage. When the moderately priced touring car first appeared owners were attracted to its engine and transmission, which provided a reliable, low-maintenance substitute for a horse; the plain, open body was not very different from a buggy. The touring car and its smaller companion, the runabout, took the place of the horse. Automobiles were used to pull plows and wagons on farms. For recreational purposes, automobiles were used in masculine sports patterned after horse events, such as racing and auto polo. On hunting, fishing, and autocamping trips, the

A Chicago family and their early 1920s house car. (Courtesy National Geographic Society)

touring car became a mechanical packhorse with bags of paraphernalia strapped to its fenders and runningboards. But in the 1920s, as middle-class men and women discovered closed cars and learned to appreciate the attractiveness and comfort of fine upholstery and handy accessories, more motorists began to use this type of vehicle on vacation trips.

Popular in the 1920s, scaled-down versions of Roland and Mary Conklin's Gypsy Van provided much more comfort than a sedan. House cars, like autocamping rigs, were enjoyed by average-income families and couples who wished to experience feelings of intimacy and cohesiveness while they "abandoned" their homes and explored America. But to house-car owners, "living like Gypsies" meant traveling in quaint homes on wheels with domestic comforts and avoiding the primitive, semiprivate conditions of tent camping. House-car owners were less interested in living informally off the land and more interested in the closed car's ability to extend and facilitate their travels with a for-mal replica of home. Elaborately furnished house cars were an accepted form of autocamping even though their owners conspicuously rejected some of the most basic autocamping principles. House-car owners enjoyed nature while being insulated from it, appeared to live a simple, nomadic existence while enjoying an abundance of material possessions, and forsook the responsibilities of maintaining a home while carrying many of their favorite comforts and conveniences with them. These contradictions grew out of autocampers' tendency to reconstruct their home environments on the road, their attachment to the enjoyable qualities of the home environment, and their attraction to versatile, comfortable closed bodies.

The appeal of house cars also reflected contemporary changes in the middle-class home. In contrast to the large, ornate, and formal homes of the Victorian era, middle-class homes in the progressive era were small, simple, and efficient, which provided for easy maintenance and a cozy, comfortable atmosphere. Historian Clifford Edward Clark Jr. found that families of the early twentieth century increasingly thought of their houses not as opulent statements of material success and social propriety but as practical, manageable staging areas for family activities.[17] The bungalow, a residential design derived from British homes in India and introduced to Americans in southern California, added openness, intimacy with nature, and rustic, natural materials. Clark further asserted that the sparseness, simplicity, and back-to-nature appeal of the bungalow were advertised by home builders as a retrenchment from urban living and conspicuous consumption in favor of a more healthful, simplistic, and pseudorural lifestyle.[18] House cars offered the same virtues as bungalows—informality and closeness to nature—with the added appeal of mobility and constantly changing scenery. Indeed, house cars were often called motor bungalows. The widespread appeal of bungalows attracted many Americans to the house-car pastime and eased the transition from living in a house to living in a compact home on wheels.

Better highways made house cars more practical and contributed to their popularity. In the 1920s federal and state governments sponsored numerous improvements in highway grading, alignment, surfacing, bridges, and signage. House cars and other heavy vehicles could travel faster and with less risk of bogging down, tipping over, or shaking uncontrollably. Roadside mom-and-pop establishments flourished; many men and women earned their living by selling gasoline or operating roadside restaurants, autocamps, tourist cabins, and produce stands. Automobile clubs and oil companies distributed road maps that were ever more detailed and accurate. In contrast to pioneer motorists of the early 1910s, motorists in the 1920s had less need for an elite establishment to blaze a trail for them across the nation. Highways were being made user-friendly by tax-supported improvements and commercial exploitation in response to the rapidly growing number of leisure and business trips by average motorists.

Unlike closed cars, mass production and mass marketing did not make house cars affordable to average-income tourists. Motorists who were attracted to the idea of a cozy home on wheels, like the Gypsy Van, designed their own house-car bodies made of wood, fiber board, metal, or canvas and placed them on new or used automobile chassis. Although several independent manufacturers sold house car-bodies in small quantities in the 1920s, most tourists preferred personalized, one-off models that they either made themselves or ordered from a nearby body maker. Motorists who enjoyed building bodies from scratch could spend as little or as much money as they wished. If they chose to commission a house car, they merely visited the nearest city or large town; the decentralized nature of the body-making business meant that qualified body makers were available everywhere. No matter how extensively house-car manufacturers advertised or how moderate prices became, relatively few autocampers became interested in factory-built house cars ordered from a catalog.

From the beginning, house-car travel, like autocamping, was a diversion that husbands and wives enjoyed together. In 1916 a young Iowa printer and his wife traveled through the West in a house car that they had made by removing the body from a touring car and replacing it with an oak-frame living compartment. The yellow, boxlike body had a swinging door, windows with cretonne drapes, lockers, and a cupboard for dishes. A canvas fly was used to cover outdoor cooking and dining. The printer and his wife carried camping equipment, including a folding table, camp stools, steamer chairs, a camp stove, white enamel dishes, and cooking utensils.[19] In the same year A. W. Robins, a printer from San Francisco, and his wife, Lucy, traveled in a 14-foot house car named the Adventurer. This vehicle's body was made of sheet metal over a pine frame and was attached to a touring-car chassis with a truck extension. The Adventurer's interior was equipped with a lounge-bed, dresser, folding table and chairs, writing desk, window curtains, washbasin with running water, ice chest, cookstove, toilet, bath, and gas and electric lights. The Robinses carried a selection of books, a medicine chest, phonograph, fire extinguisher, and "household necessities." In May 1916 they left San Francisco with their English bulldog, Monk, on an extended trip in the direction of Chicago and New York. Their objective was "wanderlust," and they carried a small printing press to earn money along the way.[20] The Robinses thought of their vehicle more as a home than an imitation of a home. In the security of their portable living space, they felt comfortable living on the road even for an extended period of time. With no particular schedule or itinerary, they preserved the feeling of nomadism that made autocamping so appealing.

Many house-car owners were connected with the automobile industry, but unlike owners of camping cars in the early 1910s, they were mechanically inclined technicians, not business executives. Some were skilled workers in the automobile manufacturing industry, which was highly decentralized and employed machinists in large factories and small shops throughout the United States. A typical automobile assembler and house-car builder was David J. H. Bacon of Wilmington, Delaware. During Bacon's varied career, he was an engineer on a pilot boat, vice president of the Delaware Marine Motor Company, a machinist at the Hagley black powder works of E. I. du Pont de Nemours and Company, and helped to build the du Pont automobile, which was introduced in 1919 by du Pont Motors. In 1921 Bacon designed a house car for his personal use, and the following year the completed body was installed on a White chassis. The walls were made of four-ply canvas and the top of California redwood. Inside were a sofa bed, bunk beds, window curtains, a two-burner cooking stove, kitchen sink, and a phonograph. Bacon, his wife, Bertha, and their two children used the house car during a vacation trip to Solomons Island, Maryland, on the western shore of Chesapeake Bay. Later they used it as a winter residence at the same location.

Another automobile maker and house-car owner was Fred Kohlmeyer, a German-born machinist and truck builder in Loganville, Wisconsin. Kohlmeyer had built a number of automobiles in Loganville in the late 1910s; he chose the name Klondike for these automobiles because he had prospected for gold in Alaska in the late 1890s. In about 1921 he built a 28-foot house car with beaver board siding and a thin, light pine interior. The house car was equipped with electric lights, a pressurized water system, and a chemical toilet. Kohlmeyer built the house car for a winter trip to Long Beach, California, but it is not known whether the journey was completed.[21]

Workers in the trucking business also became interested in house cars. Lee Scoles, a truck and charter-bus owner and operator in Fort Wayne, Indiana, built a house-car body out of wood and tin and placed it on a 1916 Federal truck chassis. In 1921 Scoles, his wife, Constance, their children, relatives, and friends—twelve people in all—visited Colorado Springs, toured Yellowstone National Park, camped in the mountains of New Mexico, and drove through the Mojave Desert and the Petrified Forest National Monument in the house car. The women in the party slept on padded boards inside the house car and the men outside on cots. A kitchen outfit was stored in the side of the house car, and a wooden table folded down from the side of the vehicle for outdoor dining. After returning to Fort Wayne, Scoles removed the house-car body and placed the chassis in his fleet of trucks for short- and long-distance hauling.

As interest in house cars grew, articles in automotive magazines provided a way to share designs and floor plans and promote the hobby of house-car building. As early as 1916 *Fordowner* published photographs and dimensions of C. W. Lindsay's Auto-Home and asked readers for their opinions and suggestions.[22] Similar articles in *Ford Owner and Dealer*, *Popular Mechanics*, and other magazines included drawings and useful tips for building a better house car—one that was safer, more convenient, and easier to drive.[23] Experienced autocampers recommended types of chassis with adequate wheelbase, power, and gearing. They also warned readers about the pitfalls of inadequate or improper house-car body design and construction. Professional body makers were also attentive to the demand for house cars, the range of experimentation, and the variety of designs that were being developed. The editors of *Motor Vehicle Monthly* wrote: "As spring approaches, thousands begin to look forward eagerly to camping trips and a good many of these lovers of the outdoors are so enthusiastic in their anticipation of their va-

Traveling to a national park in a house car was an exciting adventure for many Americans in the 1920s. This well-equipped family drove to Yellowstone National Park in 1923. (Courtesy National Park Service, Yellowstone National Park)

cations that they undertake early and elaborate preparations to insure, as far as possible, their comfort and convenience. Inquiries and orders for automobile camping bodies result in not a few instances."[24]

Technical education instructors and administrators were enthusiastic contributors of house-car plans. In 1923 Ray F. Kuns, principal of an automotive trade school in Cincinnati, Ohio, and a veteran autocamper, wrote a two-part article for *Popular Mechanics* in which he described a wooden-frame house car that he had designed and built with the help of Gustav M. Nyman, a teacher at Woodward High School in Cincinnati. Kuns traveled more than 5,000 miles in his Kamp-Kar, including a trip to the upper peninsula of Michigan. Nyman and his wife accompanied Kuns and his wife on at least one trip in the Kamp-Kar.[25] In another article for *Industrial-Arts Magazine*, a magazine for shop teachers, Kuns offered to send free plans of the Kamp-Kar to readers upon request.[26] Albert G. Bauersfeld, supervisor of technical curricu-

House-car travel combined indoor living and outdoor activities. During a trip to Yellowstone National Park in 1925, the Kinnears lived in a house car with lace curtains and other homelike furnishings, but they wore camping and hiking clothes. (Courtesy National Park Service, Yellowstone National Park)

lum for Chicago's high schools, grew tired of setting up a tent and other camping equipment during family autocamping trips and decided to build a house car. He studied other house cars and sketched what he believed would be the simplest, most practical body. Bauersfeld arranged to build the body at a Chicago technical school during a summer session; he was assisted by Victor Olsen, a woodworking teacher, William A. Sears, an auto mechanics teacher, and several students. The design was a group effort, and ideas evolved during the course of construction. Bauersfeld and his family circled Lake Michigan in the completed house car, which had a wooden body frame and beds that let down from the sides. At an autocamp near Sault Ste. Marie, they met Ray Kuns, who was traveling in his house on wheels, and the two families became close friends. Bauersfeld published photographs, drawings, and a description of his house car in *Industrial-Arts*

The Motor Chapel St. Peter carried Catholic missionaries through southern Texas in 1913. One of the earliest enclosed sleeping vehicles, it contained an altar, confessional, cooking equipment, storage lockers, and berths for three people. (Courtesy Catholic Church Extension Society)

Magazine for the benefit of teachers who might wish to build a similar house car for use in their leisure time.[27]

In addition to automotive technicians, men and women whose livelihoods depended on motor vehicles were attracted to homes on wheels. In the early 1920s Lester Rouse, an automobile dealer in Alhambra, California, traveled more than 8,000 miles in his house car.[28] In Lake City, Florida, Carroll B. Messer, the proprietor of Duval Tourist Camp, Duval Garage, and a gasoline station, owned a house car built in 1928.[29] Some automotive businessmen's house cars rivaled the Gypsy Van in their elaborateness, luxury, and completeness. In 1925 Bearl Sprott, proprietor of the Lincoln Park Auto Camp in Los Angeles, owned a buslike house car decorated with murals depicting western scenery and the official seals of California, the city of Los Angeles, and the Tourist Camp Owners Association of California.[30] Martin W.

Trester, an automobile dealer in Denver, designed the Motor Palace and had it built at a cost of about $16,000. The exterior was painted blue, and the interior was finished with gray sheet metal. The Motor Palace was furnished with beds, a folding table, silverware, glassware, nonbreakable dishes, flower vases, and window shades. Utilities included hot and cold running water, a shower, toilet, stove, and electric lights. Trester, his wife, Laura, and their poodle, Rags, left Denver in 1920 for a three-year trip. They toured Colorado, Kansas, Oklahoma, Texas, New Mexico, Wyoming, Montana, Washington, and Oregon.[31]

Enthusiasm for house cars was not limited to automotive business people, mechanically proficient men, and their wives. House-car owners were a fairly diverse group that included people from many walks of life. Farmers, ministers, bankers, realtors, and many other average-income Americans were attracted to the pleasures of owning and traveling in a home on wheels. As more families chose to spend their leisure time on the road, some felt that an elaborate house car provided just the right level of comfort and convenience. These families either built or commissioned house cars to serve as their vacation vehicles.

Farmers had formed an important market for new and used cars since the early years of the century, and many joined the ranks of motor tourists and house-car owners. Isolated farm families keenly felt a sense of detachment and deprivation and had an intense desire to see the world outside their sparsely settled communities. Autocamping provided an effective way to see the rest of the country, and house cars were the most efficient form of autocamping. As early as 1916 a midwestern farm couple built a wood-and-canvas sleeping compartment on top of a high-wheel automobile chassis and went touring in the Rocky Mountains. They carried hens for a supply of fresh eggs.[32]

Some prosperous farmers could afford to commission elaborate, fully furnished house cars. One eastern farmer paid $16,000 for a 30-foot house car on a truck chassis to enjoy during his retirement. Designed according to his specifications, the house-car body was furnished with couches that turned into beds, a kitchen, bathroom, and a porch on the rear with cots for outdoor sleeping. The owner, his family, and two guests departed on a lengthy tour of the United States and planned to remain on the road two years.[33] In about 1920 Charles A. Hyde, a farmer and Moline tractor dealer in Clear Spring, Maryland, commissioned the Crawford, an elaborate house car built according to his plans by the Crawford Automobile Company in nearby Hagerstown. Built on a Crawford truck chassis, this vehicle had beds, a stove, sink, and a dynamo that powered electric lights. The exterior was decorated with pictures of President Woodrow Wilson and General John Pershing (Hyde so revered these leaders that he named his sons Wilson Hyde and John Pershing Hyde). The house car had a rear platform with bathing equipment, including a curtain, shower, and lavatory. Hyde and his family planned to tour the West but cancelled the trip when their financial situation worsened in the postwar depression.[34]

Printers seem to have had a special fascination with house cars. One resourceful printer built a house-car body and covered the sides with discarded printing plates. Another, Wilber F. Persons of Delevan, New York, owned a house car with whimsical features including a cow-catcher and a large picture window. A newspaper publisher and president of the Empire Type and Foundry Company, Persons had his house-car body built by Wallace Cheeseman, a local cabinetmaker, and installed it on a Brockway chassis in a barn behind the Empire plant. The interior was finished in natural Philippine mahogany and had blue leather chairs that folded into beds, electric lights and fans, a kitchen with china racks, and a bathroom with washbasin and flush toilet. Special accessories included a radio, phonograph, typewriter, and an icebox with a drinking water coil. In the late 1920s and early 1930s Persons took many trips through the Northeast and enjoyed scenic spots such as Saranac Lake and the Catskill Mountains as well as Boston, New York, and other major cities.[35]

Missionaries and evangelists were attracted to house cars because they could spread the gospel to more people during an extended road trip. In 1913 a member of the Catholic Women's Auxiliary presented the Motor Chapel St. Peter to the Catholic Church Extension Society. This vehicle had an enclosed, trucklike body built by Jacob Press Sons, a wagon manufacturer in Chicago, and an Alco chassis built by the truck division of the American Locomotive Company of Providence, Rhode Island. Built for itinerant missionaries near the Rio Grande River in Texas, the truck had a fold-out chapel with electric lights and living space for two priests and a chauffeur. The mobile chapel contained three sleeping berths suspended on brass chains and two folding army cots, which could be used outdoors.[36] Five years later itinerant evangelist Nels Thompson built a house-car body, placed it on a truck chassis, and covered the exterior with hand-lettered Bible verses. He preached from the rear platform, and the interior was his home. After holding revival services in San Diego, he spoke to groups across the United States and planned to continue his ministry in Sweden.[37]

By the 1920s some religious professionals were using house cars for personal pleasure trips. Bishop Edward Fawcett of the Episcopal Diocese in Quincy, Illinois, spent the summer of 1924 touring New England with his wife and daughter in a house car.[38] Reverend Arthur G. Tippett, a minister in Odessa, Delaware, was photographed in his house car for *Motor Camper and Tourist,* an autocamping magazine that flourished in the mid-1920s.[39]

HOUSE CARS FOR WEALTHY AMERICANS

Since the early twentieth century the size, make, body type, degree of luxury, and styling of automobiles have identified the economic and social status of their owners. Packard owners and Model T owners may have shared the same roads, but they did not share the same lifestyle. In his definitive history, *Americans on the Road,* Warren Belasco found evidence that autocamping was a striking exception to this stratification. According to Belasco, autocamping was a leveling experience that commingled wealthy, middle-class, and working people, urban and rural Americans, and people from different regions. An unwritten rule of autocamping was that participants had to forget their social status and treat each other as equals and neighbors.[40]

House cars, however, tended to separate travelers because wealthy house-car owners made full use of the privacy that their vehicles offered. House-car owners of average means usually were happy to show other autocampers their "rigs" and often took them inside, but house cars of the wealthy typically carried a sign reading PRIVATE to ward off curious neighbors and those who might mistake the buslike vehicles for public transportation. Wilber Persons considered building and selling house cars similar to his "locomotive" on wheels. The brochure for his proposed Roamer included these pleas for privacy: "Look as long as you like from the outside" and "To evade answering a multitude of questions this slip is respectfully offered." Persons set a price of $10,500 for the Roamer, an amount that the average autocamper could not possibly afford.[41]

With large sums of money available, one-off house cars of the wealthy were conspicuously larger and more sophisticated than the wooden boxes on wheels of middle-class motorists. Luxury house cars were longer, more powerful, and better furnished, and their interiors resembled private railroad cars rather than homes. Walls, furnishings, and fixtures were covered with the finest woods, fabrics, and metals. Some luxury house cars even had a rear observation platform with a metal railing—an elitist design element borrowed from private railroad cars and observation cars on luxury passenger trains.

Like house-car owners of average means, many wealthy house-car enthusiasts were connected either directly or indirectly to the motor vehicle industry. One of the earliest wealthy house-car owners was Edwin J. Fithian, an industrialist in Pennsylvania's oil-producing region. Like Henry Joy and Roland Conklin, Fithian made significant contributions to the nascent motor vehicle industry. After varied careers as a carpenter, builder, contractor, and physician, Fithian began a new career in 1898 when he invented an engine clutch for pumps used in Pennsylvania's oil fields. In 1899 he and a partner, John Carruthers, formed a company to manufacture gas engines that would replace steam-powered pumps then in use at oil wells. Fithian's and Carruthers's Bessemer brand gas engines sold well in the first years of the twentieth century and were applied to many uses, including pumps, compressors, and gasoline refining.[42] Between 1910 and 1920, according to one source, nine-tenths of all gasoline refineries used Bessemer brand engines.[43]

Built by the McKay Carriage Company in Grove City, Pennsylvania, in about 1918, Fithian's house-car body was attached to a 1917 Winton touring car chassis that had been extended to a wheelbase of 221 inches. The interior was trimmed with cut velvet and had silk window shades and was furnished with a sink, water tank (under the body), icebox, washbowl with hand pump, and toilet. The exterior of the body was covered with varnished wood paneling on the lower part and leather on the upper part. Fithian used his house car off and on for eight years. In 1918 he was an unsuccessful candidate for governor of Pennsylvania on the Prohibition Party ticket; he slept and dined in the house car while campaigning across the state. He also received visitors and wrote campaign advertisements for newspapers in the house car. The house car was used during trips to Colorado and other destinations between 1921 and 1926; then it was stored on blocks in Fithian's garage.[44]

Another oil baron who owned a house car was Walter K. Campbell, president of the Western Oil Corporation of Tulsa, Oklahoma. In about 1921 Campbell hired Philip J. Lang, a body maker in Tulsa, to build a house-car body. Placed on a White chassis, Campbell's Tulsahoma had beds, cots, a sofa that also served as a bed, a gasoline stove, icebox, sink, hot and cold water, shower bath, and electric lights. Campbell, his wife, and daughter planned to spend three months traveling from Tulsa to the Pacific Ocean and back in the Tulsahoma.[45]

Truck executives were also attracted to house cars. In 1919 Charles G. Barley, president of the Indiana Truck Corporation, a manufacturer in Marion, Indiana, had his shop build a 30-foot house car named the Helomido after Helen, Louise, Mildred, and Dorothy Stephenson, daughters of company vice president J. W. Stephenson. The Barleys and their friends, Harry and Kitty Goldthwaite, traveled in the Helomido to San Francisco; their chauffeur was Albert L. Spangler, a machinist in the Indiana truck factory.[46] The Bekins family of Bekins Van and Storage Company used a one-off house car named Nav Snikeb (Bekins Van spelled backward) with a boxlike body mounted on a Reo truck chassis. The house-car interior had a walnut finish and was furnished with a sink, stove, closet, toilet, and beds for four people. In July 1925 four members of the Bekins family traveled through the Northeast in the Nav Snikeb to visit storage warehouses and locate potential Bekins agents. They mixed pleasure with business and enjoyed sightseeing, roadside and city restaurants, theatrical shows (including the Ziegfeld Follies), golf, a stroll on the Boardwalk in Atlantic City, and a dip in the Atlantic Ocean. Other members of the Bekins family used the Nav Snikeb during trips to California, Chicago, Yellowstone National Park, and other destinations.[47]

By the mid-1920s bus-sized house cars were built for wealthy Americans using actual bus chassis, particularly the White but other makes as well. From the outside these house cars resembled intercity buses. In 1925 H. H. Linn, a manufacturer of tractor-tread trucks and snow plows in Morris, New York, commissioned the Linn Haven, a long, buslike house car with tandem rear axles. Its Safeway chassis was made by the Six-Wheel Company, a manufacturer of tandem-axle buses and trucks in Philadelphia, and it had four rear drive wheels. The body was made by the Gustav Schaefer Wagon Company in Cleveland, Ohio, a wagon manufacturer that had added truck and bus bodies to its product line. Emblazoned on the side was the advertisement LINN TRACK-LAYING TRACTORS.

The interior of the Linn Haven had gray leather upholstery, sage-green curtains, a folding table and four chairs with suction-cup bases, and two folding double beds. A separate Kohler generator, added about two years after the vehicle was built, powered an electric range, water heater, fan, radio, and other appliances. The vehicle was equipped with a toilet, lavatory, and shower. Linn and his wife traveled extensively in the vehicle and were often accompanied by Linn's secretary and his wife. With an office in the rear, Linn used the vehicle to visit West Coast branches of the Republic Motor Truck Company, which acquired the Linn Manufacturing Company in 1927.[48]

Another buslike house car of the mid-1920s was the Flordellen, a 31-foot vehicle belonging to Leonard S. Whittier of Elmira, New York. Whittier was the retired secretary and part owner of the Eclipse Machine Company in Elmira, which manufactured the Bendix starter drive and other mechanical devices for automobiles, motorcycles, and bicycles. He planned to travel to Florida, Churchill Downs, New York City, and other destinations in the magnificent home on wheels, which he named by combining the first names of family members. The aluminum-paneled body of the Flordellen, which was painted two-tone green with cream and tan trim, was made by Whitfield and Sons, a maker of bus bodies in Penn Yan, New York. It was placed on a Brockway Model H bus chassis with a 200-inch wheelbase. The windows had Protex wire glass, a substitute for plate glass that would not break into dangerous shards on impact. The interior of the Flordellen had mahogany woodwork, crepe-mohair drapes with orange, green, and brown stripes, wicker chairs, upholstered chairs that converted into beds, an all-electric kitchen, and a bathroom. Following the land yacht idea literally, Whittier and his party enjoyed nautical features such as a ship's clock, chart board, and marine instruments to forecast the weather.[49]

Francis H. Buzzacott, writer, veteran, big-game hunter, and autocamping equipment dealer, drove a house car on a world tour in 1929. In Washington, D.C., he posed for a photograph at the Lincoln Memorial. (Courtesy Library of Congress)

In 1929 General Motors's truck division in Pontiac, Michigan, built a buslike house car for Paul W. Seiler, president of GM's Yellow Truck and Coach Manufacturing Company. Named the Carcajou (French-Canadian for "wolverine"), this company-owned home on wheels accommodated seven people and had upper berths and mohair-upholstered seats that converted into beds. The interior was finished in brown mahogany with maple inlay. The kitchen had a sink made of Monel Metal, hot and cold running water, a gasoline stove, and a refrigerator. The Carcajou also had heaters, electric fans, and a radio.[50]

By the mid-1920s some wealthy Americans who had no connection with the automobile industry or the promotion of highway travel were turning to house cars as an alternative to railroad travel. An elaborate, fully equipped house car provided most of the amenities of a private railroad car but was more personalized and flexible. One of the best-known examples of a wealthy businessman's house car was the Ark, owned by Will Keith Kellogg. The man who put cornflakes on America's breakfast tables enjoyed the latest recreation vehicle, a plush, bus-like house car designed to his specifications. Kellogg loved to travel to broaden his knowledge, ease his insomnia, and escape the pressures of his business. Of his vacation home on wheels, he said, "When tired of making Kellogg's Corn Flakes, I find the Ark an incentive to rest."[51]

The dark blue body of the Ark, which was made of aluminum sheeting over an ash frame, was built in 1923 by the Bender Body Company of Cleveland, Ohio, a maker of automobile, truck, and bus bodies. The body was placed on a White Model 50 chassis, the first chassis designed especially for buses (instead of trucks) and mass produced for the bus market. The 5.5-ton vehicle moved at speeds of 30 to 35 miles per hour and averaged 7.5 to 8 miles per gallon of gasoline. Inside the Ark, Kellogg, his wife, and their relatives enjoyed a handsome interior finished with mahogany panels, maroon Spanish leather upholstery, folding tables, and a nickel washbasin. They rode in four adjustable swivel chairs upholstered in taupe mohair, which converted into sleeping berths at night. In addition to a kitchen and a bathroom with shower, they enjoyed such extras as a radio, ice machine, sliding glass partition between the chauffeur and the passenger compartment, and a telephone that linked the passengers to the chauffeur. The Ark also carried a 16-foot folding boat with a gasoline motor.[52]

Like all house cars, the Ark especially attracted attention wherever it went, and the promotional opportunities did not escape Kellogg. In 1928, after five years of occasional use for pleasure trips, the Ark was converted into a mobile sales unit for Kellogg's products. In 1928 and 1929 it toured eleven states offering samples of breakfast products that were, like the Ark itself, real eye-openers.

HOUSE CARS AS HOUSING

By the 1920s house cars had become so common that people of average means were using them as portable housing. Living on the road in the personalized, protective surroundings of a well-furnished house car no longer seemed extraordinary; migrating families, writers, entertainers, and other peripatetic Americans found house cars to be a practical, or at least expedient, home away from home. Although house-car dwellers enjoyed traveling and sightseeing, they especially sought the mobility that a house car provided. House-car dwellers went beyond vacationing and actually took up residence in remote communities

In about 1919 Norman M. Mason moved his family from New Jersey to California in a house car that he made by attaching a bus body to an Oldsmobile truck chassis. After arriving on the West Coast, Mason lived in the house car and commuted to work in it. (Courtesy George T. Mason)

and rural areas for weeks or months at a time. At the end of each day they found the familiar space inside the house car, combined with the abundant resources of small towns and local people along the way, quite comforting.

For families who moved to new, distant homes, a house car, with its familiarity, individuality, and self-sufficiency, was a modern prairie schooner. During the last three months of 1920, Thomas B. Slate, an inventor who had patented improvements to airplane propellors, internal combustion engines, ball bearings, crankshafts, and other transportation devices, lived with his wife, Edith, and their two small children in a homemade house car in the Maryland suburbs near Washington, D.C. Built on a Ford chassis, the house car had two beds, a dresser, wardrobe, curtains, window shades, a kitchen, and a bathroom. The Slates were struggling with illness and financial insecurity;

By the 1920s some Americans lived in house cars and used their enhanced mobility as a way to a better future. For several months in 1920 Thomas and Edith Slate and their children lived in a homemade house car near Washington, D.C. The following year, they set out for a new home in Oregon in their modern prairie schooner. (Courtesy Oregon Historical Society, neg. OrHi 74778)

their most recent residence had been the Women's Commonwealth Farm near Washington, where Edith recovered from tuberculosis. In April 1921 the Slates left Washington in the house car to move to a new home in Oregon, Edith's native state. Unfortunately, after four months of leisurely sightseeing, the vehicle overturned in Nebraska and was damaged beyond repair.[53]

Another migrating family who lived in a house car were the Masons of Glen Rock, New Jersey. Norman M. Mason lost his wife in the 1918 influenza epidemic and lived with his mother, Amelia, and his small children, Norman, Robert, George, and Elisabeth, in a house in Glen Rock. In about 1919, after Mason's own health began to deteriorate, he decided to move to California to improve his health and start a new life for his family. A skilled machinist, factory worker, automobile mechanic, and chauffeur, Mason removed the cab and body from an Oldsmobile truck, lengthened the chassis, and placed a bus body on the chassis. He bolted bunk beds, chairs, and a dresser to the floor and furnished the body with removable hammocks, a phonograph, music

A mobile lifestyle facilitated the careers of some writers and other professionals. In the 1920s Mary Chapman and her husband, Stan, traveled extensively in their Nomad and gathered ideas for juvenile novels and nonfiction articles. (Courtesy Maristan Chapman Collection, University of Oregon, Division of Special Collections)

box, medicine chest, and other furnishings. He also installed a sink with running water, a kerosene stove with detachable oven, an icebox, and a fireless cooker with pieces of concrete that were heated in the stove.

Leaving their home in Glen Rock, the Masons traveled across the United States in the house car, which he named Marty Coast to Coast after a woman he was dating. Following the Lincoln Highway most of the way, the Masons stopped at autocamps or visited friends and relatives. In the West they spent some nights at private ranches. The ranch owners were happy to have visitors and conversation, and the Mason children played with the ranchers' children and looked at animals. On the road many people wanted to see the house car. The Masons distributed picture postcards of it.

After their arrival in California, the Masons temporarily lived in a camp near Malibu. Mason and his mother slept in the house car and the children in a tent. He also commuted in the house car to Santa Monica, where he had purchased a service station. A California resident the rest of his life, he later purchased a Pierce-Arrow truck and operated a trucking and heavy equipment business. He sold the house car in the 1920s and last saw it in 1931 in Burbank, where it was serving as an office for a junkyard.[54]

Some entertainers chose to live in homes on wheels because of the itinerant nature of their work. In the early 1920s Charles and Helen Polley toured with a vaudeville show and lived with their child in a house car. For the Polleys, a private, homelike vehicle was an appealing alternative to one-night stays in hotels and boarding houses that catered to show people.[55] For less than $500, John Bowers, a dramatic actor who starred in silent films in the 1910s and 1920s, designed and built a house car on a Ford chassis for his professional and recreational activities. Like a versatile stage set, the one-room interior had furniture and hinged boards that shifted to convert the space into a living room, dining room, bedroom, kitchen, or bathroom. Bowers used the house car for pleasure trips, as a residence in his hometown, and at his "localities of business"—presumably filming locations.[56] Chief Two Moon (Chico Meridan), a Hispanic-American medicine-show operator who posed as a Blackfoot Indian, capitalized on widespread popular belief in the natural healing powers of native Americans and toured the country in a well-equipped house car, selling laxatives, cough elixirs, and other health remedies. His entourage traveled in luxury automobiles and slept in portable tepees.[57]

Charles G. Phillips, a traveling tent show producer in Cortland, Ohio, owned an ornate house car in the early 1920s. Built at a cost of more than $4,000, the 22-foot, cream-colored vehicle had wooden exterior panels, stained glass and beveled plate-glass windows, silk drapes, twin beds, and a table. Utilities included a stove, lavatory, and lights operated by a portable electric light plant. From the 1890s to the 1920s Phillips owned and operated a tent show that toured extensively in wagons and presented the play *Uncle Tom's Cabin* as well as motion pictures. In later years Phillips led the wagon procession in his house car. He also used the house car to travel to Florida each winter. On the way to Florida in November 1931, the house car was struck by a train at a crossing near South Charleston, Ohio. Phillips suffered severe injuries and died two days after the accident.[58]

Several fiction writers absorbed the colorful surroundings and cul-

In the 1920s Charles G. Phillips managed a traveling theatrical show and led a procession of wagons in an ornate house car with stained glass windows and silk drapes. He also drove the house car to Florida each winter. (Courtesy Library of Congress)

tures of rural America in house cars. Traveling in a house car enabled them to live for extended periods in small towns and rural places. Another bonus was that the house car invariably attracted local citizens. These glimpses of everyday life often provided inspiration for entertaining literary works. Pearl Doles Bell, an author of juvenile novels, took trips in an 18-foot house car with her husband, George Bell. Erle Stanley Gardner, a California attorney and a prolific writer of pulp detective stories and crime mystery novels, often took off alone into the desert in his house car to find solitude, relaxation, and inspiration. He hunted with a bow and arrow, took photographs, looked for old mines, wrote manuscripts, and gathered ideas for future works. In mining camps he would "switch on the electric lights, get out the drinking whiskey, and entertain characters who let their reminiscences fall on fertile soil."[59]

Stan and Mary Chapman, a notable husband-and-wife writing team, gathered material for novels and articles while roving in their house car, which they named the Nomad. Using the pseudonym Maristan Chapman, they jointly wrote more than thirty novels, including juvenile adventure stories, mysteries, and novels set in Mary's home state of Tennessee. They also wrote short stories, poetry, technical and business articles, and articles on diverse subjects such as agriculture, literature, and camping and touring. The Chapmans also wrote works of fiction under several other pseudonyms, including Jane Selkirk, Dent Ilsley, and Kirk Connell.

The Chapmans' transatlantic romance began in their youth. John Stanton Higham Chapman was born in London. As a teenager he worked as an apprentice in automotive and general engineering. He then became an aircraft engineer, working for the Grahame-White Aviation Company and Geoffrey de Havilland's Aircraft Manufacturing Company in the early 1910s. During World War I, Chapman served in the British Army Reserve as an aircraft production engineer. In 1917 he was detailed to the United States Army Signal Corps to speed up production of de Havilland airplanes, and he was assigned to the Dayton-Wright Airplane Company in Dayton, Ohio. On February 26, 1917, he married Mary Ilsley, who he had met as a child during one of her visits to England. Born in Chattanooga, Tennessee, Ilsley received a degree in literature from the University of Chicago in 1913. That same year she moved to England, her mother's native country, and during the next several years Mary worked as a secretary, first to a member of Parliament and then in the British aircraft service. She was also a schoolteacher and volunteered for the Women's Service Corps during World War I.

After the war ended, the Chapmans spent some time traveling around the United States in an automobile. In the early 1920s they settled in Jacksonville, Florida, where Mary, an aspiring writer, opened a literary agency. The agency was not financially successful, and in 1923 the Chapmans moved to St. Louis, where Stan had accepted a job with Curtis and Company Manufacturing Company, a maker of air compressors, garage compressors, air hoists, clutch discs, traveling cranes, and circular saws.

Stan lost his left hand in a shop accident in 1923 and quit the engineering profession. The couple decided to resume their touring and literary efforts on a grand scale. They commissioned a house car, the Nomad, and they decided to travel around the United States and write books and articles as a team. The Nomad was built and furnished between October 1923 and February 1924. The body, which was made of Vehisote panels on an oak frame, was built to the Chapmans' specifications at a cost of $450 by F. L. Ruzicka, a St. Louis shop that originally made wagons but had switched to making automobile, truck, and bus bodies. The Nomad's body was attached to a Ford Model TT truck chassis purchased for $435 from the Mendenhall Motor Company, an automobile dealer in St. Louis. Among the costs of adapting the body to the chassis were $125 for a chassis frame extension, $111 for an auxiliary transmission, and $28 for external brakes. The body was furnished with a daybed, Morris chair, movable table, kitchen, and their "tools of the trade," including a bookcase, typewriter, and steel letter file.

The Chapmans left St. Louis on March 12, 1924, and lived in the Nomad, writing articles, gathering material for novels, and "doing odd jobs" for two years. They visited Ohio, New York, the North Carolina mountains, Florida, Tennessee, and the Pacific coast. Later they recalled that they had crossed the United States several times and had visited half of the forty-eight states in their home on wheels. The Nomad provided an easy way to attract and meet local citizens; in every town citizens turned out to see the house on wheels, and some thought that the boxy, lumbering vehicle heralded the arrival of a circus. In 1928 the body of the Nomad was removed from the Model TT chassis and placed on a more powerful Graham truck chassis purchased from the Citizens Auto Company, a Dodge dealer in Chattanooga, Tennessee. The Chapmans wrote at least two novels, *Homeplace* (1929) and *The Weather Tree* (1931), in the modified Nomad.[60]

ON THE ROAD IN A HOUSE CAR

What was it like to live in a house car during an extended trip? Unfortunately, few firsthand descriptions of such trips exist. A study of diaries, logbooks, memoirs, newspaper interviews, and oral history interviews sheds some light on food preparation, personal hygiene, daily chores, child care, leisure and play, and other aspects of a house-car voyage. Most important, though, these descriptions reveal interesting similarities and differences between house-car travel and autocamping, and between the house-car environment and the home environment.[61]

In some ways house-car living was similar to autocamping. House-car owners, like autocampers, bought groceries at local general stores, produce stands, and farms. Both groups obtained drinking water from public faucets and washed their clothes in streams. Both groups followed their daily rituals of personal hygiene, cooking and eating, work, rest, and play as they did at home. House-car owners and autocampers alike stopped for the night at autocamps, parks, fields, schoolyards, and other large lots.

There were important differences between perceptions and expectations of house cars and autocamping rigs. A house-car owner was more inclined to think of his or her vehicle as a home, with all of the security and convenience that a home provides. House cars were sealed against the elements and had real furniture, tableware, indoor plumbing, and electric lights; some also had heating. House-car occupants neatly stored their belongings in drawers, cabinets, closets, and compartments instead of tying them to the fenders and runningboards as autocampers did. Edith Slate referred to their vehicle as "our warm little house." She busied herself with household chores such as scrubbing the floor, cleaning the kitchen, and ironing and folding clothes. When she came down with chicken pox, she retreated to her snug bed in the house car. Such domestic activities were not possible in a touring car or a tent.

Food preparation and consumption were also easier in a house car. House-car owners could "eat in" whenever they wished. House cars were quite self-contained, so when stopped, their occupants could begin cooking and eating without unpacking tables, chairs, and a cookstove, as autocampers had to do. Some house-car owners, such as the Slates and the Masons, began preparing meals in the morning and cooked the food slowly as they rolled along.

House cars and autocamping rigs could be used for short trips, but only house-car owners were equipped to take sightseeing trips that lasted months or years. A house car meant the use of fewer roadside services, reducing the inconveniences associated with a long trip. Un-

Gustav de Bretteville (right), a San Francisco real estate agent, introduced a forerunner of the pickup camper in 1916. The Automobile Telescope Touring Apartment, which fit on a Ford Model T, included a bed, cooking equipment, and drawers for clothing and other paraphernalia. (Courtesy California History Room, California State Library, neg. 23,710)

like autocampers, house-car motorists often stayed in one place for days or weeks at a time. During visits with friends and relatives, house-car owners often parked on the lawns of friends' houses, the house car becoming a convenient guest cottage. Some house-car owners even found jobs during their trips. In San Antonio Harold Holloway, a college student who had purchased a used house car for pleasure trips, found work as an electrician, and Norman Mason repaired automobiles while living in Chicago for a month en route from New Jersey to California.

A house-car body was safer and more convenient for small children to sleep and play in than a touring-car body. The Slates often put their children to bed early in the evening and continued driving until they found a resting place for the night. Bathing the children was easier in the privacy and comfort of a house car than in an autocamp. And it was easier to preserve family rituals in a house car, like bringing a pet along or gathering around the phonograph for indoor entertainment.

Autocampers enjoyed socializing with other autocampers, but only house-car owners socialized with house dwellers. Local residents often knocked on the doors of the strange vehicles and asked permission to look inside. The Slates, Holloways, Masons, and other house-car owners made many friends with nearby home owners who were curious about their vehicles. Residents often reciprocated by inviting house-car owners inside their homes for dinner or conversation. Some of these temporary neighbors were concerned about the motorists' safety because they were sleeping in a vehicle instead of a house.

Life in a house car may have been closer to home life than tent camping was, but furnished vehicles differed from houses in significant ways. A typical house car had only one room that served many purposes, and there was little flexibility regarding the arrangement of furniture and use of space. Furniture and accessories were carefully positioned to make maximum use of available space. The furniture in a house car, though similar or identical to domestic pieces, often was bolted or hooked to the floor for safety. Dining tables and beds sometimes were hinged so that they folded flat against a wall when not in use. Occupants had assigned places and had to remain seated while the vehicle was in motion.

Although cramped by late twentieth-century standards, a house car of the 1920s was a marvel to its owners and admirers. Its compactness and completeness were highly regarded as virtues and examples of ingenuity. Unlike Gypsy wagons, house cars were part of the mainstream of American culture and were accessible to all curious motorists. House cars epitomized how automobiles were extending the reach of ordinary Americans. They showed how motorists themselves were helping to change the nature of personal travel. With a house car, a family could visit and live in places they had only read about. In 1929, when juvenile literature magnate Edward Stratemeyer added *Tom Swift and his House on Wheels* to his list of novels about amazing inventions, he placed house cars in the same league as airships, submarines, and other unorthodox means of transportation that enabled humankind to reach remote places and take journeys that once were merely fantasies.[62]

FACTORY-BUILT HOUSE CARS

House cars were not mass produced during the autocamping craze of the 1920s, but builders of truck and bus bodies and other firms made small quantities of house-car bodies for the growing number of auto-campers who preferred indoor comforts. A lack of statistics makes it impossible to determine the number of manufactured house cars that were on the road. Photographic evidence, however, suggests that only a small percentage were chosen from manufacturers' brochures; the majority were one-offs made by shops and individuals. Even house cars that emerged from factories were made by hand. Although their exteriors generally conformed to catalog illustrations, their interiors were often custom fitted with options selected by the buyer from the manufacturer's list. Typically, there were so many options regarding size and furnishings that it is likely that few if any manufactured house cars of a particular make were identical. Some manufacturers even permitted customers to purchase empty body shells and install their own furnishings.

Occasionally manufacturers introduced innovations that made house cars more useful or appealing. As early as 1916 Gustav de Bretteville, a San Francisco real estate agent, introduced a collapsible, all-steel camp-ing attachment that replaced the rear portion of a Ford Model T. Named the Automobile Telescope Touring Apartment, this odd unit— the forerunner of the pickup camper—resembled a large tin can and was equipped with a bed and accessories for cooking and dining. It had a fold-out cooking surface and pantry, an oil stove, kitchen utensils, a detachable, folding dining table with two folding chairs, drawers for clothing and other essentials, bedding for two or three people, and elec-tric lights. The whole unit collapsed to a length of about 3 feet and ex-tended to 6 feet to provide a fully enclosed sleeping space. At least one prototype was made. De Bretteville set up an office in San Francisco to manufacture and sell the units, but it is not known whether his plans ever came to fruition.[63]

In 1921 the Tourist Camp Body Company of Chicago advertised a collapsible house-car body that seated five passengers and could double as a truck. Two beds folded out from the sides, and the top raised to provide 6 feet of standing room inside the vehicle. The owner covered the skeletal outline of the trucklike frame with sheets of khaki cut to the proper sizes and fitted with windows made of glass or celluloid. The rear porch, also enclosed with khaki, served as a dressing room. The company offered Brewster green bodies in two sizes: the Model A for automobiles with a 100-inch wheelbase, including Ford, Dodge, and Maxwell, and the Model B for automobiles and trucks with a 124-inch wheelbase, including Buick and Reo Speed Wagon. The Model A was priced at $400 and the Model B at $500. Furnishings included a folding table (with the beds as seats), a three-shelf cupboard, gasoline stove, 7-gallon water tank, and electric lights.[64]

One of the earliest documented producers of standard, boxlike house-car bodies was William P. Norrington Jr., a British-born automobile body maker in San Francisco. In 1920 or 1921 he completed a one-off house-car body for R. C. Johnson of San Francisco. Johnson, his wife, and their child planned to take an extended pleasure trip in this vehicle, which had a couch bed, folding upper berth, folding glass doors between the living area and the driver's compartment, and western landscapes on the interior walls. After deciding to manufacture house-car bodies, Norrington issued a brochure for the Norrington Auto-Home, which was offered in four sizes ranging from 9 feet to 20 feet in length, and 5 feet to 8 feet in width, for use in extended touring or as a permanent home. The Rough and Ready model was furnished with a single or double folding bed and "other conveniences as may be desired." The Pullman model was more elaborately furnished; it could accommodate two to seven persons and had heat, a kitchen, running water, icebox, shower bath, and electric lights. In 1970 Norrington's son, Ross, recalled that his father made and sold approximately twelve house cars with Dodge chassis.[65]

One of the few nationally advertised house cars originated at an industrial equipment firm in St. Louis. In 1919 George F. Steedman, vice president of Curtis and Company Manufacturing Company, a maker of air compressors, hoists, cranes, steel castings, and saws, commissioned a one-off house car for his personal use. The Road Cruiser Wampus had fold-out beds, a table, kitchen with sink, gas stove, and icebox, closet, and fire extinguisher and was mounted on a Dorris automobile chassis, another St. Louis product. Steedman toured the West in the house car, and in 1920 Curtis president Edwin H. Steedman, his wife, and their two daughters spent six months touring western parks in it.[66] In the early 1920s George F. Steedman and Arthur W. Lambert served as vice president and president of the Camping Car Company, which was formed to manufacture a body similar to that of the Road Cruiser Wampus. The Camping Car Company built another house-car prototype named the Lamsteed Kampkar, which they displayed at an automobile show in Kansas City early in 1921. The body of this prototype, which was mounted on a Ford chassis, was made of poplar and high-carbon, cold-rolled steel panels painted a khaki color. It had sleeping accommodations for four people, two inside and two on beds that folded out from either side. Each bed measured 6 feet 4 inches long by 3 feet 6 inches wide.[67]

The Camping Car Company moved into a former wagon factory in St. Louis. By late 1921 it had issued a brochure for the Lamsteed Kampkar body, which had a poplar frame with light sheet-iron panels. Standard equipment included an icebox, folding table, Prentiss-Wabers Kamp-Kook stove, and aluminum pots, pans, and tableware. The body, including all accessories, was priced at $735, a little less than the price of a Ford Model T sedan. It was designed to fit a Model T chassis.[68]

It is not known how many Lamsteed Kampkar bodies were built, but production continued for several years. By 1923 Lamsteed Kampkar bodies were being built by Anheuser-Busch, a St. Louis brewer. After prohibition took effect in January 1920, the vehicle department at Anheuser-Busch, which repaired beer wagons and trucks, accepted orders from outside customers and built bodies for a wide variety of commercial vehicles—refrigerated milk, ice cream, and meat trucks, armored cars, horse carriers, passenger buses, school buses, and others. The Lamsteed Kampkar was added to this line of special-purpose bodies. Anheuser-Busch advertised the Lamsteed Kampkar in *Field and Stream* and issued a new brochure. The bodies could be ordered to fit many different automobile and truck chassis and the price was reduced to $535, about the price of a Ford Model T coupe. The stove, cooking utensils, and tableware were offered as an option package priced at $30. Little else about the Lamsteed Kampkar had changed under the new management.[69]

Another well-known house-car body was built by Wayne Works, a

Henry Ford, the nation's most famous autocamper, did not manufacture camping vehicles, but house car bodies could be purchased from other companies and mounted on a Ford chassis. Some house cars were surprisingly affordable; a Lamsteed Kampkar body cost about as much as a Ford Model T sedan. (Courtesy National Automobile Museum, the Harrah Collection)

manufacturer of truck and bus bodies in Richmond, Indiana. Established in 1868, Wayne had manufactured horse-drawn road carts and wagons and changed to motor vehicle bodies in the early twentieth century. In the early 1920s company officials learned that motorists were purchasing Wayne bus bodies and furnishing them as house cars. "For several years we have noticed the sale of increasing numbers of our body shells—bodies without upholstering or furnishings—to be fitted out for touring bungalows," Wayne Works president John W. Clements wrote in a brochure for prospective house-car dealers. "Year by year with the development of better roads we sensed the growing demand for a touring body equipped to give every comfort of home. With this incentive we determined to build a touring 'Home' that would meet this popular demand and fulfill every touring requirement."[70]

The Touring Home was placed on the market after vacationers began purchasing empty bus bodies from Wayne Works and furnishing them as campers. The Touring Home came equipped with everything from a heating system to a coffee percolator. (Courtesy National Museum of American History, Smithsonian Institution)

According to a 1923 price list, Wayne Touring Home bodies were available in standard lengths from 11 feet 8 inches to 19 feet 5 inches, and custom bodies as small as 9 feet 1 inch long were available upon request. Vehicle heights varied from 56 inches to 66 inches, and prices ranged from $795 to $925. Wayne promised to fit any automobile chassis, but two models of the Touring Home were designed to fit a Ford truck chassis. They also sold a frame-extension kit for other types of chassis.

The Touring Home body had a steel-reinforced hardwood frame made of oak, ash, and hickory, with plywood panels and roof and a natural interior finish. There were folding beds inside; a tent-covered bed could be lowered by chains from the rear of the vehicle. Standard equipment included interior electric wiring for lights, air vents, a dropleaf table, gasoline stove, sink, pressurized water system, window curtains, and interior divider curtains. According to Wayne sales literature, the exterior of the Touring Home was painted deep Brewster green with black trim and a single gold stripe. Upon request, the owner's name could be painted on both sides in gold-bronze letters shaded in red.[71]

The Touring Home bodies could be purchased fully furnished, partially furnished, or unfurnished. The complete set of optional equipment included everything from electric lights and under-floor heat (from the engine exhaust) to an icebox, blue and white enamelled steel tableware, coffee percolator, tea kettle, baking utensils, broom, washboard, clothes line, tool compartment, towing cable, radio, toilet, and medicine cabinet. When the accessories were packed away, the interior of the Touring Home was sterile in appearance and not very homelike. The Wayne sales brochure even urged owners to leave their furnishings at home: "Don't substitute your home things. . . . A touring home has enough space for convenience and comfort and no more. There's a place for every bit of equipment the factory supplies, and that equipment fits in that place. It can hardly be expected that your things will fit in a like manner and consequently keep from jostling around in a way that is likely to prove annoying."[72]

Another noteworthy house-car body manufacturer was George P. Wiedman, a manufacturer of bus and truck bodies in North Tonawanda, New York. In 1925 Wiedman applied for a design patent for a house-car body with a clerestory roof and fold-out beds on the sides. He received patent number 69,420 for this design in 1926. The Wiedman Body Company of North Tonawanda, operated by George and Edward Wiedman, advertised a body of this type in the mid-1920s.[73] According to their sales brochure, the Wiedman house-car body was available in three sizes with lengths of 13 feet 6 inches, 16 feet, or 20 feet. The interior could be furnished by the customer, or they could have the manufacturer install optional furnishings such as wicker chairs, a daybed, a steel and leather driver's seat, and a folding dining table with storage space for dishes. Included in each body were a kitchen, washbasin, shower bath, chemical toilet, electric lights, a linen cupboard above the windshield, and garment cradles suspended from the ceiling. Testimonial letters from owners of Wiedman house cars were quoted in the sales literature. Several Wiedman house cars exist today in private collections.

Frank Zagelmeyer of Bay City, Michigan, was one of the few camping vehicle manufacturers who had no previous experience as a body maker, yet his name became prominent among makers of house cars and tent-style camping trailers. A manufacturer of cast concrete blocks and the machinery to make this type of block, Zagelmeyer built and sold house cars and tent trailers as a sideline. In the mid-1920s the Zagelmeyer Auto Camp Company sold a tentlike body that attached to the back of an automobile. This body was based on a patent requested by Zagelmeyer in 1922 and issued in 1925 as number 1,527,105. Zagelmeyer also sold a house-car body called the Kamper-Kar, an enclosed body that attached to the buyer's automobile chassis. At night, two canvas-covered beds could be folded out from the sides of the Kamper-Kar, and the top rose to provide extra headroom. By the late 1920s Zagelmeyer was advertising in *National Geographic* and selling buslike, fully enclosed house cars with berths, a drop-leaf table, icebox, stove, and electric lights. A 1928 Zagelmeyer catalog included the 11 foot 5 inch Gypsy Cruiser house-car body, with a dark oak interior, black, imitation leather sofa bed, kitchen, and table, and the 15.6-foot Pullman Touring Coach body, with a mahogany interior, optional mohair or velour upholstery, berths, desk, wardrobe, and sink with running water. The Gypsy Cruiser was mounted on a Chevrolet truck chassis, and the Pullman Touring Coach was mounted on a Reo Speed Wagon chassis, but either body could be built to order for other truck chassis.[74]

At least one motor vehicle manufacturer built house cars only for wealthy vacationers. In the mid-1920s the Pierce-Arrow bus catalog included a house car named the Caravan with a base price of $15,900. This vehicle had a Pierce-Arrow Model Z bus chassis and a body made by the Buffalo Body Corporation, a bus-body manufacturer in Buffalo, New York. The standard body had an ash frame covered with aluminum; the interior walls were covered with uncut plush below the belt line and imitation leather above the belt line, and the floor was covered with linoleum. The heated interior was furnished with four armchairs that converted to berths, as well as folding tables, bookcases, dome lights, reading lights, drawers, closet, radio, drop windows with copper screens, fans, curtains, rug, cigar lighters, and a searchlight. Utilities included a kitchen, water tank pressurized by the engine, shower bath, folding washbasin, and toilet.[75]

The Caravan could also be custom ordered. In 1926 O. O. Norwood, a municipal securities broker in Austin, Texas, paid between $25,000 and $30,000 for the Longhorn, a custom-designed Caravan with three-tone blue exterior, black walnut interior, white enamel kitchen and bath, and full-length French mirrors. After taking possession of the 10-ton vehicle, Norwood and his wife, Calie, hired a driver and traveled from Buffalo to Austin by way of Yellowstone National Park, the Pacific coast, and the Grand Canyon.[76]

Authors of autocamping manuals debated the pros and cons of manufactured house cars. Frank E. Brimmer, managing editor of *Outdoor Recreation* and a prolific author of books and magazine articles about autocamping, had a favorable opinion of house cars. In *Motor Campcraft* (1923), he described a typical house-car body and added, "This style of camping car is especially recommended for extended trips afield. It is easy enough to add many other articles, such as a phonograph, typewriter table, radio receiving set, shaving stand, sewing kit, and a dozen things that one needs on long trips where this type of camp car will literally be home for months at a stretch." But Brimmer admitted that house cars had their drawbacks. "The single disadvantage felt universally where this special body has been used," he said, "is the fact that the camping outfit sticks like a leech. With a car outfit or a [tent] trailer one may leave the whole impedimenta in permanent camp for the day, while he makes side trips with the car."[77] Elon Jessup, associate editor of *Outing* magazine and author of *The Motor Camping Book* (1921), advised against traveling in "expensive and luxuriant 'land yachts'" and recommended the use of tent trailers. House cars, Jessup wrote, were "not nearly such workable outfits as the ordinary camping trailer. A two-thousand pound palace car is likely to come to grief when wallowing through a bad mudhole."[78]

Whether factory built or homemade, house cars of the 1910s and 1920s were the most conspicuous innovations in the burgeoning field of vacation travel by car. A symbol of Americans' enthusiasm for motor vehicles, their impatience with slow, labor-intensive tent camping, and their zeal for extended travel, house cars provided a novel way to combine the furnishings, equipment, and comforts of home with the invigorating pleasures of the outdoors. House cars represented a desire to enjoy cottagelike accommodations on the road; in the late 1910s and early 1920s roadside tourist cabins were few in number and sparsely furnished. Well-equipped, privately owned house cars were the most efficient way to mediate between home and countryside and transform the roadside into a comfortable place to spend the night. In the 1930s the changing social environment of the road would bring a swift end to roadside camping and the house-car craze, but both activities had fundamental appeal to vacationers and would reappear in many different forms during the next several decades.

3 HOUSE CARS BECOME STREAMLINED

During the Depression, the appeal of autocamping waned as migrating workers, the impoverished, and the dispossessed took to the road in search of shelter, jobs, and sustenance. Makeshift camps beside the road were filled with men, women, and children who were traveling from job to job or from abandoned homes to an uncertain future, many living in dilapidated sedans. Sleeping in the car and lashing one's possessions to the fenders and runningboards no longer symbolized romantic adventure but disadvantaged Americans' struggle to survive. Only designated autocamps in government-owned parks and forests, established in the 1910s and 1920s, remained popular enclaves for motorists who chose to sleep outdoors for pleasure.

Searching for motifs that reflected their buying power and their growing enchantment with stylish consumer products, thousands of middle-class tourists purchased colorful, well-furnished house trailers in the 1930s. Enclosed trailers were not common in the 1920s; there were a few one-off examples, and there were the Motor Bungalo and Aerocar, both designed by airplane pioneer Glenn Curtiss, on the market. The house trailer manufacturing industry was one of the few bright spots in the American economy during the Depression; for the first time, consumers could choose from a wide selection of vacation vehicles produced by hundreds of large and small manufacturers and sold at approximately the price of a new car.

House trailers had modern exteriors and fully equipped, cottagelike interiors, and unlike house cars, their tow cars could be detached and driven on side trips. Trailer parks were designed and priced to attract tourists, not transients. The finest parks were landscaped and had amenities to please and pamper their customers and make them feel at home. Ollie Trout's luxury trailer park in Miami had palm trees, hibiscus bushes, manicured lawns, lawn chairs, neon lights, a playground, slot machines, and valet parking for trailers.[1]

Americans who built their own homes on wheels also preferred trailers over house cars. Some homemade vacation trailers were designed from scratch, while others were based on plans chosen from popular magazines or do-it-yourself trailer plan catalogs. Owners of homemade trailers experienced both the pride of owning a unique creation and the pleasure of owning the latest type of recreation vehicle, one that compared favorably with factory-built trailers. Even migrant workers, retirees, and other low-income, itinerant Americans preferred house trailers; documentary photographers who visited roadside camps in the 1930s found that many people were holding onto their battered automobiles and living in makeshift boxes on two wheels.[2]

Wealthy Americans bought a number of custom, self-propelled house cars in the 1930s. Most of these vehicles either resembled buses or were actually converted buses. In 1930 Anita Johnson, granddaughter of California businessman and philanthropist O. T. Johnson, purchased a new Twin Coach transit bus and had the interior remodeled and furnished as a house car by the Pullman Company in Chicago. This vehicle, which Johnson named the Californian, was paneled in walnut and had complete utilities, quarters for a maid and chauffeur/cook, and elegant sleeping and dining quarters for Johnson. She took four trips around the United States, often carrying camping equipment on top of the vehicle and towing a Ford Model A automobile so that she could camp in remote places off the main road. The 12-ton house car was a giant in a world populated by small cars, and often it foundered in mud or ditches and had to be pulled out. Johnson's chauffeur used the Model A to seek permission from local authorities to cross spindly bridges; if permission was denied, the Californian and its party had to follow detours as long as two hundred miles.[3]

During the Depression, autocamps were filled with impoverished Americans living in makeshift car homes. In 1932 World War I veterans in the Bonus Expeditionary Force occupied this ragtag camp in Washington, D.C., and demanded cash bonuses promised to them by the federal government. (Courtesy Theodore A. Ongena)

In about 1932 Johnson sold the Californian to film comedian Buster Keaton. The massive house car, which Keaton called his "land yacht," provided a welcome distraction at a low point in the actor's life. His career fading because of his inability to adapt to talkies, his screen character "warped" (as he put it) by MGM, his marriage ruined, and his mind and body succumbing to alcoholism, Keaton hardly knew what to do next. The Californian became a refuge from his problem-filled world. With it, he could indulge conspicuously and extravagantly in fun and relaxation, and he could show the world through newsreels and photographs that he was still a funny, successful man. Actor Lew Cody became Keaton's cohort during hunting and fishing trips in the Californian as well as some merry pranks. On one misadventure they parked in Harold Lloyd's driveway in Beverly Hills and prepared dinner. On another occasion they pulled up at a hotel in San Francisco and demanded room service and a telephone connection. Keaton and Cody dressed in nautical uniforms borrowed from MGM's costume department, and Keaton named himself an "admiral." Keaton was fortunate to have retained his sense of humor and his fascination with visual comedy involving vehicles, a fascination that he often displayed in films. Although Keaton owned the Californian only a short time, the house on wheels helped the film star through his difficulties and contributed, if only in a small way, to his resilience and ultimate comeback.[4]

Business executives still constituted a small but steady market for bus-

In the mid-1930s cowboy film star Tom Mix accompanied his own traveling circus in an elaborate home on wheels. Luxurious house cars and house trailers were conveniences and status symbols for many film stars, including Buster Keaton, W. C. Fields, Ray Milland, and Ginger Rogers. (Courtesy Merle G. Norris)

type house cars. Edward Thomas Strong, president and general manager of the Buick division of General Motors, enjoyed a company-owned house car. Built in 1931 by GM's Yellow Truck and Coach Manufacturing Company in Pontiac, Michigan, the massive, 33-foot vehicle had the same body shell and chassis as a Yellow model Z-250 intercity bus. The interior, which accommodated eight people, had chairs, a sofa that converted into beds, an elegant dining table, kitchen, bathroom, and radio.[5] In about 1941 Anheuser-Busch, the St. Louis brewing company, purchased the house car and named it the Adolphus in honor of Adolphus Busch, cofounder of the company. It was used by August A. Busch Jr., Adolphus's grandson and general manager of the firm. With the Adolphus at his disposal, Busch could mix business with pleasure. During long trips, the luxurious house on wheels typically was filled with business associates, friends, and family members. Busch often presided

The popularity of homemade house cars declined in the 1930s, but the custom-made, luxury bus home was still king of the road. A 1931 General Motors bus was transformed into the Adolphus, the rolling home of Anheuser-Busch executive August A. Busch Jr. (Courtesy Museum of Transportation, St. Louis, Missouri)

over marathon card games or stopped at horse shows en route to his destination. In about 1946 Anheuser-Busch sold the Adolphus to Robert Baskowitz, Busch's close friend and bottle supplier, and purchased a new, converted bus that was also christened the Adolphus.[6]

Self-propelled campers did not become popular again until special, manufactured vehicles reached the market. By the late 1930s automobile manufacturers managed to put some measure of respectability back into recreational car-sleeping by introducing optional, built-in bed kits for their new sedans. The Nash bed, introduced in the 1936 model year, became a best-seller. It was deployed by lifting the rear seat back cushion, hooking it to the walls, and leveling the lower portion of the

In the late 1930s mechanical engineer Alexius R. Pribil and race car driver Ray Harroun built this streamlined house car in an effort to popularize self-propelled campers. Pribil planned to manufacture the Aircar, but he died in 1938. (Courtesy G. K. Mulholland)

rear seat with blocks. A mattress completed the convertible double bed, and the rear window provided a convenient "skylight." The Edwards Iron Works of South Bend, Indiana, sold a bed conversion kit called the Slumber Coupe for the 1940 Studebaker. Hudson sedans from 1939 through 1942 could be purchased with the Hudson Sleeper Kit, which was similar to the Nash bed. Also called the Hudson Hotel, this kit had straps that fastened the back rear seat cushion to the ceiling and a contoured felt mattress that spread over the rear seat and trunk.

Several mechanically inclined individuals tried to revive the small house car by applying similar streamlined styling used for exotic one-off automobiles and some production automobiles. In 1935 Alexius R. Pribil, president of the Saginaw Stamping and Tool Company in Saginaw, Michigan, designed a teardrop-shaped house car named the Aircar.

Trained as a mechanical engineer in his native Austria, Pribil had worked for manufacturing companies in Cleveland, Pittsburgh, and Detroit, including the Ford Motor Company, before joining Saginaw Stamping and Tool in about 1917. With the assistance of veteran race-car driver Ray Harroun, an employee of Saginaw Stamping and Tool, Pribil completed a prototype of the Aircar by 1937. The prototype had a vanadium steel frame, a steel shell, and mica insulation. Inside were a divan that converted into a bed, a folding table, sink, and radio. The editors of *Modern Mechanix* magazine pointed to the Aircar's compactness, simplicity, and maneuverability and speculated that house cars similar to the Aircar might replace house trailers. The Pribil Safety Aircar Company was formed to manufacture Pribil's brainchild, but his death in 1938 put an end to this venture.[7]

A prolific builder of one-off, streamlined house cars was J. Roy Hunt, a motion picture cameraman in Hollywood. Hunt began his career working as a newsreel photographer and later became a feature cinematographer. During a career that lasted from 1916 to 1953, he filmed more than 150 movies, including *Beau Geste* (1926), *Flying Down to Rio* (1933), and the science fiction classic *She* (1935). House cars fascinated Hunt. In his spare time, for example, he equipped a 1935 Willys sedan delivery car with a bed, folding table, and electric power generator. Several years later he hired a southern California body shop to make a streamlined steel body, which he attached to a 1937 Ford truck chassis. Named the Turtle, this house car was furnished with a sofa bed, chairs, kitchen, shower bath, and bar, and it sported a metal turtle for a hood ornament.[8] Several more streamlined house cars were built according to Hunt's designs, including a 1941 model with a two-cylinder steam engine in the rear. This 2.5-ton vehicle was 17 feet long and had an aircraft-type body with tubular steel frame, duralumin body, and wraparound windshield. Inside were beds, a kitchen, sink, and shower bath. The house car had an oil heater and a gasoline generator to provide electricity for a cooking stove, water heater, refrigerator, and lights. Hunt claimed to have spent about $29,000 on this vehicle.[9]

By the early 1940s the streamlined look was applied to long, bus-size house cars built for wealthy motorists. Designed and built by professional body makers, these custom-designed vehicles combined the spaciousness and modern appearance of a house trailer with the maneuverability of a house car. But streamlined house cars were not patterned after trailers or buses; they tended to be highly original in appearance, and their distinctive exteriors and luxurious appointments set them apart from all other recreation vehicles on the road. In 1940 Ray Peterson commissioned the Bungalow Bus, a 35-foot, streamlined house car, to commute between the R. G. LeTourneau plants in Peoria, Illinois, and Toccoa, Georgia. Peterson was vice president and plant manager of LeTourneau, which made heavy grading machinery for road building and other construction projects. The massive house car, which cost $15,000, had a General Motors chassis and a body by Schelm Brothers of East Peoria, Illinois, a manufacturer of truck bodies and trailers. By 1942 the Bungalow Bus was being used as a roving "gospel bus" for the LeTourneau Evangelistic Center in New York City. Schelm built fifteen or twenty bodies similar to the Bungalow Bus for other customers.[10]

One of the nation's most prominent industrial designers applied his streamline-styling ideas to a house car in 1938. S. C. Johnson and Son, a nationally known wax manufacturing company based in Racine, Wisconsin, commissioned Brooks Stevens to design a combined house car and mobile laboratory that would be used to test the quality of Carnauba palm trees in Brazil and the waxy substance that they yield. The consumer-oriented wax company was well aware of the advertising value of the exotic-looking house car. In the 1920s and 1930s S. C. Johnson and Son had captured the public's attention with exciting initiatives such as air delivery of its products in company planes, company president Herbert F. "Hib" Johnson's amphibious airplane journey to Brazil in search of Carnauba palm trees, sponsorship of the popular network radio comedy show *Fibber McGee and Molly*, and the building of a modern, skyscraper-style headquarters designed by Frank Lloyd Wright. Like these exciting events, the bulbous house car helped attract media attention. Finished in Cherokee red, the corporate color chosen by Wright, the house car's gleaming body even showed off a new product, Johnson Wax-O-Namel.[11]

Brooks Stevens was a contemporary of Raymond Loewy, Norman Bel

Geddes, Henry Dreyfuss, Walter Dorwin Teague, and other leading figures in the newly established industrial design profession. Stevens was one of the few nationally prominent industrial designers who was not located in New York City. After studying architecture at Cornell University in the early 1930s, he returned to his native Wisconsin, where he opened a design office in Milwaukee. One of Stevens's specialties was automotive design. In the late 1930s and 1940s he designed several streamlined Western Clipper product-display cars for the Western Printing and Lithographing Company of Racine. His flair for forward-looking vehicle design caught the attention of the Willys-Overland Company of Toledo, Ohio, and they brought him on board. During a sixty-one-year career, Stevens contributed to the styling of many popular automobiles, including the Willys Jeep, Studebaker Hawk and Lark, and AMC Ambassador and Gremlin, as well as numerous prototype and limited-production automobiles.[12]

Stevens was one of the few top-ranked industrial designers who turned his attention to recreation vehicles. In 1936 he designed a teardrop-shaped tow car for a streamlined Curtiss Aerocar house trailer owned by William Woods Plankinton Jr., wealthy heir to a Milwaukee meat packing and real estate fortune. The tow car had sleeping quarters for a chauffeur and a trailer attendant. Plankinton often traveled between offices in Milwaukee and New York, and in his spare time he enjoyed hunting, fishing, photography, and travel. He wanted a car and trailer capable of high speeds; the Stevens-designed tow car, which was built by the Badger Automobile Body and Trailer Corporation in Milwaukee, originally had an International truck engine, but Plankinton replaced it with a supercharged Mercury automobile engine rated at 137 horsepower. Stevens also specified cosmetic changes to the lightweight wood, fabric, and wire trailer so that it would match the tow car.[13]

The Stevens-designed Johnson Wax house car was built in 1940 by the Linn Corporation of Oneonta, New York, a trailer manufacturing company founded by H. H. Linn, owner of the Linn Haven house car. After Linn's death in an airplane crash in 1937, Arthur R. Perkins, a former garage mechanic, body shop operator, and house trailer manufacturer, took over management of the Linn trailer firm. He would eventually purchase the company. Perkins added front-wheel-drive trucks with monocoque bodies to the Linn product line and built special-purpose, front-wheel-drive units such as mobile broadcast stations and dental clinics.[14]

The front-wheel-drive design of the Johnson Wax vehicle eliminated the drive shaft housing on the floor, which allowed for 6 feet 2 inches of standing room. Aside from a laboratory, the 23-foot vehicle was equipped with two beds, a sofa that converted into a bed, a kitchen with sink, gas stove, and gas refrigerator, desk with built-in radio, folding table, and bathroom with shower. It also had an oil furnace, hot-water heater, air conditioning, and electrical outlets for lamps and small appliances such as fans, toasters, and razors. Under the sofa was a place to store guns and fishing rods—Hib Johnson was a lifelong hunting and fishing enthusiast and also used the mobile laboratory as a recreation vehicle.

On the house car's first trip, Hib Johnson and Brooks Stevens drove from Oneonta to the Thousand Islands, then to the New York World's Fair, where the house car was put on television at the RCA pavilion, studied at the Ford pavilion, and examined by the High Commissioner of Brazil at the Brazilian pavilion (later the house car would take an exploratory trip to Brazil). Johnson and Stevens picked up Adolph Peterson, an S. C. Johnson and Son sales manager and the company's representative at the fair, and the three men traveled to Racine in the house car via Buffalo and Detroit. The Johnson Wax house car was made available to civilian defense officials in Racine County, Wisconsin, during World War II for use as a mobile casualty station by the Emergency Medical Service. Equipped with pharmaceutical, surgical, and medical supplies, it had a driver on call in the event of emergencies involving injuries to Racine County residents. It also traveled throughout Wisconsin for examination by county chiefs of the Emergency Medical Service and was displayed in Madison during the war sessions of the American College of Surgeons. The house car was featured in many newspaper articles in the early 1940s and excited readers with its novel look and functions.

The appearance of another modern house car in the 1941 Paramount motion picture *Sullivan's Travels* further stimulated public interest in self-propelled houses on wheels. This classic comedy, written and directed by Preston Sturges, is about a film director named John L. Sullivan who is known for comedies but yearns to make a "socially conscious" film about the dark side of everyday life—the poverty and misery that afflicts millions of Americans. He prepares for this great work by pretending to be a hobo and living among the poor. He is stalked by overly solicitous aides traveling in a streamlined house car. When Sullivan hitches a ride in a motor vehicle, his aides chase after him at high speed; dishes, pans, and food fly about in the house car's kitchen, and the aides tumble around in its compartments. The house car was identified in Paramount's publicity as "a specially constructed land yacht built before the present war."[15]

The house car's positive image in the media and its streamlining makeover of the late 1930s and early 1940s reflected resurging public interest in this "new" type of recreation vehicle. Despite favorable publicity, house cars were not part of the idealistic vision of technology and family life presented at the New York World's Fair of 1939 and 1940. Affordable house trailers still had a firm grip on middle-class Americans' travel tastes, and trailer sales would continue to dominate the recreation vehicle market for decades. Homemade house cars would become more popular after World War II, and a few odd-looking production house cars—essentially house trailers with motors—would emerge from the drawing boards of trailer engineers. The world of recreation vehicles had changed almost overnight, and the future of house cars now lay in the bulky shadow of manufactured house trailers.

4 AUTOCAMPING IN THE POSTWAR ERA

n the late 1940s and 1950s a new autocamping boom created more demand for recreation vehicles as families, hunters, anglers, and others discovered the pleasures of outdoor living in their leisure time. Materials and housing shortages eased, and veterans and their families were settling into new, suburban homes. At the same time, people returned to the highways in search of fun and adventure. Sleeping in campgrounds and other outdoor settings promoted family intimacy, satisfied a desire to be close to nature, and eliminated motel bills and a nightly search for clean rooms with appropriate furnishings. Like their forerunners in the 1920s, many autocampers of the 1950s used tents, but some preferred the comfort and convenience of a home on wheels.

Many vacationers who became interested in recreation vehicles wanted ones that were more maneuverable than house trailers (now called travel trailers) and had the tight handling and responsiveness of the family car. A small number of vacationers made their own house cars, but more often postwar vacationers modified manufactured vehicles to meet their needs. Car sleeping was once again an accepted form of recreational travel by the late 1940s, and many families made or purchased fixtures that enabled them to sleep, cook, and eat in their sedans or station wagons. Other families, especially those with many children, preferred to travel and sleep in spacious, con-

Inventor Larry Vita built two Vita-Home Cruisers in the 1950s. The design of the 1951 prototype epitomized the suburban ranch house on wheels, an ideal that inspired postwar manufacturers of motor homes and travel trailers. (Courtesy Larry Vita)

verted buses. By the 1950s owning a bus was no longer a privilege of the wealthy; bus homes had become family vehicles and were driven by anyone who had enough time and imagination to convert them. Cars and buses shared qualities that trailers lacked; they were easier to turn, back up, and park, and unlike trailers, the occupants could ride together and use the vehicle's facilities while in motion. The growing popularity of car and bus vacation homes indicated a large market for a new type of recreation vehicle, one that was self-propelled and self-contained.

IT'S A BOAT! IT'S A PLANE! IT'S SUPERCAR!

A modest revival of interest in homemade house cars occurred in the 1940s, but most designs were closer to Roy Hunt's streamlined, metal vacation homes than the wooden boxes on wheels of the 1920s. Engineers, pilots, manufacturers, and others who were involved with aircraft design and production during World War II built one-off house cars using airplane fuselage materials, including tubular steel frames, aluminum sheeting, duralumin, Lucite, and wood laminated with plastic. Few of these vehicles had the excellent strength-to-weight ratio of a fuselage, but they indicated renewed interest in house cars as an alternative to travel trailers and a desire to build larger house cars made of materials that were stronger and more durable than wood.

During the war, Albert R. Krause, a supervisor at Lockheed Aircraft in California, designed a house car with a tubular steel frame and aluminum outer sheeting. Krause began working at Lockheed in 1938; in the early 1940s he was a supervisor in the experimental department and worked on the P-38 Lightning fighter plane and Constellation passenger and transport plane. In his memoirs, he wrote,

> Trips through the years with the best in tents, cots, folding tables, gasoline stoves, and all equipment made me dream of a way to rough it in comfort, without spending half the time setting up camps and packing to go. . . . I began dreaming of a motor home while in high school in Oklahoma in the 1920s. . . . [In the 1940s] I researched trailers and what few motor homes existed all over southern California. During the war years, there were a few motor homes around and I saw them all. Several were made with steel tubing frames, aluminum skins and streamlined, but most were heavy and crude.[1]

In 1944 Krause began building his house car in a garage in Burbank. His brother, Fred, an aircraft stress engineer, helped with the structural design. Although metals were rationed and in short supply, Albert Krause was able to purchase enough steel tubing for the frame. Aluminum sheeting came from war surplus stores, and a fully adjustable B-25 bomber pilot's seat served as the driver's seat. Chassis parts came from a 1933 LaSalle sedan and a 1941 Ford truck. In 1946 Krause's son, Jimmy, a master mechanic, was discharged from the navy and helped him rivet the aluminum sheeting onto the exterior. The interior had sleeping accommodations for six people, a kitchen with an electric refrigerator, and a bathroom. By March 1947 Krause was ready for a shake-down trip to visit some relatives in San Francisco. Although the house car was built for pleasure trips, Krause, his wife, Esther, and their

Some house cars of the 1940s resembled aircraft and had riveted aluminum sheeting, tubular steel frames, and other aircraft materials. Humorist Herb Shriner named his bulbous, streamlined vehicle the Graf Zipalong. (Courtesy Wil Shriner)

children lived in it in the San Fernando Valley from March 1948 to March 1949. Albert and Esther Krause took pleasure trips in the house car until the 1980s.[2]

In 1946 Lloyd Rounds, an army pilot who learned to fly in World War I and flew B-17 and B-24 bomber planes in World War II, began building a mammoth house car using war surplus materials. His 40-foot, 7.8-ton vehicle had front-wheel drive, a Ford V-8 engine, riveted aluminum sides, a plexiglass and Lucite windshield, infrared heaters, and an air conditioner. It took Rounds three years to complete the machine, which he named the Nomad III. In the 1950s he made several trips to North Dakota and Arizona in the house car as well as short trips in California. The Nomad III was also Rounds's home for long periods between trips.[3]

Another aircraft enthusiast who built a house car for pleasure trips was Otto W. Timm, an airplane manufacturer in Van Nuys, California. Trained in mechanical engineering, Timm learned to build airplanes in about 1910 and started his own aircraft construction and remodeling shop in Glendale in 1928. During World War II, the Timm Aircraft Corporation of Van Nuys built plastic-bonded, plywood training monoplanes for the army and navy. Among the virtues that Timm claimed for his Aeromold material were ease of manufacture, high strength-to-weight ratio, a smooth, aerodynamic surface, low maintenance cost, ease of repair, and conservation of critical metals, particularly aluminum. In the late 1940s Timm spent $28,000 to build the Ruffinit, a rear-engine house car with a body similar to his wartime monoplanes. Designed in 1946 and completed in 1949, the Ruffinit had twenty-eight laminated spruce ribs circling the inner surface of its body with laminated stringers connecting the ribs. An outer layer of mahogany plywood covered with plastic formed a stressed-skin enclosure with unusual strength. Aircraft-type hydraulic lines connected the driver's controls with the engine. The house car was furnished with foam rubber beds, a butane cook stove, sink, refrigerator, folding table, toilet, shower, and clothes closet. Otto and his wife, Caroline, used the Ruffinit for pleasure trips in the West.[4]

Another one-off house car influenced by aircraft design was built in 1952 by Hayward Powell and his brother, Channing Powell. The Powell brothers had begun manufacturing radios in Los Angeles in 1924; in the late 1930s they began producing motor scooters, and in 1940 they built a scooter factory in Compton, California. During World War II, they manufactured hydraulic aircraft valves and gun parts, and after the war they resumed production of motor scooters. In about 1950 the Powell brothers and their wives and children designed a self-propelled, aircraft-type camp car. Dorothy Powell, Hayward's wife, later recalled,

> It even became a bedtime story, with Daddy sitting on the bed telling [their daughter Linda] what it would be like, what would be in it, where we would go, and as work progressed, what the latest additions had been. And believe me, the children had their ideas, too, as to what should be incorporated into our vacation [home] on wheels. . . . Drawings were made at practically any hour of the day on calendars, blotters, newspaper margins, grocery tapes, or any scrap of paper available at the time.[5]

Aircraft manufacturer Otto W. Timm patterned the Ruffinit after plastic-bonded plywood training airplanes that he built for the army and navy during World War II. Timm and his wife, Caroline, toured the West in the Ruffinit, which was completed in 1949. (Courtesy Peter Brower)

Hayward and Channing obtained a Cadillac sedan chassis and built a body frame out of welded square steel tubing in their factory in Compton. "When the house car was just a framework still only clamped together," Dorothy Powell said, "we'd slip inside and with shipping crates and boxes in the position of our anticipated stove, refrigerator, table, etc., we'd visualize what it would be like."[6] Duralumin exterior sheeting and full sleeping, cooking, and dining facilities rounded out the house on wheels. Working far into the night—their wives calling themselves "camp car widows"—the Powell brothers rushed the house car to completion in the late summer of 1952. In late August the two families traveled to San Francisco and the redwood groves of northern California. Driving a car as well, the two families took turns living and traveling in the house car. They continued to use the house car for vacation trips, still taking turns, until the late 1960s.[7]

In the mid-1950s George W. Crise of Danville, Ohio, built a 28-foot house car that he named the Landyacht. An inventor and manufacturer, Crise had grown up on a farm in eastern Ohio and learned to appreciate mechanical objects from his father, who was a civil engineer as well as a farmer. George Crise studied engineering at Ohio State University but dropped out to design, build, and sell radios. He had an eclectic and inventive mind: he also built a glider plane out of wood, plywood, and fabric and owned and operated several private planes. In 1940 he submitted a design for an attack plane to the National Advisory Committee for Aeronautics, and in 1950 he patented a rotating vane parachute for dropping heavy equipment from airplanes. Leaving the radio business, he obtained patents for thermostatic controls, electric warming devices, and other devices and established companies to manufacture thermostats, electric motors, and electric bed warmers.

Crise built the Landyacht for winter trips to the Florida Keys. The body, which Crise built with the help of a local carpenter, resembled a travel trailer but was made of plywood glued and stapled to poplar ribs. It rested on a steel tube so that shock and torque from the chassis would not be transmitted to the body frame; this assembly was further stabilized by a vertical "mast." The vehicle had a modified 1953 Dodge school bus chassis with the engine mounted in the rear. Completed in 1955, the Landyacht was equipped with a front seat that converted into a sofa bed, a folding table, two bunks with inflatable foam-rubber mattresses, a stove, sink, electric refrigerator-freezer (cooled by frozen brine at night so that the auxiliary engine and compressor did not have to run), cupboard, closet, bathroom with shower, heater, and air conditioner. There was 6 feet 2.5 inches of standing room. Aside from the Florida Keys, the Crise family used it for trips to Yellowstone National Park, Mount Rushmore, and other places. Crise considered manufacturing vehicles similar to the Landyacht and even formed the Landyacht Company for this purpose, but after consulting with his family he decided that it would not be a successful venture.[8]

Occasionally, watercraft served as sources of design concepts for postwar homes on wheels. The analogy of house cars and yachts was an easy one to make; both embodied a sense of independence, adventure, and a wayfaring spirit. In practical terms the streamlined shape of a boat hull cut resistance in air as well as water. Some boat builders began manufacturing travel trailers, and others built one-off land yachts by using boat materials and shapes for trailers and house cars. In the late 1940s Paul Prigg, proprietor of the Prigg Boat Works in Miami, designed a house car with a wood plank roof that resembled an inverted boat hull. Prigg's house car had a wooden grille and aluminum sides with round windows that resembled portholes. Inside were sofa beds for two people, a dinette, hot and cold running water, closets, and other furnishings and equipment. Prigg, his wife, and their two small children took trips to New York and Texas in the unusual vehicle.[9]

THE SUBURBANIZATION OF AUTOCAMPING

A simpler approach to do-it-yourself motor camping was the revival of the automobile sleeper. As communities reshaped themselves around the automobile after World War II, families flocked to highways for a varied array of leisure activities, many of which focused on the interiors of their cars. At drive-in theaters family cars became living rooms on wheels and at drive-in restaurants mobile dining rooms. In contrast with the social dislocations and seedy autocamps of the Depression era, the automobile as extended living quarters became a symbol of the prosperity and good times of the 1950s.

In the late 1940s many autocampers slept in their automobiles in order to make their camping trips easier, faster, less expensive, and more comfortable. The best-known manufactured automobile with a built-in bed, the Nash sedan, was reintroduced in 1946. Advertised as an inexpensive, convenient form of lodging for weekend tourists, vacationers, hunters, anglers, and traveling business people, the optional Nash Convertible Double Bed featured a mattress and metal window screens. To install the bed, the motorist lifted the rear seat back and fastened it to the walls with straps and hooks, pulled the rear seat cushion up and forward until it rested on folding metal arms, pulled down a hinged, auxiliary rear cushion to fill the gap where the seat cushion was, and laid the mattress over the entire trunk and rear seat area. Beginning in

1949, Nash replaced the seat-and-trunk bed with a design that resembled reclining-seat sleepers of the 1910s and 1920s. The 1949 Nash Airflyte sedan had reclining front seat backs that folded down to form a double bed consisting of the front seat, seat backs, and rear seat. In the 1950s the Nash sedan with Airliner reclining seats was advertised extensively in *Field and Stream, Outdoor Life, Sports Afield,* and other magazines read by outdoor recreation enthusiasts. The seat-bed was standard on some Nash sedans and optional on others. A mattress and window screens were offered as options with the bed. After Nash and Hudson merged in 1954 and formed American Motors Corporation, the seat-bed was available in some Hudson, Rambler, and AMC automobiles.[10]

Some motorists converted their cars into sleeping vehicles by making and installing their own beds. Unlike the hinged front seats in modified touring cars of the 1910s and 1920s, one-off beds of the late 1940s and 1950s resembled the 1946–1948 Nash bed, which filled the rear seat and trunk. One homemade bed consisted of a double mattress placed on the rear seat and trunk floor extended onto a sheet of plywood attached to the rear bumper. A wooden stick propped up the trunk lid.[11] Another bed, made by Matthew Howard of Minneapolis, comprised three seat cushions on the rear seat and trunk floor, plastic window screens for nighttime ventilation, and a plywood car-top carrier for the spare tire and luggage displaced from the trunk.[12] Seattle freelance writer Howard Jackson removed the rear seat and trunk partition of his automobile and built a plywood bed and table outfit. David and Kavvy Barish, a peripatetic army couple who lived in a trailer, decided to use their tow car for weekend pleasure trips. They slept on an innerspring twin mattress that took the place of the rear seat and extended into the trunk. Their son, Craig, slept on the front seat. Kavvy Barish reported, "The rear window slants just enough to provide a wonderful view of the sky—so our indoor bed is as outdoorsy as a cot." The Barishes took turns dressing inside the car.[13]

Autocamping with tents became very popular in the 1950s, and a new generation of folding tents, tables, chairs, and other pieces appeared on the market. Much of this equipment was similar in form and function to wood-and-fabric 1920s autocamping gear, except the new products were made of light, durable materials such as aluminum, plastic, and nylon. A wide selection of lightweight stoves burned gasoline, propane, kerosene, or Sterno. Some modern lanterns had a battery and fluorescent tube instead of gasoline and a mantle. Instead of khaki or army green, camping accessories of the 1950s came in rainbow colors that harmonized with brightly-hued automobiles and clothing. Some autocamping accessories of the 1950s, such as charcoal grills, picnic baskets, paper plates, and paper cups, were identical to those used in suburban backyards. The new accessories added the convenience of modern materials, the aesthetic appeal of stylish designs, and the pleasures of family living in a patio setting on wheels.[14]

Automobile travel accessories of the 1950s reflected the growing technological sophistication of the American home. Postwar consumers had grown accustomed to a wide range of electrical appliances and conveniences that saved time and effort in every room of the house. Naturally, they began to equip their automobiles in much the same way for vacation trips. The editors of *Ford Times*, a company-sponsored travel magazine, observed, "The makers of gadgets know full well that to the average American, an automobile is more than a vehicle of transportation. It is a living space as well. It's a parlor, a library, a kitchen, a clothes closet and a bedroom. It has lights and an electrical outlet. Almost anything that can be built for a house can be tailored down for the inside of an automobile."[15] By the late 1950s household gadgets such as a coffee pot, shaver, bottle warmer, and even a small refrigerator could be purchased and plugged into the cigarette lighter of an automobile.[16]

The most famous one-off automobile sleeper of the postwar era epitomized consumers' desire to take the gadget-laden American home on the road. The Fabulous Car, a white 1947 Cadillac owned by Elias ("Louie") Mattar, had a custom interior filled with pop-out appliances and plumbing fixtures. In order to prepare more convenient accommodations for his wife, Rose, and their three children during camping trips, Mattar, an automobile mechanic and owner of Louie's Garage in San Diego, decided to add cooking, washing, and hygiene facilities to their Cadillac. He turned to a friend, Joe Mitchell, for help. A mechanical engineer with General Dynamics's Convair Division, Mitchell had learned to design and build airplane components as an Army Air Corps mechanic during World War II. Every evening for six years, Mat-

Many postwar Americans installed comforts of home in their automobiles before taking long trips. The Fabulous Car, a 1947 Cadillac sedan modified by Louie Mattar and Joe Mitchell for camping and transcontinental marathons, was equipped with the works: a television, tape player, radio, clock, bar, hookah, and other devices. (Courtesy Louie Mattar)

tar and Mitchell labored over the Cadillac in Louie's garage, adding a sink, toilet, and manifold water heater. Downsized versions of an electric stove, refrigerator, washing machine, and iron were installed in the rear seat area and slid in and out of the trunk. Mitchell's mechanical ability and inventive mind turned Mattar's ideas into reality. Mitchell even installed a shower in place of the radio antenna and a drinking fountain that spurted from a rear fender.[17]

Louie's garage employees joked that with all of its built-in conveniences, the Cadillac could be driven from coast to coast without stopping. Mattar took the suggestion seriously, and he and Mitchell prepared the car for such a journey by installing retractable runningboards so that they could change tires and service the engine while in motion. Then they carefully planned rolling refueling stops (using tank trucks)

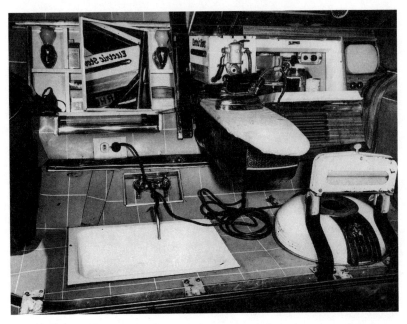

The rear seat of Louie Mattar's Fabulous Car concealed a sink, stove, iron, ironing board, refrigerator, washing machine, and toilet. (Courtesy Louie Mattar)

and police escorts through towns along the route. On September 20, 1952, Mattar, Mitchell, and Andy Bashara, a gas station owner, left San Diego in the Fabulous Car. Driving in five-hour shifts, they took turns cooking, eating, and sleeping in the back seat. They reached New York City, and without a pause they turned around and headed for Hollywood, arriving on September 27. Mattar exultantly reported that the wheels never stopped turning during the 6,320-mile trip. The story was reported in *Life* and other magazines.[18] In 1954 Mattar staged an international, nonstop run from north to south in the Fabulous Car with his son, Leroy, and Joe Henderson, an automobile salesman. The three men left Anchorage, Alaska, on August 10 and arrived in Mexico City eight days and 7,482 miles later. For this trip Mattar and Mitchell fitted the Cadillac with retractable, auxiliary wheels that lifted the car while in motion when it was necessary to change a tire.[19]

Not all motorists required the complexity of the Fabulous Car for touring, but many needed a vehicle that was larger and better equipped than a sedan. Increasingly, station wagons filled this need. Thousands of postwar Americans purchased station wagons for their everyday transportation and slept in them during pleasure trips. Station wagon owners fitted their vehicles with dozens of accessories and devices used in food preparation, equipment storage, personal hygiene, and other daily needs. The station wagon became a cozy home on wheels for many vacationing families who learned to sleep in the cargo area and cook on the tailgate.

At mid-century the station wagon underwent a dramatic transition from a commercial to a personal vehicle. Its attractive steel and wood-panel body had evolved from motorized depot hacks of the 1920s—tall, open, workaday vehicles that carried people and cargo—which were patterned after horse-drawn delivery wagons. By the 1930s enclosed "woody" wagons had become workhorses and pleasure vehicles of wealthy Americans and were commonly found at country estates, country clubs, inns, private schools, and other rustic, upper-class settings. The traditional wooden body of the station wagon harmonized with its rural, conservative environment and was an anachronistic ornament in an industry that otherwise had converted to all-steel bodies by 1937. The station wagon of the late 1940s was still a boxy, limited-production, wooden-body vehicle with seats that could be removed or inserted to carry small groups of people, luggage, recreational equipment, or cargo.[20] But strong demand for used "woodies" among postwar, middle-class families alerted automobile manufacturers to the larger market. Soon this handsome status symbol was transformed into a ubiquitous family car tailored to America's mushrooming suburban lifestyle.

The introduction of all-steel bodies on the 1946 Willys, 1949 Plymouth, 1949 Chevrolet, and 1952 Ford station wagons eliminated laborious refinishing and waxing of wooden panels, a task that busy suburbanites disdained, and sales soared. The addition of fold-down rear seats and a roll-down tailgate window instead of a hinged window made it easier to haul cargo. Sedan-type styling made the station wagon look at home in suburban driveways, thus completing its transition from a truck to an automobile. The use of imitation woodgrain siding and trim perpetuated its rural, elitist image. As suburban families found utilitarian and recreational uses for their station wagons—taking children to school, picking up lawn and garden supplies, carrying home project materials, and enjoying day trips and vacations—it quickly became a symbol of family activity and intimacy in the outdoors.

It did not take long for couples and families to discover that they could sleep in their station wagons and enjoy an inexpensive, intimate form of pleasure travel. Shortly after World War II a veteran named Russell Rosene and his wife, Nita, purchased a 1942 Ford station wagon and converted it into a camper. Using inexpensive materials, items from their garage, and scrap materials, they removed the rear seats and installed a bed, curtains, shelves, towel rack, thermometer, camp stove, washtub, axe, lantern, and kitchen utensil kit. The total cost of the conversion was $25. The Rosenes traveled through California, Nevada, Yellowstone National Park, and the East. Like earlier autocampers, they pretended to forsake their home while clinging to some of the security that it provided. "Ours was the carefree Gypsy life," wrote Rosene. "Home was wherever night overtook us and our front yard stretched to the horizons that forever lay ahead. We ate hot meals by the roadside, we washed clothes in campgrounds, we bathed in rivers and hot springs. We carried our water in a waterbag hanging on the tailgate, and even when icicles formed beneath, as they did at Lake Tahoe, we were snug and warm and comfortable without the need of a heater."[21]

Station wagon camping offered several practical advantages over tent camping. Unlike a tent, a station wagon enclosure was above the ground, where insects, snakes, and animals could not intrude. The windows kept out rain and wind, and they could be adjusted to control the amount of fresh air. Doors could be locked to keep others out. Camping in a rigid vehicle was faster and easier than setting up and breaking down a tent, table, chairs, or tent trailer; invariably, the tailgate served as a convenient cooking surface or dining table. And it was no longer necessary to find a campground, because a level site was all that was needed. Station wagon campers often slept in roadside rest areas or other places that were not designated for their use.

Offsetting the station wagon's virtues were the limitations of its cargo space. In most models, there was too little room between the wheel wells for two adults to sleep comfortably. And in virtually all station wagons, there was not enough headroom to sit up and dress. Campers quickly found that they needed to modify their station wagons to overcome these disadvantages. Many motorists built wooden storage cabinets that fit between the wheel wells and placed bedding over the full width of the cabinet and wells. A tarp or curtain attached to the station wagon's exterior provided a simple dressing room. A radical solution was a homemade, car-top tent, reached by a ladder, which provided more space for above-ground sleeping.[22]

Automobile manufacturers soon responded to the wagon-sleeping trend. Chrysler promoted station wagon sleeping in a 1949 Plymouth Suburban sales brochure that suggested, "Take a hotel with you! Fold the rear seat into the floor, spread out your mattress or bedding rolls—and you have a real bedroom!" Although the design of these vehicles did not change to accommodate campers, Ford, the leading manufacturer of station wagons in the early 1950s, actively promoted station wagon camping, fostered the development of special station wagon camping equipment, and publicized commercially made accessories that made it easier to sleep and cook in and around Ford wagons. In 1952 the editors of *Ford Times* entered into an agreement with inventor, professor, and visionary R. Buckminster Fuller to develop a new generation of camping equipment. With funding from Ford, Fuller's students at the Massachusetts Institute of Technology designed a lightweight tent made of aluminum and orlon and a sliding kitchen cabinet for station wagons.[23] Ford hired an engineering firm to make additional prototypes of car camping accessories, including a lightweight fiberglass boat that fit on top of a station wagon, a smaller, lighter utility cabinet, a double-deck sleeping accommodation for the interior of a station wagon, and a tent supported by compressed air. Descriptions of these and other camping devices were published in *Ford Times*, and readers also sent in descriptions of their own homemade contrivances.

Recreation Unlimited (or alternately the Station Wagon Living Program), Ford's effort to stimulate and improve station wagon camping, was directed by Franklin M. Reck, a frequent writer for *Ford Times*, and C. William Moss, a designer of camping and recreational equipment.[24] As the program grew, Ford writers and editors supervised the development of additional station wagon camping accessories (including a sunshade made of canvas and fiberglass) and tested manufactured camping accessories that came on the market. They also toured the United States, studying and photographing station wagon autocampers and their equipment. In addition to the articles in *Ford Times*, the editors published their field reports, color photographs, and commentaries in book form in 1957.[25] The proliferation of manufactured camping accessories and the growing popularity of station wagon camping led to the publication of a second book in 1958 and a third one in 1964.[26]

Changes in the middle-class home help to explain the popularity of station wagon sleeping. The one-story, suburban ranch home, which combined indoor and outdoor living in ways that were more direct than a bungalow, became extremely popular after World War II. Sliding-glass doors, patios, and spacious backyards enabled middle-class Americans to mix domestic and nature experiences more thoroughly than ever. On vacations, sleeping in or beside the family car became an extended form of backyard living as millions of Americans discovered the sensory pleasures, intimacy, and economy of autocamping. The family sedan or station wagon became a ranch house on wheels; long and low, close to the outdoors but protected from it, the family car served as a secure platform for bedding, cooking, and dining facilities, storage units, portable showers, and other conveniences. The qualities that the station wagon contributed to suburban living—utility, easy access, and family cooperation—were readily transferred to vacation living.

As the popularity of station wagon camping grew, a number of independently designed accessories made this type of travel easier, more enjoyable, and more homelike. There were slide-in kitchen units such as the Kamp Kitch'n, Camp-N-Wagon, and Port-A-Camp, mattress pads and air mattresses, nylon window screens and mesh "porches," clothes racks, car curtains, rear hatch covers, freestanding fabric dressing rooms, and seat-back car trays.[27] Suburbanites took their patios with them as they gathered around the tailgate for meals on colorful paper or plastic tableware. Station wagon camping miniaturized the carefully controlled nature experience of backyard recreational living, which depended on the security and conveniences of the home for a pleasant, risk-free environment.

Even the second-story camping outfit became a commercial product. A car-top tent and ladder kit, such as a Sky-Vue or a Tour-a-Tent, gave a station wagon an upstairs "bedroom" and a downstairs "bedroom" and conserved space in crowded autocamps. A combination car-top tent and side tent, such as the Touri-Camp or the Heilite Car-Topper, provided two lower "rooms" and one upper "room."[28] In 1961 Edmonds L. Guerrant, a mechanical engineer in Fort Worth, Texas, and president of the Ready Hung Door Corporation, began manufacturing and selling a complete living unit that attached to the rain gutter around the top of a station wagon or sedan. Guerrant had designed and built a station wagon rooftop sleeper for his family's use during trips through the West, and he believed that a market existed for this type of unit. The Guerrant Camp'otel Car Camper included a folding, car-top tent and several optional accessories: a 5-gallon water tank, vinyl shower enclosure that hung from the rain gutter, and a dining kit for ground use with an aluminum table, benches, Coleman gasoline stove, and two plastic sinks. Guerrant formed a corporation to manufacture Camp'otel units. They were sold through Sears, Roebuck, J. C. Penney, Western Auto, and other retail stores. The Camp'otel became quite popular among owners of station wagons, automobiles, and vans, especially in Texas. Camp'otel owners in the Fort Worth area formed the Penthouse Campers Association in 1963; they took trips together and published a newsletter, *Penthouse Poop*. The Camp'otel Corporation flourished through the 1960s but fell victim to the gasoline shortage of 1973 and the disappearance of rain gutters on new cars.[29]

The pièce de résistance of specially equipped station wagons was the Ford Pushbutton Camper. William Moss and a team of designers created a 48-inch working model of a 1958 Ford station wagon with electrically deployed accessories, including a folding car-top tent with a double bed, aluminum power boat on mechanical davits, slide-out tailgate kitchen unit, and projecting rear canopy. The Pushbutton Camper was a highlight of Ford's station wagon advertising campaigns in the late 1950s and early 1960s; several full-sized, working prototypes were made, and one was displayed in the American Road Show, a Ford vehicle sales show that traveled to shopping centers between 1957 and 1960. The Pushbutton Camper was displayed in "Design for Station Wagon Living," a section of the show that included Ford wagons and a wide array of camping equipment. Other sections of the show included "Design

for Suburban Living," which featured Ford automobiles, patio entertainment, and mechanical devices for suburban homes, and "Design
for Country Living," which featured Ford tractors, farm implements,
and farming techniques.[30]

The autocamping boom of the 1950s may have echoed the material
sophistication, wanderlust, and family intimacy of 1920s autocamping,
but the romance of spending the night on the roadside did not fully return. Most designated campgrounds of the 1950s were located not beside highways but deep within national or state parks, forests, reservoir
properties, or other government-owned natural enclaves. Mid-twentieth-
century government autocamps were tailored to the needs of mobile
families who slept in station wagons, trailers, cars, or tents. These camps
had hot showers, laundry rooms, outdoor lighting, electrical outlets,
and other conveniences. Some had electrical, water, and sewage connections for trailers.[31]

The demand for commodious, efficient autocamps was so great by
the late 1950s that many park systems struggled to cope with overcrowding while maintaining the physical integrity of their camp facilities and acceptable standards of service and sanitation. Over 47.8 million Americans visited national parks in 1954, more than twice the
number of visitors in 1941. In Florida state park authorities reported an
increase from 5,244 campers in 1949 to 14,299 in 1954 and 89,493 in
1957.[32] In Illinois the number of campers rose from approximately
76,000 to 400,000 during the same period.[33] Overcrowding in many
camps led to tighter rules and regulations, higher camping fees, time
limits on visits, advance reservations, and the construction of new
campgrounds. In 1956 the National Park Service launched Mission 66,
a program aimed at expanding and improving visitor services by 1966,
the fiftieth anniversary of the National Park Service. The major purposes of Mission 66 were to maintain public interest and support for national parks, contain motor traffic within designated areas, and keep
park tourism a higher priority than dams, reservoirs, and other passive
uses. Among the results were thousands of miles of newly built, paved,
straightened, or widened roads and more than 1,500 new parking lots.
Critics claimed that national parks were being "urbanized," and indeed,
scenic parkways or "motor nature trails" attracted thousands of addi-

tional motorists to an experience that combined the wonders of nature with the sedentary pleasures of a drive-in theater.[34]

THE FAMILY BUS

One-off adaptations of station wagons reflected a growing tendency to equip the interiors of factory-made vehicles for camping instead of building camper bodies from scratch. After the motor vehicle manufacturing industry changed to all-steel, closed bodies for automobiles, buses, and small trucks in the 1920s and 1930s, almost any vehicle would provide a strong, waterproof environment that lent itself to autocamping. By the 1940s there was a wide range of vehicles with amazing durability, capacity, and versatility. Because these vehicles could not be dismantled and rebuilt as easily as a Ford Model T, few postwar motorists chose to remove the body and replace it with an original creation. Instead, they thought of ways to use its interior.

The transition of privately owned buses from playthings of the wealthy to middle-class vacation vehicles in the 1950s was one of the most dramatic changes in recreation vehicles. In the 1930s and 1940s motor-bus homes were conspicuously upper-class, luxurious, and custom-made homes on wheels. In the 1950s and 1960s, however, hundreds of families of average means discovered the pleasure of making simple modifications to bus interiors for vacation trips. Baby-boom families, especially those with many children, preferred converted buses because of their spaciousness, and a plentiful supply of used buses made them affordable. Unlike autocampers of the 1920s, who imitated the rich by building scaled-down versions of elaborate house cars, postwar campers furnished full-sized buses themselves or sought the help of professional body shops. The enjoyment of motor buses by middle-class families revealed a growing market for self-propelled sleeping vehicles that were considerably larger than a station wagon.

In the late 1940s converted intercity buses still appealed to the tiny segment of travelers who could afford custom-furnished sleeping vehicles. Anheuser-Busch replaced the aging Adolphus with a new, converted ACF-Brill intercity bus for the use of August A. Busch Jr. when he became company president in 1946.[35] A Dayton, Ohio, businessman, Otto L. Spaeth, commissioned a similar house bus in the same year. A former Ford tractor salesman, Spaeth was president of the Dayton Tool and Engineering Company from 1935 to 1946 when the Spaeths moved to a large apartment on Park Avenue in New York City. Spaeth was attracted to yachts and considered purchasing one, but he refrained because (as he joked) he could not swim and became seasick easily. Instead, he ordered an intercity bus from ACF-Brill and had it outfitted to his specifications as a land yacht by the Consolidated Shipbuilding Corporation of City Island, New York, a yacht specialist. Eloise Spaeth, Otto's wife, specified the interior decor.

Few recreation-vehicle owners took the yacht analogy as literally as the Spaeths. The land yacht's space was divided into a "forward lounge," "stateroom," and "after lounge," with a "galley," two lavatories, a shower, and three closets in between the main rooms. The lounges and stateroom had sofas that converted to double beds for the Spaeths and their four children. The galley was finished in stainless steel and was equipped with a sink, oil stove, electric refrigerator, cupboards, and an electric sign labeled TURN AND BANK INDICATOR that warned the cook of an approaching turn. The massive vehicle, which was painted battle-ship gray, measured 35 feet in length and weighed 18.5 tons. Spaeth called it an executive coach, but his friends dubbed it the Otto Bus or the Spaeth Ship.[36]

The land yacht was delivered to Otto Spaeth in New York on December 30, 1947. The next day he and his son, Otto L. ("Tony") Spaeth Jr., and two crewmen traveled to Cincinnati, Ohio, where Spaeth was building two Howard Johnson restaurants. From there the Spaeths traveled to Fort Wayne, Indiana, for the wedding of Otto's nephew, Bernard L. Spaeth, and Florence G. Swanson. The Spaeths returned to New York nonstop, two drivers alternating so that the vehicle could run day and night. During the next two years, the Spaeths traveled to forty-seven states in their land yacht, sightseeing, playing golf, visiting friends, and playing host and hostess to a variety of guests. Spaeth entertained the directors of many art museums on board the land yacht. He was president of the Spaeth Foundation, which assisted young artists and actively promoted the arts and architecture within the Catholic church. A collector of modern paintings and sculpture, Spaeth advocated the placement of art works in communities, religious organizations, and businesses. The walls of the land yacht were decorated with watercolors by American artists Charles Sheeler and Walt Kuhn.

During a visit to Washington, D.C., Spaeth stopped at the White House to see an old friend, Charles G. Ross, a former contributing editor of the *St. Louis Post-Dispatch* and now President Harry S. Truman's press secretary. The Associated Press reported, "Ross found the large bus so interesting that he brought the President out to the White House driveway for a look. Mr. Truman saw the small but complete kitchen, the fully equipped bathroom, the sleeping compartments, and the lounges. 'I don't think I would want to pay for the tires and the upkeep,' the President said."[37] President Truman politely signed the logbook of the Spaeth Ship.

A leading bus manufacturer responded to the small but steady market for luxury homes on wheels by producing complete vehicles on order. In 1948 the Flxible Company of Loudonville, Ohio, a manufacturer of intercity buses, introduced the Land Cruiser, a standard, twenty-nine-passenger bus shell with an elaborately furnished interior custom designed to the purchaser's specifications. In nearby Millersburg, Flxible's Special Products Division began building Land Cruisers in addition to mobile post offices, portable darkrooms, product display coaches, mobile television camera units, and other special vehicles that comprised its diverse product line.[38] According to James Dudte, a Flxible executive who was involved with sales of the company's buses in the 1940s, the Land Cruiser was the brainchild of Arthur L. Perkins, president of the Linn Coach and Truck Corporation of Oneonta, New York, which manufactured trailers and front-wheel-drive vehicles. Under Perkins's supervision, Linn had built the 1940 Johnson Wax house car in Oneonta. Dudte recalled that Perkins persuaded Flxible to enter the house-car business, and Perkins designed much of the interior layouts of the first Flxible Land Cruisers.[39]

Aimed primarily at business executives, more than a dozen Land Cruisers were sold for uses ranging from personal pleasure trips to corporate outings and mobile business activities. Goodyear officials used a Land Cruiser during the 1948 National Air Races in Cleveland, and a Flxible executive completed a six-month, 30,000-mile trip in one. The

Land Cruiser could be fitted with an office, radio with speaker system, telephone intercom, or radio-telephone for busy executives. A typical Land Cruiser measured an impressive 33 feet in length and was equipped with a rear-mounted Buick engine rated at 144 horsepower. A separate engine powered a generator, which provided electricity for a cookstove, refrigerator, hot water heater, and automatic coffee maker. The tiled bathroom had a shower stall, folding lavatory, and toilet with holding tank. At the touch of a button, a dinette, sofas, and chairs converted into sleeping berths for six or seven persons by means of electric motors. Each Land Cruiser was heated and air-conditioned. The walls were paneled with Honduran mahogany, and accordion-type folding screens separated the compartments. Prices ranged from about $18,000 to $33,000.[40]

One of the earliest Land Cruiser owners was J. C. Long, an attorney, developer, and city councilman in Charleston, South Carolina. Delivered in April 1948, Long's $30,000 vehicle had sleeping space for seven, seats for seventeen, and a rooftop deck for observation and lounging. The front was lettered ISLE OF PALMS after one of Long's residential developments near Charleston. Long used the home on wheels for visits to building sites, short recreational trips with his family and associates, and trips to the Kentucky Derby. In May 1952 six Charleston civic and business leaders borrowed Long's Land Cruiser for a tour of eastern states and the nation's capital to promote Charleston as a tourist destination. The novelty of the Land Cruiser helped to draw attention to the group and its mission. The vehicle was stocked with displays, literature, and audiovisual material about Charleston and was lettered CAROLINA LOWCOUNTRY SPECIAL for this trip.[41]

By the early 1950s Flxible was busy filling orders for the United States Army and urban transit companies and was less interested in building bus homes and other specialized vehicles. In 1955 Flxible sold its Special Products Division to Miles Elmers, former president of Detergents, Inc., of Columbus, Ohio. Elmers, who had owned a Land Cruiser since 1952, renamed the division Custom Coach Corporation and moved it to Columbus. He retained the name Land Cruiser for new or used buses (including Flxibles and other makes) that his company converted into custom homes on wheels.[42] By the 1960s the

A strong postwar market for recreation vehicles prompted the Flxible Company to furnish some of its intercity buses as luxury bus homes and sell them to affluent vacationers. J. C. Long (left), an attorney and real estate developer, purchased a Flxible Land Cruiser in 1948. (Courtesy The Beach Company)

prices of these modifications ranged from $10,000 to more than $50,000.[43]

Tourists who could afford to acquire and remodel their own intercity buses enjoyed advances in bus design and features, including reclining seats, storage compartments, and air conditioning. When Ernest Scrivener Jr., the owner of a building materials company in San Antonio, Texas, converted a Greyhound bus into a home on wheels, he retained several reclining seats and the convenient under-body luggage bays.[44] In 1955 Anheuser-Busch leased a split-level Greyhound Scenicruiser and converted it into a house car named the Anheuser; it was converted back into a bus the following year when the lease expired. The upper level of the bus was higher above the road than a conventional bus passenger compartment, which helped provide a smoother, quieter ride. Under-body luggage bays provided ample storage.[45]

Owners of do-it-yourself bus campers in the 1950s enjoyed doing chores that crew members performed in bus homes of the wealthy. Ernest Scrivener Jr. made the most of his role as chief cook and driver of his converted Greyhound bus, in which he escorted friends and relatives to fishing spots. (Courtesy Ernest Scrivener Jr.)

Postwar entertainers discovered intercity-bus conversions to be a convenient, expressive form of luxury travel. Bandleader Tommy Dorsey purchased a used White bus and had it remodeled as a home on wheels. He named the vehicle the Sentimentalist after his professional nickname, "The Sentimental Gentleman of Swing," and used it on band tours in the 1950s.[46] In about 1960 Elvis Presley purchased a Greyhound Scenicruiser and had it converted to a house car by George Barris, a well-known car customizer in southern California. The floor was lowered to provide more standing room and was covered with lead sheets to reduce engine and road noise. The lavish interior, which was decorated by Shirley Barris, George's wife, featured a main lounge with two sofas upholstered in red and sand striped velvet, an electronic entertainment console with color television, tape deck, and phonograph, and a "sky lounge" in red velvet and crimson carpet. Elvis's "royal suite" had porthole windows, an L-shaped bed upholstered in violet and gold, purple carpet, an entertainment console, makeup dresser, folding bunks, kitchen with automatic hot drink maker and refreshment bar, and a bathroom. Elvis used the vehicle on tours and trips between Graceland, his home near Memphis, Tennessee, and Hollywood. He often drove the vehicle himself and had a two-way radio system so that he could talk to business associates in cars following the bus.[47]

In the 1950s a new type of private sleeper bus began to outnumber luxury bus homes on America's highways. A do-it-yourself bus conversion was an attractive alternative for families and couples who wanted spacious, comfortable, low-cost accommodations. A used transit, intercity, or school bus could be purchased for a few hundred dollars and furnishings and equipment installed by the owners. Furnishings were far simpler and less expensive than those in buses for the wealthy. Converted buses were especially popular among large families, who often had difficulty finding adequate, affordable lodging. With a bus camper, budget-breaking motel bills disappeared, and there was as much space as in a motel room. A converted bus offered many advantages over a trailer or an automobile. Instead of squeezing into a tow car, as trailer families had to do, bus campers rode in their roomy vehicles and could walk from the living quarters to the driver's compartment. A bus was especially convenient in the rain; there was no need to go outside to change compartments or hitch a trailer to a tow car.

As early as 1949 Howard C. ("Bud") Stone, a mechanic who worked for the highway department in the town of Auburn, Massachusetts, purchased a 1934 Mack bus and converted it into a home on wheels. He had seen a converted school bus parked near his shop and decided that this type of vehicle would be ideal for pleasure trips. Stone and his wife, Audrey, removed most of the seats in the Mack and installed a double bed, kitchen, cupboards, and toilet. They retained two bus seats for a breakfast nook and hung curtains Audrey made out of sugar sacks. Lettered on the outside of their bus was THE ROLLING STONES. The Stones enjoyed many trips in the Mack and a succession of other converted buses, including a 1950 Marmon-Herrington and a 1948 Flxible. Their buses were especially handy when their children traveled with them in the 1960s.[48]

A typical bus camping family of the 1950s were the Youngs of North Hollywood, California. Lawrence Young, the manager of a printing business, purchased a used, thirty-five-passenger bus so that he, his wife, and their five children could avoid motel bills and crowded conditions in the family car. Young built bunks inside the bus. The Youngs spent their summers touring the United States, Mexico, and Canada in the bus.[49]

One of the most colorful family buses belonged to Stanford and Loyola Bardwell of Baton Rouge, Louisiana. In 1953 Stanford Bardwell, a realtor and insurance agent, purchased a new, 32-foot Blue Bird school bus with a Chevrolet chassis and had it converted into a sleeper bus by James Ponder, a trailer builder in Baton Rouge. A pun on wheels, the yellow bus was named the Collegiate Caravan, and its exterior was decorated with painted college pennants representing Stanford, Loyola, and their seven small children: Stanford Jr., Duke Kane, T'lane, Harvard, Princeton, Auburn, and Cornell. The bus had ten beds with privacy curtains for the Bardwells and their maid, Bea Houston. It also had tables that slid under the beds, a kitchen, bathroom, Kohler gasoline generator for the electrical appliances, and a 100-gallon water tank mounted on the roof. In the summer of 1953 the Bardwells toured the West in the Collegiate Caravan, and the following summer they visited Florida. They used the vehicle for vacation trips until about 1962.[50]

Many sporting enthusiasts also found bus campers convenient. In 1952 Harold Putzke, a General Motors dealer in Minnesota, purchased a 1941 Flxible intercity bus for $350 and converted it into a mobile hunting lodge named the Hunter's Den. He cut off the roof, raised it one foot, and added round windows in the roof extension for additional light. He equipped the bus with bunks for four people, an electric stove, propane-gas refrigerator, and freezer. A boat rested on the roof rack. Putzke and two friends, Dale Bast and Tom Vanderpool, used the Hunter's Den to hunt Canada geese in Saskatchewan. Putzke also drove the bus to Washington State, Alaska, and the East Coast.[51] In the early 1960s nine deer hunters in Maine formed the Nine Natives Club

Some baby-boom families traveled in spacious, converted buses during their vacations. The Collegiate Caravan, a 1953 Blue Bird school bus, belonged to the Bardwell family, whose given names matched colleges and universities. The Bardwells also appeared on Art Linkletter's House Party *on television. (Courtesy children of Stanford and Loyola Bardwell)*

and converted a 1948 Reo school bus. They removed the seats and installed bunks made of welded pipe and canvas, a sink, 30-gallon water tank, gas cookstove, gas space heater, and gasoline generator for lights, electric shavers, and the heater fan. The floor was covered with carpet removed from a room in Maine's state capitol. The men built a long wooden dining table and wooden benches with storage underneath for canned goods. The overhead book racks already in the bus were used to store various types of gear. Each year, the nine sportsmen lived in Maggie, as they affectionately named the bus, on deer hunting trips in the Maine woods.[52]

Owners of converted buses formed several organizations to socialize and share travel and technical information and ideas about interior conversions. The earliest organizations were local. In the late 1950s a group of converted-bus owners began meeting regularly in Minnesota, and in California owners of converted Flxible buses formed the Royal Coachmen.[53] Eight Michigan couples who owned converted school buses formed the Michigan Courtesy Coach Club in 1963; at their first meeting in McCurdy Park in Corunna, Michigan, they examined each other's coaches and discussed objectives of the new organization. Foremost among these objectives was establishing rules of conduct on the road, exchanging information about overnight parking places, and sharing tips on converting and maintaining the buses.[54]

The rapidly growing popularity of converted buses and bus organizations led to the formation of a national organization in 1963. A Massachusetts couple, Robert and Jean Richter, enjoyed trips in a 1940 General Motors intercity bus, which they had purchased in 1962 for $600 and converted into a vacation home on wheels. In 1962 the Richters obtained the names and addresses of eight other owners of bus campers, some of whom, like themselves, had purchased their vehicles from the Metropolitan Coach Company in Belmont, Massachusetts. The Richters sent handmade Christmas cards to the eight owners, inviting them to a get-acquainted party. Word spread quickly, and invitations were sent to more than one hundred owners of self-propelled homes on wheels. On July 18–21, 1963, some twenty-six camper vehicles, built between 1940 and 1963 and converted in the 1950s and early 1960s, rolled onto the campus of the Hinckley School, a private school in Hinckley, Maine. Sixteen vehicles were former intercity or transit buses, seven were former school buses, and three were manufactured motor homes. The 133 occupants, most of whom lived in the Northeast, came to socialize, witness a total eclipse of the sun, and consider the need for an organization to represent their interests.[55]

At the Hinckley gathering, the Family Motor Coach Association (FMCA) was formed "to promote and facilitate the ownership and use of self-propelled vehicles having self-contained cooking, sleeping and sanitary facilities as mobile living accommodations." The association's name, which was coined by members Raymond and Anna Fritz, sent a clearly democratic message: converted buses were affordable to middle-income Americans and filled a niche between the rolling palaces of wealthy tourists and small camping vehicles such as pickup campers and station wagons. A private bus was an acceptable, even superior way for an average family to see the country, and to FMCA members, it was as much a part of middle America as backyard barbecues and drive-in movies.

In contrast with makers of one-off house cars in the 1920s through the 1940s, the FMCA's founding members were not engineers, mechanics, or tinkerers but white-collar workers. Among the officers and directors were an electronics design engineer, an assistant superintendent of public schools, a business manager for a public school system, a farm service adviser for an electric utility company, a bakery equipment sales manager, and a physician. Robert Richter, an electronic components sales representative and former newspaper editor and printing executive, was elected president of the fledgling organization. The Richters' home in Hanson, Massachusetts, served as the first headquarters of the FMCA.[56]

By 1964 the FMCA had more than six hundred members from every region of the United States and Canada, and by 1965 approximately one thousand members from forty-nine states and several foreign countries.[57] Local bus owners' organizations either ceased to exist or became chapters of the FMCA. *Family Motor Coaching* magazine, founded by the Richters in 1964, became the association's official organ and featured technical and travel information, vehicle descriptions, advertisements, and notices of association meetings. The FMCA continued to grow and flourish in the next several decades to include tens of thousands of members.

The bus-conversion hobby attracted more and more families in the 1960s. In 1962 Richard Pierce, a fireman in Moline, Illinois, and his wife, Bess, converted a 1948 International school bus into a vacation home on wheels named the Omnibus. They obtained some parts and furnishings for the interior from a local pickup-camper distributor and made others by hand. The Pierces and their three children traveled to New York, Washington, D.C., Florida, and many other places in the eastern United States and Canada.[58] Roy Bucklew, operator of the La Jolla Motel in Islamorada, Florida, paid $400 for a transit bus that had operated between Brownsville, Texas, and Matamoras, Mexico. He removed the seats and installed an icebox, freezer, running water system, bathroom with shower, and holding tank. The I Kontiki was furnished with a double bed and a dinette that converted into a double bed. Bucklew, his wife, Joy, and their daughters, Sandi, Kristi, and Panchi, were musically inclined, so they installed an organ in the bus and took a flute, trumpet, guitar, maracas, and claves on their trips. The Bucklews traveled to New Orleans, Carlsbad Caverns, the Grand Canyon, Las Vegas, and Mexico City in the I Kontiki.[59]

Arthur and Dorothea Baker of Philadelphia grew tired of tent camping in uncertain weather conditions, and they sought a more comfortable means of travel for themselves and their seven small children. In 1963 Baker, a tractor-trailer driver, purchased a 1949 General Motors school bus for $450 and converted it. He removed the seats, built triple-deck bunk beds out of pipe and fabric, and installed a double bed that also served as a table. He also installed a stove, a Coca-Cola chest for an icebox, and a playpen that fastened to the floor. The Bakers frequently traveled in the home on wheels, which they named the Baker's Doze-In. On their first journey in August 1963 they visited Niagara Falls and Quebec. And on subsequent trips to relatives' homes in southeastern Pennsylvania the bus served as a guest house.[60]

A more expensive option for middle-class vacationers was to commission a bus conversion by a professional body shop. The Thomas F. Moroney Company, a body conversion shop in Shrewsbury, Massachusetts, modified school buses, delivery trucks, and other vehicles for recreational use at prices in the $5,000–$6,000 range. Moroney recalled, "People came in with a dream, and we built it." Typically, these one-off vehicles were used in New England and for trips to western parks. Moroney advertised his conversion services and considered manufacturing recreation vehicles, but the estimated retail price of $25,000 for a specially designed vehicle discouraged him from entering the business.[61]

No matter how they obtained their vehicles, many Americans of the 1950s and early 1960s came to prefer the intimacy and maneuverability of a self-propelled camper over the cramped riding conditions and difficult driving characteristics of a tow car and travel trailer. With the prosperity of the 1950s, the roadside environment continued to improve, and families felt comfortable traveling for extended periods of time. But self-propelled vacation vehicles were lacking in some important respects. One problem was the range of available sizes; a bus was too large for most families and a station wagon too small. Another problem was the popular image of recreation vehicles. In a few years station wagon styling had changed to fit consumers' tastes and harmonize with family sedans, but the same was not true of buses. A bus was still a commercial vehicle and was not always a welcome sight in the driveway. Before self-propelled campers could be widely accepted, their designers had to transfer the modern furnishings and ranchlike exterior of a travel trailer to a vehicle that was smaller than a bus but larger than a station wagon. With the right balance of vehicle size, outward appearance, furnishings, and maneuverability, vacationers could be lured away from travel trailers and motels. A few alert manufacturers who believed that motorized homes would appeal to many vacationers designed and produced several new types of house cars in the 1950s and early 1960s.

5 HOUSE CARS REVISITED

ost–World War II house-car owners were attracted to the strength and simplicity of factory-made, metal bodies and integral chassis. Pickup trucks with mounted campers, converted delivery trucks, and van campers appealed to thousands of vacationers because they were relatively inexpensive, easier to drive than a car towing a trailer, and could cover rough terrain more easily than bus-size recreation vehicles. Truck campers were not subject to reduced speed limits as were trailers and could be licensed as automobiles in many states. Unlike travel-trailer owners, families with truck campers could ride together without crowding into a tow car. Increasingly, vacationers chose to use small, self-propelled work vehicles for pleasure trips because of their driveability, affordability, and comfort.

For the first time, a sizable self-propelled camper manufacturing industry developed. By the late 1950s scores of independent pickup camper manufacturers in California, Michigan, and elsewhere were turning out camper bodies at prices that vacationers of average means could afford. Unlike house cars and buses, pickup campers were not imitations of recreation vehicles owned by wealthy tourists; instead, they were the realization of Gustav de Bretteville's concept of a versatile, add-on camper box that could be manufactured and sold at a modest price, a concept that he promoted in 1916. In the early 1960s automobile manufacturers were selling specially designed pickup trucks for use with camper bodies as well as complete van campers and delivery truck campers. With its simplicity and conveniences, the factory-built truck camper promised to become everyone's recreation vehicle.

SMALLER IS BETTER: THE PICKUP CAMPER

The most popular type of truck camper in the postwar era was the pickup camper—a pickup truck with a fully furnished body mounted on the cargo area. The pickup camper was made possible because of the increased size and strength of postwar pickup trucks. A small, personal truck, the pickup had evolved from both light trucks and automobiles. By 1910 many light trucks with express or box bodies were on the market.[1] In the 1910s and 1920s aftermarket cargo beds made by independent manufacturers were added to touring cars and runabouts. Mass-produced pickups soon followed; in 1925 Ford introduced the Model T Runabout with Pick-Up Body, and other manufacturers soon marketed similar vehicles. The pickup truck became a staple of small businesses, manual trades, and farming, carrying a wide variety of small goods, equipment, farm produce, and other cargo. By the 1940s, in response to the pickup's versatility and popularity, pickup-truck beds had become longer, wider, and capable of carrying heavier loads. For recreational purposes, it seemed more practical to build a camper body that rested on the truck bed rather than dismantling and replacing the cargo-carrying portion of the truck.

Pickup campers offered many advantages over travel trailers and converted buses. Not the least of these was the camper body's low purchase price, which was much less than that of a trailer or bus. Maneuverability was another advantage. Due to its relatively small size, a pickup truck was easy to steer and back up and could be driven faster than an automobile towing a trailer, a major advantage in states that limited trailer speeds. Light, powerful, and designed with superior road clearance and traction (because of the added weight on the rear drive wheel), a pickup camper could travel in rough areas where other vehicles might get stuck. This was especially appealing to people who sought remote spots off the highways for hunting and fishing. Perhaps most appealing of all, the camper body could be removed and stored between trips, and the truck could be used for other purposes.

Like other types of recreation vehicles, the earliest pickup campers were one-off vehicles designed and built by motorists who wanted to sleep in their pickup trucks. Unlike house-car owners of the 1920s, who started with bare chassis and built boxlike bodies, autocampers of the 1940s typically started with a complete pickup truck. Some early pickup-truck campers simply placed a fabric cover over the cargo bed. In 1941, for example, Thomas Pugh, a farmer near Lawrence, Kansas, covered the back of his Studebaker pickup truck with metal bows and a tarpaulin during a pleasure trip to Cody, Wyoming, and Yellowstone National Park. The tarpaulin was put on each night, and Pugh, his wife, Emma, and their daughters, Barbara and Verna, slept in the vehicle, which was parked beside or behind gasoline stations or in city parks.

In 1944 or 1945 Pugh, then in his sixties and semiretired, built a more substantial plywood enclosure for the same pickup truck so that the family could spend the winter in the warm climate of the Rio Grande Valley in Texas. The wooden enclosure rested on the sides of the truck's cargo bed. The only furnishings in the camper body were a large mattress on boards, a Coleman gasoline lantern, and a kerosene cookstove, which was used outdoors or inside a tent. The Pughs spent the nights at gasoline stations or roadside parks. At Mission, Texas, their final destination, the Pughs and their children, Barbara and Thomas Jr., lived in the camper for about six months. Barbara's half sister, Margaret, and her husband, Delbert Steele, and their two small boys lived in a tarpaulin-covered pickup camper near the Pughs. The men worked for a local well driller, and the women cooked for their families and worked as maids for the well driller and his wife.

After returning to Kansas, Thomas Pugh removed the camper body from his pickup whenever he needed the truck for other purposes. In 1947 the camper body was reattached, and all four of the Pughs took another trip to Cody and Yellowstone in the Studebaker. They were joined by Charles Warren, Emma's uncle, who owned a truck camper similar to the Pughs'.[2]

Influenced by the domestic furnishings and the smooth outward appearance of travel trailers, early commercially made pickup campers

In the 1940s some outdoor enthusiasts furnished boxlike bodies with camping equipment and mounted them on the backs of pickup trucks. Manufactured versions like this Cree Truck Coach became popular because they offered comfort, traction, and maneuverability at low prices. (Courtesy Dorotha Cree Bent)

were essentially miniature trailers placed on pickup trucks. A Michigan trailer park owner became one of the pioneer manufacturers of pickup campers. Howard L. Cree, a native of Brownsville, Pennsylvania, had worked in a coal mine and operated an ice cream shop with his wife, Lillian, before moving to Detroit in 1929. In the late 1930s and early 1940s the couple operated Cree's Log Cabin and Trailer Court on U.S. 24–25, 7 miles from downtown Detroit. Thirty furnished cabins stood beside a restaurant, general store, laundry, and travel-trailer campground. Soon Cree began selling Covered Wagon and Silver Moon trailers on the side. During World War II, he sold the cabins and trailer park and moved to Marcellus, Michigan, where he purchased the local Ford dealership.[3]

Cree was an avid sportsman and planned to hunt and fish in Alaska. It occurred to him that a truck and camper combined in a single vehicle would be more stable, compact, and maneuverable on Alaska's back roads than an automobile towing a travel trailer. His trailer park had been well patronized by sportsmen, vacationers, and others, and Cree drew on his observations of homemade and manufactured trailers to design an "ideal" pickup camper for his own use. He and some friends built a camper body out of Masonite and installed it on a Ford pickup truck.

As it turned out, Cree did not have time to go to Alaska. He made some improvements to his camper, built two additional campers at the request of acquaintances, and displayed a wood-and-aluminum version at a sports and travel show on Navy Pier in Chicago in 1945. Public response at Navy Pier encouraged Cree to hire some carpenters and cabinet makers to build pickup campers in Marcellus, and he set up dealers in several states. In 1950 he finally drove to Alaska to deliver two campers to the Cree dealer in Anchorage and a third one to a customer in Valdez. While in Alaska, Cree hunted bear and elk and fished for salmon and trout on the Kenai Peninsula.

In the early 1950s, as demand for camping vehicles grew, Cree publicized his pickup-camper body in sales literature, popular magazine articles, and displays at fairs. Originally marketed to sportsmen, the Cree Truck Coach soon attracted a wide range of motorists, including vacationing families, retirees, and itinerant workers. The rugged, compact truck and camper unit especially appealed to those who chose to live, work, or play in remote areas and needed room for only two or three people. Among Cree's customers were retired businessmen, farmers, and teachers who enjoyed cross-country sightseeing trips, as well as pipeline inspectors, oil exploration teams, sheepherders, contractors, fire and game wardens, and salesmen who needed portable housing.[4]

The appeal of the Cree camper had more to do with practicality than aesthetics. It had all of the homeliness and simplicity of a Model T; a bread box on wheels, it was covered with aluminum, Masonite, or Homasote on the exterior and varnished plywood on the interior, with fiberglass insulation in between. Most of the comforts of a travel trailer—cushioned seats that converted into a 6 foot 6 inch double bed, a folding table, curtains, gas range, cabinets, clothes closet, sink with running water, icebox, and 6 volt DC/110 volt AC electrical system for lights—were packed into an 8-foot unit. An electric refrigerator and 10-foot body were available as options.

By the 1950s Cree was well known as a pioneer manufacturer of pickup campers and as an explorer and lecturer. In 1957 Pablo Bush Romero, his dealer in Mexico, accompanied him in a Cree pickup camper during a five-month hunting safari in Africa. Cree took 16-millimeter film footage of the expedition and turned that into a movie titled *Bwana M'bogo (Master of the Buffalo),* which he presented free of charge at schools and corporate and civic meetings in the United States.[5]

The founder of the west coast pickup camper industry was Walter King, a former railroad worker and shipyard foreman who manufactured small "teardrop" trailers in Torrance, California, a suburb of Los Angeles. An avid outdoorsman, King drove his pickup truck on a hunting trip to Idaho in the fall of 1944 with a Kampmaster teardrop trailer in tow. Struggling through an early snowstorm, he got an idea: why not put the trailer on the back of the pickup to improve traction and driveability? After he returned home, he designed a pickup camper and, when materials became available after the war, built a prototype. In the fall of 1945 King and his wife, Eleanor, traveled in the prototype pickup camper to Montana during elk hunting season. There they met a sheepherder who admired their rig and ordered five pickup campers for himself and other itinerant sheepherders. The Kings added pickup campers to the product line, and Sport King campers, made of aluminum sheeting over a wooden frame, soon attracted many who wanted a small, rugged, and maneuverable recreation vehicle.[6]

In the 1950s the Los Angeles area became a major center of pickup-camper production as more manufacturers followed King's initiative. Southern California's temperate climate, population density, and proximity to mountainous areas created strong demand for rugged, maneuverable camping vehicles. By the end of the decade, one estimate placed the number of pickup-camper manufacturers nationwide at more than eighty, with about fifty located in southern California.[7] The Dreamer, made by Coons Custom Coach in Pomona, the Sports Cab, made by Highway Cruisers of California in Azusa, the Travel Queen, made in Norco (later in Pomona), and the Pullman, made by the Downey Sheet Metal Shop in Downey, were among the early units produced in this region.

Pullman founder Virgil Maidl had seen several other pickup campers before deciding to build one for camping, hunting, and fishing trips with his wife, Mabel, in 1955. He built another camper for a friend, and in 1956 the Maidls set up a pickup-camper display at the H. Werner Buck sporting-goods show in Los Angeles. After receiving twenty-seven orders at the show, they decided to close their sheet-metal business and manufacture campers. The distinctive design of the Pullman camper included a slide-out canopy at the rear that protected occupants from sun and rain while they rested or used the fold-out table and pantry. Mabel Maidl became a well-known "wagonmaster," leading camper treks or "caravans" to scenic locations in western states as well as Canada and Mexico.[8]

In Compton, a suburb of Los Angeles, Hayward Powell and his brother, Channing Powell, who had built one-off house cars, manufactured pickup trucks and pickup campers from 1954 to 1957. The Powell brothers wanted to build an inexpensive pickup that looked and handled like an automobile but had the utility features of a truck. Their slogan was "Built like a battleship, drives like a sports car, rides like a sedan."[9] Every Powell Sport Wagon had a used 1941 Plymouth automobile chassis and a squarish, colorful body made in the Powell factory. The Powell pickup was available with an optional camper body made of plywood and metal. The camper top flipped up on hinges to provide more headroom, and the camper contained two mattresses on folding plywood supports. Some models had a pull-out cabinet for a cookstove and storage space. Another product, the Powell Station Wagon, featured an optional bed for the rear cargo area. A unique feature of both the Powell Sport Wagon and the Powell Station Wagon was a metal tube that slid into a rear fender for fishing rods, guns, tools, maps, or other narrow objects.[10]

Despite their growing popularity, pickup campers had several disadvantages that limited their appeal. Most pickup-camper bodies were too small to accommodate a large family; the width at floor level was limited to the space between the wheel wells in the pickup-truck bed and most could accommodate only two to four people. The ride inside the truck cab and camper body was not very comfortable. Furthermore, family members were separated from each other on the road. There were handling problems as well; the camper body was not always compatible with the pickup truck's size, weight, and suspension, often making the vehicle tail-heavy. Many pickup-camper owners drove half-ton pickup trucks, which were too light for the average camper body and tended to sway or even overturn with a camper attached. Undersized pickup trucks also tended to develop tire and chassis trouble with the added weight of a camper. The tall camper body created wind resistance at the front and sides, which decreased stability and increased fuel consumption.

As the market for pickup campers grew, some camper manufacturers tried to overcome space limitations by building bodies that were larger and better equipped. They accepted width limitations, but in order to increase space, they built longer units. The cab-over body, a design that originated on moving vans and delivery trucks, added sleeping space above the pickup cab. A rear overhang added storage space and made entry and exit easier. Trailer amenities such as showers and toilets were added. The larger, better furnished models were given a new product name, the pickup coach, to distinguish them from the simpler pickup camper.

Another way to increase interior volume was to build a taller unit. Among the most visually impressive examples of a tall, spacious pickup coach were Kamp King Koaches, made by the McNamee Coach Corporation in southern California. Merle D. McNamee, a former construction worker and owner of a sheet-metal shop in Rosemead, California, began making custom sheet-metal covers for pickup trucks in 1952. Within a few years he began building fully furnished pickup campers in response to growing demand. In 1957 he moved to a factory in South El Monte, California, and built stylish cab-over models that soared over the pickup truck and featured front observation windows. In the early 1960s Kamp King Koaches epitomized the trend toward larger pickup coaches. One of their three-level giants was mounted directly on a 1-ton truck chassis and had a walk-through connection between the

The Penthouse pickup camper, made by the McNamee Coach Corporation, had a folding upper story and a deck. Suburban families of the 1960s felt at home with these inexpensive, houselike features. (Courtesy Merle D. McNamee)

cab and the camper, sleeping accommodations for six people, a combination den and dining room, and a wood-burning fireplace.[11]

Building a camper body that telescoped vertically was a clever way to increase height without adding wind resistance. In 1953 Robert Donald ("Don") Hall and his wife, Irene, designed and built a pickup-camper body divided into a fixed lower portion and an upper portion that could be raised or lowered hydraulically.[12] Don Hall was a sheet-metal worker at Brady's Sheet Metal Shop in Burbank, California, and built his special camper during evenings and weekends in his garage. Irene's only instructions to her husband were, "Make it go up and down." By 1955 the camper was ready for testing. Two years later the Halls drove the camper to Alaska, where Don could enjoy his favorite sports, hunting and fishing. They met many people who expressed interest in their unusual vehicle.

When the Halls returned to California, the owner of Brady's Sheet Metal Shop borrowed their camper and was so impressed that he encouraged them to go into production. The Halls began producing telescoping campers in 1958, first naming them Hi-Lo, then Alcan (after the Alaskan Highway), and finally Alaskan. By the 1970s the R. D. Hall Manufacturing Company was operating a factory in Sun Valley, California, and six franchised manufacturers were operating Alaskan camper factories in Pennsylvania, Texas, Colorado, South Dakota, Washington State, and Alberta. Don Hall was in charge of production at Sun Valley, and Irene managed sales and promotion, including frequent displays at sports and recreation vehicle shows.[13] Other manufacturers soon applied the telescoping concept to the Tuk-a-Way, Turnpike, and other pickup campers.

Some camper builders in the 1950s and early 1960s increased the stability and volume of pickup coaches by mounting the coach body directly onto the truck chassis, without a cargo bed in between. These "chassis-mounts" were basically spruced-up versions of 1920s house cars. One Florida couple, the Rhynes, purchased a new Chevrolet pickup truck chassis, had it extended, and built a boxlike living unit with trailer-type windows and screens, sliding back door, innerspring mattresses, bottled gas stove, and complete kitchen and bathroom. They removed the seat from the cab and installed a more comfortable, reupholstered seat from an Oldsmobile car. They traveled to Florida, the Great Smoky Mountains, the Gulf of Mexico, and many other destinations in their vehicle.[14] Kenn Hore, a retired bookseller, purchased a Dodge pickup-truck chassis and built a plywood-box body to serve as a house car and "semi-permanent vacation home in the woods."[15] By the early 1960s several pickup coach manufacturers, including Mitchell, Roll-A-Long (Roll-A-Long Sportster), Jaclen (Turnpike Cruiser), and Bermar (VagaBondia) offered models that bolted directly onto the truck chassis. Some chassis-mounts had passageways that made it possible to walk from the driver's compartment to the camper. Despite the passageway and extra space, chassis-mounted pickup coaches were less versatile than slide-ins and accounted for only a small percentage of pickup camper production. A chassis-mounted camper could not be removed as easily as a slide-in, and the rear half of the pickup truck could not be used for farm and house chores between vacation trips.

Despite growing consumer interest in pickup trucks and campers, pickup-truck sales were sluggish in the late 1950s, falling from a total of 537,299 in 1955 to 344,110 in the recession year of 1958.[16] Essentially a work vehicle, the pickup truck was not widely accepted as a family vehicle and was not a common sight in suburban driveways. Since the 1920s the pickup truck had been a workingman's tool. Farmers, ranchers, mechanics, plumbers, and many other people who worked with their hands depended on the tough, versatile cargo carrier for their everyday needs. In the 1940s pickup-truck camping was merely a leisure-time activity for workingmen. But in the late 1950s and early 1960s a new market for pickup trucks emerged as consumers, including families and single women, bought them for use as primary or secondary cars and, in some cases, specifically for recreational travel. By the early 1960s pickup-truck manufacturers offered features that supported the weight of campers more gracefully and provided better handling on the road. A pickup truck with a longer wheelbase shifted the center of gravity forward of the rear axle, increasing stability. Better suspension helped smooth the ride. The 1965 Chevrolet Custom Camper, for example, had heavy-duty shock absorbers, auxiliary rear springs, and a front stabilizer bar for better steering. The 1965 Ford Camper Special had independent front suspension and coil springs for a sedanlike ride.

Some new pickup trucks featured automotive styling meant to appeal to middle-class consumers. Broad, square hoods, chrome trim, whitewall tires, sculpted sides, two-tone paint schemes, designer upholstery, and other touches personalized the pickup truck and made it look more at home beside the family car. The most conspicuous examples of trucks with car styling were the 1955 Chevrolet Cameo, which had stylish upholstery, a chrome grille and trim, a two-tone paint scheme, and automobile-type wheel covers, the two-tone 1957 Ford Styleside, and the 1957 Dodge Sweptside, which had automobile-type tail lights, a two-tone paint scheme, and tail fins like some Dodge automobiles. All of these models remained in production several years. The 1959 Chevrolet El Camino and 1960 Ford Falcon Ranchero were actual passenger automobiles with cargo beds instead of trunks, thus completing a circle that began with Ford Model T touring cars converted into pickups. By 1960 the pickup, like the station wagon, was evolving from a truck to an automobile, and consumers were learning to make the most of its virtues as a recreation vehicle. Even camper shells for the El Camino and Ranchero were sold in the early 1960s.

As more consumers discovered the advantages of pickup trucks, a sales boom of historic proportions began. Pickup-truck sales had increased in 1959 and almost doubled by the mid-1960s, growing from 538,349 units in 1960 to 1,015,219 units in 1965. Pickup-camper production rose from 15,800 units in 1961 to 44,300 units in 1965.[17] A new focus on the health benefits of outdoor activity, stimulated by the President's Council on Physical Fitness and well-known health advocates such as bicyclist and cardiologist Paul Dudley White, helped popularize outdoor recreation and recreation vehicles.

Perhaps the most famous pickup-camper owner was Pulitzer Prize–winning novelist John Steinbeck. The social aspects of mobility fascinated Steinbeck; several of his best-known novels, including *The Grapes of Wrath* (1939) and *The Wayward Bus* (1947), focused on migration, motor vehicles, and the highway as a social environment. He often drew on firsthand observations of people in motion in the California valley where he was born and raised. In the 1960s he began writing nonfiction books and articles about American society as a whole, but he felt that he was looking at the nation through the prism of his New York City home, the media, and memories of trips that he had taken in the 1930s. At age fifty-eight he decided to travel around the United States in a recreation vehicle and record his observations of the land and its people, noting regional differences, changes, and idiosyncracies. "What I'll get I need badly," he wrote to friends, "a re-knowledge of my own country, of its speeches, its views, its attitudes and its changes. It's long overdue—very long."[18] Steinbeck's factual travelogue was published serially in *Holiday* and in book form as *Travels with Charley: In Search of America* (1962).[19]

In order to get in touch with grassroots America, Steinbeck insisted on anonymity. He wanted the freedom to mingle inconspicuously with people in their own environments and hoped the camper would help him blend in. The novelist thought of the pickup camper not as a consumer's plaything but as a workingman's vehicle. He also liked the voyeuristic access that a pickup truck allowed and believed that only a pickup camper could take him to the figurative heart of America. In a letter to a friend Steinbeck wrote,

> Motels and bus routes are on the main highways. One cannot leave the highways. At a motel or tourist house you have made an inroad—your coming is noted—your name registered, your intentions and plans subject to question or curiosity.
>
> I chose a truck for several reasons. First, a truck is a respectable and respected working instrument as apart from a station wagon or an automobile or a trailer. Second—in a truck I can get into a countryside not crossed by buses. I can see people not in movement but at home in their own places. This is very important to me.
>
> Now my reason for wanting to be self-contained is that I also will be at home. I can invite a man to have a beer in my home, thereby forcing an invitation from him.[20]

Steinbeck was no stranger to truck campers. In 1936, while visiting migrant farm laborers in California in preparation for a series of articles for the *San Francisco News*, he lived in a former bakery truck equipped with a mattress, blankets, food, and cooking utensils. He later reminisced, "I traveled about in an old bakery wagon, double-doored rattler with a mattress on its floor. I stopped where people stopped or gathered, I listened and looked and felt, and in the process had a picture of my country the accuracy of which was impaired only by my own shortcomings."[21]

In preparation for the trip through the United States, Steinbeck wrote to General Motors and outlined in specific terms what kind of pickup camper he thought he would need. With GM's help, he ordered a 1960 GMC pickup truck and a camper made by the Wolverine Camper Company of Gladwin, Michigan. The camper was equipped with a double bed, stove, refrigerator, heater, interior lights, and chemical toilet. Steinbeck named the trip Operation America, but when friends described the project as quixotic, he began calling it Operation Windmills and named the truck camper Rocinante after the protagonist's horse in Miguel de Cervantes's satirical novel *Don Quixote*. Shirley Fisher, a friend of Steinbeck's, painted ROCINANTE on the side of the camper body in sixteenth-century Spanish script.[22]

Steinbeck suffered a mild stroke in late 1959. His wife, Elaine, and some of his acquaintances were openly apprehensive about him traveling alone. But Steinbeck insisted on going. For companionship, he asked Elaine for permission to take Charley (Charles le Chien), a French poodle he had given her. Elaine agreed and jokingly said that Charley would take care of him. After loading the camper with books, hunting rifles, supplies, and emergency equipment, Steinbeck left his Long Island fishing retreat on September 23, 1960, and drove north through Massachusetts and Vermont. As the trip progressed, his attitude toward the compact home on wheels changed from bold anticipation to gritty acceptance. Before the trip, he euphemistically compared the camper to "the cabin of a small boat or the shell of a learned snail."[23] On the road he endured a grinding regimen of driving, cooking, cleaning, and taking care of Charley. Often he ate in restaurants to escape the monotony. He longed for a bathtub and telephone and often stayed in a motel to enjoy those conveniences. During one of many long-distance telephone calls to Elaine, she commented on his letters describing the journey. "They remind me of *Travels with a Donkey*," she said, referring to Robert Louis Stevenson's travelogue about southern France. "I think of them as *Travels with Charley*." Steinbeck replied, "You've just given me my title."[24]

As Steinbeck had hoped, his truck camper attracted curious people. Before inviting them in, Steinbeck fastidiously polished the stove, washed the refrigerator, and scrubbed the floor. "Talking with people is easy because everyone loves the truck," he wrote to Elaine. "It's stopping like this that gets talk going. Everyone wants to see the inside of the truck."[25] The truck camper also allowed him to rub shoulders with transient workers. Before the trip, Steinbeck did not consider travelers worthy of his study. "They are not *home* and they are not themselves," he wrote to a friend. "There is a change that takes place in a man or a woman in transit."[26] But during the trip, he discovered that the road *was* home for many workers. In Wisconsin, for example, he parked behind a truck stop and mingled with truckers in the coffee shop. And in Minnesota a gas station attendant invited him to park for the night in a row of tractor trailers that were hauling cattle. He talked to a truck driver at breakfast and watched the truckers load cattle into the trailers.

Although Steinbeck thought of permanence and mobility as opposite lifestyles, he obviously could conceive of his truck camper as a portable home and truck stops as a form of community. But he harbored deep antipathy toward vehicles as permanent housing. After visiting a residential trailer park, Steinbeck railed against the synthetic, sterile qualities of the immobilized metal boxes. In a letter to Elaine, he sarcastically wrote:

> This trailer business is very important. It means you will throw away a house the way you consign a car to the junkyard.
>
> These [trailer dwellers] are Martians. I wanted to ask them to take me to their leader. They have no humor, no past and their future is new models. . . . I said to the owner [of one trailer,] "That looks like an architect's office." He said, "It's my home!" That's dreadful! A home accumulates. A home has a roof of hope and cellar of memories. That's our kind of home. But there's a new kind. That man meant it. That plywood and aluminum thing is his "home."[27]

After rolling through the northern tier, Pacific coast, Southwest, and deep South, Steinbeck's own home on wheels had become little more than a refuge from his exhaustion and stupefaction. Of the last leg of the trip he wrote, "My bed was unmade. I slipped into it for naps at long uneven intervals. My stove was unlighted and a loaf of bread gathered mold in my cupboard. The miles rolled under me unacknowledged."[28] The trip, overall, was productive and successful. In February 1961, soon after his return to Long Island, John and Elaine went to Barbados, where John began writing *Travels with Charley* from his notes and letters. Published in July 1962, *Travels with Charley* was a best-seller. This was a happy period in Steinbeck's life; in October 1962 his accomplishments were given the highest recognition when he was awarded the Nobel Prize in Literature.[29]

DELIVERY TRUCKS

Although the delivery truck was never accepted by consumers as an all-purpose family vehicle, stand-up delivery-truck campers could be found at campgrounds from coast to coast. Many of their interiors were installed by the owners themselves, but professionally made versions were available from several leading truck manufacturers. Approximately the size of a pickup truck, a stand-up delivery truck had several advantages over a pickup-truck camper: it was built as a single, well-balanced unit, had an aerodynamic shape, and the driver's compartment was connected to the living quarters, adding a sense of togetherness that a pickup camper lacked.

Introduced in the 1930s, the stand-up delivery truck had a streamlined, capsule shape, snub-nosed front, and tall body. Although smaller than a strandard delivery truck, the stand-up truck had plenty of head room, and the driver could walk easily from the front seat to the rear of the vehicle. By the 1940s several makes of stand-up trucks, including the Ford Vanette, Chevrolet Dubl-Duti, Chevrolet Step-Van, Dodge Route-Van, and others, were familiar sights in commercial areas of cities and in residential neighborhoods. Drivers delivered milk, bread, and other baked goods to stores and residences, picked up and delivered laundry, and performed many other consumer-oriented services. Many stand-up trucks were used by plumbers, radio repairers, and other technicians to carry parts and equipment.[30]

Because of its spaciousness and standing room, a stand-up truck camper readily lent itself to dressing, sleeping, and cooking. Like most recreation vehicles, demand among individual consumers preceded the manufacture of campers with this type of body. In about 1946 one of the earliest manufacturers of stand-up delivery-truck bodies, the Boyertown Body and Equipment Company of Boyertown, Pennsylvania, installed a camper interior in a delivery-truck body and placed it on a Dodge truck chassis at the request of freelance writer Wallace R. Boren. Boren was best known for his long-running column "Wally's Wagon," a feature in *This Week* magazine that served up bits of homespun humor and philosophy in a mythical lunch-wagon setting. Boren, his wife, Blanche, and their daughter, Elaine, used their truck camper for pleasure trips in the late 1940s.[31]

Sensing a potential market for a camping vehicle that was smaller, lighter, and easier to maneuver than a travel trailer or a converted bus, Boyertown introduced the Tour Wagon in 1949. This vehicle consisted

Wallace R. Boren (left), a writer and outdoor enthusiast, asked the Boyertown Body and Equipment Company to furnish a small delivery truck as a camper for trips with his wife, Blanche (right), and their daughter, Elaine (center). From the 1950s to the 1980s, Boyertown sold hundreds of Merchandiser trucks equipped as Tour Wagons. (Courtesy Elaine Boren Dodge)

of a Boyertown Merchandiser stand-up delivery-truck body with a special interior and a Ford chassis. The 18.5-foot welded-steel bodies were taken from the Merchandiser assembly line and furnished with two seats that formed a double bed, a kitchen with sink, gas range and icebox, a folding table, gasoline space heater, clothes closet, storage lockers, dome lights, and bathroom with washbasin and chemical toilet. A portable shower could be installed in the front door, and the rear opening could be fitted with double doors or a hatch that opened to form either a "porch" or a ramp. The price of a complete Tour Wagon was approximately $4,600, less than the cost of a custom-bus conversion but three times the cost of a travel trailer of similar size. The Tour Wagon body could be purchased separately for $3,070 and mounted on the purchaser's truck chassis. A demonstrator unit was displayed at automobile shows in the Northeast.[32]

The Tour Wagon was novel and appealing because of its small, streamlined metal body. Aesthetically and functionally, it was the realization of one-off, teardrop-shaped house-car prototypes of the late 1930s such as the Pribil Aircar and the Turtle. Although a Tour Wagon could not accommodate a large family, Boyertown anticipated a broad market encompassing vacationers, sporting enthusiasts, traveling salespeople, itinerant hobbyists, surveyors, explorers, geologists, entertainers, and others. The Tour Wagon was popular and continued selling well in the 1960s, when the two-bed Custom 202 model, priced at $6,995, and the four-bed Custom 204 model, priced at $7,295, were available on Chevrolet, Dodge, or Ford chassis. Interior appointments in the 1960s included modern home furnishings such as a stainless-steel sink, Formica counter top, dinette, and upholstery, and draperies in "decorator" colors.[33] Several hundred Tour Wagons were built, most on Ford chassis, before production ended in the 1980s.

Some tourists and sporting enthusiasts found it less expensive to buy a stand-up truck and convert it themselves. In 1957 Eugene Lewis, a mechanic and welder in Indiana, installed a camper interior in a Chevrolet Step-Van. He and his wife toured many parts of the United States in their truck camper.[34] In 1959 Gerald Hatfield and other members of the Bellflower Sportsmans Club near Los Angeles converted a 1953 Ford Vanette into a camper. Hatfield used it for hunting and fishing trips and vacations until 1965, when he bought a Seeburg Music demonstrator truck and converted it into a home on wheels. Several other members of the Bellflower club also converted stand-up delivery trucks for their own use.[35]

One of the largest concentrations of custom, stand-up delivery trucks was at Cape Cod on the Massachusetts shore. In the 1940s and 1950s hundreds of adult recreational anglers camped on the beach in converted automobiles, "woody" wagons, and panel trucks equipped with beds, food cabinets, and cooking facilities. These third- and fourth-hand vehicles had large tires for better traction, and some had extra layers of paint to protect against blowing salt and sand in 1950. Some of the sand campers formed the Massachusetts Beach Buggy Association (MBBA), a mutual aid organization dedicated to the promotion of safety, compliance with traffic laws, removal of litter, and enjoyment of social activities. A converted stand-up delivery truck became the vehicle of choice for many MBBA members. Most trucks were emblazoned with fanciful names such as SAND SCHOONER and CONTINENTAL CRUISER. These trucks, along with converted vans, pickup campers, converted buses, and manufactured motor homes, were a common sight on Cape Cod's beaches.[36]

Some affluent motorists hired body shops to design and build interiors for their stand-up delivery trucks. In the early 1950s Walter Glascoff Jr., a cannery owner in Waupun, Wisconsin, purchased a used International Harvester laundry truck with a Metro body and had it converted. Glascoff was a close friend of Brooks Stevens, the internationally known industrial designer and vehicle stylist who had designed the 1940 Johnson Wax house car. He hired Stevens to design a custom interior and exterior for the truck. Leonard Stam of Stam Auto Body in Waupun remodeled the truck for Glascoff at a cost of approximately $2,000, including raising the roof to provide more standing room. Glascoff purchased many of the appliances and furnishings in Milwaukee. For several years he used the camper for hunting and fishing trips, family excursions, and trips to University of Wisconsin football games.[37]

A striking indication of the practicality and growing consumer acceptance of stand-up delivery-truck campers was General Motors's entrance into the market. In 1961 Chevrolet added the Traville, a modified Chevrolet Step-Van delivery truck, to its truck-options catalog. Marketed by the Traville Corporation of Detroit, this vehicle had a Chevrolet delivery-truck chassis and a special Step-Van body shell built by the Union City Body Company of Union City, Indiana, which built standard Step-Van delivery-truck bodies. The interior of the Traville was built and installed by Cree Coaches in Marcellus, Michigan. Sold through Chevrolet dealers, the Traville was promoted as a vacation vehicle for families, sporting enthusiasts, and retirees. GM also planned to market it as a mobile office for contractors, traveling executives, and other itinerant professionals. The steel body of the Traville, which measured 20 feet 4 inches long, had double walls with fiberglass insulation and large windows with safety glass. Inside were two sofas that converted into beds for four people, a folding table, roof vents, and storage compartments. The kitchen was equipped with a gas refrigerator, oven, and range, and a stainless-steel sink. An electric water pump and 30-gallon water tank serviced the kitchen and bathroom, which had a lavatory and toilet with septic tank. An optional gas space heater, water heater, shower, and air conditioner could be purchased at additional cost. Chevrolet continued to advertise and sell the Step-Van camper conversion through the 1960s.[38]

VAN CAMPERS: AUTOMAKERS CATCH THE BUG

At first glance, the boxy, rectangular van looked like a small, spartan delivery truck. Like the station wagon, however, it served as both a passenger and utility vehicle. Vans were marketed as a consumer as well as a business vehicle. Because of its shape and intermediate size, the van proved to be more versatile than its nearest cousins—the stand-up delivery truck, panel delivery truck, and station wagon. By the 1960s its utility, ease of handling, and dual use as a cargo and passenger vehicle made it as much in demand as the depot hack had been in the 1920s.

The van was developed by Volkswagen in Wolfsburg, West Germany, in 1948 and 1949. Production models were built and marketed in 1950 as the Volkswagen Bulli, later called the Transporter in the United States. The Transporter's design was simple but revolutionary: a rectangular steel box with side and rear doors and an air-cooled engine in the rear. The absence of a drive shaft meant that the floor was close to the ground, which made loading and unloading cargo easier than with a conventional truck. Within a few years, the Transporter was available in several configurations: the Panelvan for cargo only, the Kombi with removable seats, the Samba, the upscale Micro Bus, and a pickup version. Special models were built to serve as ambulances, postal delivery vehicles, and other special-duty vehicles.[39]

Recognizing the potential market for a small, self-propelled recreational version of the Transporter, Westfalia-Werke of Wiedenbrück,

West Germany, a leading manufacturer of camping trailers, began making the Camping-Box option for Volkswagen's van in 1951. Founded in 1844 by Johann Bernhard Knöbel, a blacksmith, Westfalia had built farm implements, carts, and carriages before switching to utility trailers and camping trailers in the 1930s.[40] The VW camper with interior by Westfalia was equipped with sofa beds made of plywood and foam rubber, a folding table, door-mounted cabinet with washbasin, drawer, storage cabinet, heater and cookstove, rooftop luggage rack, and side awning. The sofa beds accommodated three adults, and the driver's seat converted into a bed for two children.[41] In 1955 the price for this ingenious, compact living unit was only $525, in addition to $2,095 for the Transporter.[42]

Like pickup campers, the manufactured van camper generated strong demand after it appeared on the market. Between 1951 and 1959 more than one thousand VW-Westfalia campers were built, and by 1969 the total number built reached more than fifty thousand.[43] By 1956 VW campers were being sold in the United States by Volkswagen of America through its dealers.[44] The success of the VW camper inspired other European auto makers to test the American market; the Mercedes-Benz Executive Coach, also made in West Germany, and the Hillman-Commer Caravan, made in England, were among the imported, van-sized campers available in the United States in the early 1960s.[45]

By 1963, when the VW van camper was sold in the United States as the Volkswagen Campmobile, Westfalia interior kits came in six versions with prices ranging from $465 to $730, plus $1,895 to $2,655 for the van. The campers included birch paneling, seats that turned into beds, folding tables, side-door shelves, clothes closet with door mirror, wall-mounted electric lamps, foam-rubber cushions covered with vinyl or nylon, food storage compartment, magazine cabinet, and other storage cabinets and compartments. The more expensive kits had a two-burner gas stove, water tank with chrome pump and swivel spigot, icebox, and chemical toilet. At additional cost, optional accessories provided extra pleasures, comforts, or sleeping space; among these options were an awning tent, a free-standing tent that fit onto a roof carrier for transport, a shower unit and canvas shower enclosure, a sundeck

*Handy and affordable, the Volkswagen van camper became popular among
vacationers in the United States and Europe. This 1964 Volkswagen Campmobile
was one of 50,000 VW campers built in the 1950s and 1960s. (Courtesy Volkswagen
of America)*

with ladder, a roof-mounted tent named the Campette, and a hammock sling for a child that fit over the front seat. Some of the camper
kits were made by Sportswagon Conversions of El Paso, Texas, a subsidiary of El Paso Canvas Products.[46]

Despite the popularity of Volkswagen vans and van campers, it took
American automobile manufacturers a full decade to develop and market similar vehicles. Seeking an attention-getting "dream" truck for its
annual Motorama traveling exhibition, General Motors developed a
van prototype in 1954 and 1955. Called Vehicle XP-39 during the planning stages, this front-wheel-drive vehicle was conceived by GMC and
Chevrolet truck stylists and endorsed by two powerful advocates: Harley
Earl, vice president in charge of GM's styling division, and Philip J.
Monaghan, vice president and general manager of the GMC truck and
bus division. GM stylists and engineers examined a Volkswagen Micro

Bus and designed an easy-to-load vehicle with the cargo-carrying capacity of a van and the handsome appearance of a station wagon. The finished prototype, named L'Universelle ("all-purpose or versatility of application"), was unveiled in January 1955 as part of the GM Motorama show in New York City and toured the United States in the traveling exhibition of GM production cars, experimental "dream" cars, engineering displays, and Frigidaire household appliances.[47]

The automotive press immediately noticed the unorthodox L'Universelle, particularly its vertically lifting cargo doors, low floor, and engine located behind the driver's seat. The press also noted GM's expectation that the van would be adapted for camping, carrying groups of people or cargo, and other uses. "Although its basic design is a panel delivery," Philip Monaghan explained, "minor manufacturing changes can convert it into a small bus, taxi, station wagon or sportsman's car."[48] At the San Francisco Motorama venue, GM's president, Harlow Curtice, announced that L'Universelle would "go into production as soon as possible."[49] Within a year, however, plans for marketing the radical vehicle were dropped because projections indicated high production costs and a small market.

Several years after L'Universelle was shelved, GM developed another van that reached the market as cargo- and passenger-carrying versions of the Chevrolet Corvair. In an attempt to compete with Volkswagen one-on-one in the compact car market, GM introduced the air-cooled, rear-engine Corvair in the 1960 model year. The popularity of the Volkswagen Transporter prompted General Motors to introduce three rear-engine Corvair vans in 1961: the plain, utilitarian Corvan panel delivery van, the stylish Greenbrier Sports Wagon, and the Greenbrier De Luxe Sports Wagon. All of these models were based on the same body, which was engineered like the Transporter but with some of L'Universelle's sculpted styling.

As sales of imported van campers and domestic pickup campers grew, Chevrolet dealers began selling Corvair Greenbrier vans with optional camper interiors available from General Motors. In 1961 and 1962 the Greenbrier camper had sofa beds, a kitchen counter with Formica top, drawers, cabinets, drapes, Coleman stove, cooler, and jug.[50] For the

1963 through 1965 model years the revised interior featured sofa beds, an adjustable table, stainless-steel sink, water tank and pump, ice chest, cabinets, drawers, and wardrobe.[51] Chevrolet dealers continued to sell camper conversions of the Greenbrier Sports Wagon until the 1965 model year, when the Corvair vans were discontinued. The Chevy-Van, which replaced the Corvair van, and the GMC Handi-Bus also came with optional camper interiors.

Another version of the Greenbrier van camper was made and sold by the Lone Star Motor Company, a Chevrolet distributor and Chevrolet and Cadillac dealer in El Paso, Texas. In the early 1960s W. Kent Elliott, Lone Star's president and manager, assembled and distributed camper interiors with the assistance of Marcus J. Simon, his parts manager. Simon purchased bunks, windows, refrigerators, stoves, and other components from suppliers and coordinated them as camper packages. Lone Star installed these packages in Greenbrier vans and sold the conversions directly to individuals. Elliott also distributed the camper interiors to Chevrolet dealers nationwide to install in Greenbrier vans for their customers. Some of the interiors were partially customized according to the purchasers' wishes. Elliott advertised the conversions in Chevrolet dealer magazines and managed the financial side of the business.[52]

By 1962 several independent body companies were making camper interiors for Greenbrier vans and selling their conversions through Chevrolet dealers. These small, creative companies contributed a significant new feature that provided additional headroom, sunlight, and ventilation: a pop-up top. There were several types of pop-up tops. The Traville Corporation of Detroit offered the Vista Camper, a Greenbrier van with a trapezoidal dome. Royden Industries, a subsidiary of Stewart Coach, made the Travelcar, a Greenbrier van camper with a raisable, rectangular top. The Travel Equipment Corporation of Elkhart, Indiana, sold a Greenbrier van camper conversion with a flip-up, rounded metal dome. Maurice Calthorpe had introduced the latter type of dome in England in 1956; he filed a United States patent claim the following year and received patent number 2,926,042 in 1960. The Calthorpe dome had become quite popular throughout Europe, and the inventor penetrated the American market by licensing the Travel

Equipment Corporation to manufacture his top. Originally named the Calthorpe Home Cruiser with Travel-top, this converted van was renamed the Travel Wagon by 1963.[53]

Unlike the Corvair vans, the 1961 Ford Econoline Delivery Van and Ford Econoline Station Bus came equipped with a water-cooled engine (the same engine as in the Falcon, Ford's entry in the compact-car field) in the front and conventional rear-wheel drive. In 1961 Einar Miller of San Bernardino, California, designed an interior that converted an Econoline Station Bus into a Sportswagon camper. On special order, Miller's workers installed Kamperkit units in customers' vans at Ford dealerships. The interior had mahogany-paneled walls, sofa beds, table, ice chest, water tank, faucet, Coleman stove mounted on the side door, and an optional awning.[54] For the 1962 models Ford sold an accessory Ford Camper Kit that fit its full line of vans, including the Econoline Van and the redesigned (and renamed) Falcon Station Bus, Falcon Club Wagon, and Falcon Deluxe Club Wagon. This slide-in unit had sofa beds, a table, underseat storage, and a stove mounted on a folding utility shelf attached to the side door. A supplementary kit, available separately, added two large storage cabinets and a wardrobe closet.[55] Some of the Ford van-camper interiors were built by Sportsmobile in El Paso, Texas, and were shipped to Lorain, Ohio, for final assembly.[56]

Beginning in the 1965 model year, the Dodge Sportsman van, with front bucket seats, could be purchased from Dodge dealers as a Camp Wagon with a pop-up aluminum "cupola" and interior conversion by the Travel Equipment Corporation.[57] Another pop-top van camper, the Dodge Freeway Traveler, was available from Freeway Traveler of Elkhart, Indiana.[58] The Corey Cruiser, a modified Dodge Sportsman van with a longer body and a molded, stationary fiberglass top that provided standing room, was available from Corey Cruiser Conversion of Pasadena, California.[59] So many Dodge van owners purchased camping packages that Dodge introduced a more powerful V-8 engine and heavy-duty transmission and suspension as options midway through the 1965 model year.

Van campers had many virtues that enticed vacationers. Chief among these were their versatility and relatively low purchase price; for about $3,000 the owner had a vehicle that served as a station wagon, truck, and camper. A van handled like a station wagon, and in most states it could be licensed as an automobile. Because of its relatively small size and slim profile, a van camper was faster and easier to maneuver than larger recreation vehicles. American-built vans had more powerful engines than the Volkswagen Transporter, an advantage on rough back roads. Higher-priced models had colorful, automobile-type upholstery and decorative trim.

But the van camper's disadvantages inevitably limited its market appeal. Even with an expandable top, its interior was cramped compared with a travel trailer or a converted bus. Only two adults and two children could sleep comfortably in a van—an auxiliary tent beside the van was preferred by many users and necessary for large families. Because of the van's compact interior, it was not possible to walk from the front seat to the living quarters; it was necessary to stop the vehicle and open the side doors. There was limited storage space inside; a rack on top could compensate for this shortcoming but precluded a dome.

Some motorists built their own van-camper interiors to save money, make better use of space, or install furnishings that they found more desirable than standard options. Harold Bryant and his wife, Lola Mae, "fell in love" with a Volkswagen Campmobile displayed at an auto show and considered purchasing one for vacation trips. Instead, they decided to buy a Volkswagen Transporter and build their own interior. Working on Sunday afternoons for six months, Bryant and his father built a plywood unit with seat-beds, table, food storage cabinet, water pump, and bathroom, all at a cost of only $202.31. The finished vehicle had trailer-like features not found in ordinary vans, including fiberglass insulation and inlaid linoleum floor covering.[60]

Another family's homemade van camper illustrated both the appeal of a do-it-yourself interior and the advantages of a carlike, self-propelled camper over a tent or a trailer. The Geraci family of Langley Park, Maryland, a suburb of Washington, D.C., became disenchanted with outdoor living after seven years of tent camping and wanted the comfort and convenience of a recreation vehicle. "The Florida trip [in 1961]," Philip Geraci wrote, "taught us the folly of making an extended trip with an umbrella tent, which must be packed and unpacked each day. For a long while we deliberated, balancing the lightness of a tent trailer against the convenience of a four-man travel trailer." But either option presented a problem regarding the tow car. "Our 1957 Ford already had begun to show signs of age," Geraci noted. "We had trouble with it last summer returning from Florida, and I was hesitant to commit it to a [western] trip nearly three times as long."

The Geracis decided to buy a single, self-propelled vehicle that they could use as a camper. They went to the 1962 Washington auto show, where they too "fell in love" with the Volkswagen camper. But there was a problem. "We had been campers for seven years," Geraci wrote, "and had managed, piece by piece, to acquire considerable gear. Unwilling to part with it, we compromised. We bought a standard VW station wagon [Transporter] instead of the camper and made our own camper out of it." The Geracis removed the rear seat of the Transporter and replaced it with two seats facing each other, with storage compartments underneath. A small table was placed between the seats. They also installed a removable wooden platform with foam cushions to serve as beds. A battery-powered fluorescent light illuminated the interior of the vehicle at night, and a 12-volt battery, alternator, and converter powered a 110-volt refrigerator, shaver, and vacuum cleaner. Geraci built a clothes closet along the rear wall and a set of wooden shelves to serve as a kitchen unit. He installed a 12-volt pump to pressurize the water in a 25-gallon tank and devised a spray unit and shower curtain that hung just outside the Transporter's front door. The Geracis used an alcohol stove for cooking when the weather precluded a campfire.

After living in the van camper at home for five weeks to adjust to it, Philip Geraci, his wife, Dottie, and their children, Philip and Ronnie, took shakedown trips to Williamsburg, Virginia, and the Atlantic Ocean. In the summer of 1962 they took a long-planned trip to the West Coast, stopping at Hannibal, Missouri, Royal Gorge, Colorado, Rocky Mountain National Park, Grand Teton National Park, Yellowstone National Park, Mount Rainier, Devil's Tower, and the Badlands en route to the Century 21 Exposition in Seattle. At night they stayed in state-park campgrounds, a town park, a meadow, lakeside campgrounds, and a trailer park sponsored by the Exposition. Some campgrounds had few campers, and others were crowded. Often the Geracis were directed to the "overflow" area and had to squeeze between two other recreation vehicles.

The Geracis cooked, played games, and lived inside their camper. "We played a round of pinochle, cozy and warm inside our Volkswagen, while a damp wind raged outside," Geraci wrote. They were fascinated by the wide variety of FM radio broadcasts, which formed a continuous musical accompaniment to their trip. They were impressed by the superior reception on mountaintops and drifted to sleep by the sounds of nature and artificial music. Geraci wrote, "It was a great comfort to lie in bed late at night, surrounded by mountains or covered by pines, with the forests nearby full of wildlife, and turn the switch on the radio and find music to match the surroundings. It was almost like camping with sound effects."[61]

Like station wagons in the early 1950s, vans, stand-up delivery trucks, and pickup trucks shed their workaday image by the early 1960s and were widely used for family camping. The transition of small trucks from work vehicles to pleasure vehicles was brought about by strong consumer demand for an affordable, maneuverable, intimate camping vehicle, new features that enhanced the usefulness of trucks as living quarters, and features that improved stability and driveability. Manufactured pickup campers were heavily influenced by the travel-trailer industry in terms of their design, equipment, and production origins, but the simplified interiors of van campers and delivery-truck campers were more efficient than homelike. A compact delivery-truck camper or van camper was, in essence, a rigid tent with a hard shell for protection and built-in chairs, tables, and cooking accessories that saved time and effort.

While these features satisfied many vacationing families, most recreation-vehicle enthusiasts still preferred the spaciousness and complete furnishings of a travel trailer. A few ingenious trailer manufacturers and mechanically inclined people combined the advantages of travel trailers and the maneuverability and intimacy of trucks, buses, and vans and created a new type of vehicle that was as revolutionary as the horseless carriage itself: a travel trailer that needed no tow car because it had its own engine and transmission. The self-propelled trailer, or motor home, emerged during the 1950s, and the few examples on the nation's highways invariably turned heads. In the 1960s a flourishing motor home industry would develop, and the skyrocketing popularity of motor homes would change the image of recreation vehicles to a degree unmatched since the trailer boom of the 1930s.

6 EARLY MANUFACTURED MOTOR HOMES

n the 1950s a new type of manufactured, self-propelled vacation vehicle offered an appealing alternative to modified trucks and buses. These redesigned house cars, or "motor homes" as they were called by the early 1960s, were among the most expensive recreation vehicles, but they combined the best features of a travel trailer and a converted bus without their limitations and drawbacks. A motor home, like a bus, was spacious, easy to maneuver, and had adequate power, gearing, and suspension. But a motor home was more aesthetically pleasing than a bus and more acceptable in the suburban driveway. Like trailers, motor homes were ranch houses on wheels; they were long and low, had aluminum siding and picture windows, and were equipped with contemporary furniture, modern kitchens with built-in appliances, and forced-air furnaces. But a motor home was easier to park than a trailer because it did not need to be jockeyed, unhitched, or leveled, and it was less likely to bounce or sway on the road. Family members could ride together without feeling crowded and use many of the motor home's facilities en route. Within a short time, affluent vacationers embraced the motor home with the same affection that they felt for the family car.

The manufactured motor-home revolution did not begin in the backyards of tinkerers and vacationers. Unlike one-off house cars of the 1940s, which were patterned after airplanes, boats, or buses, manufactured house cars of the 1950s had trailerlike bodies grafted onto truck or bus chassis. Travel trailers still dominated the recreation vehicle market after World War II because of their relatively low prices and homelike furnishings. Thousands of Americans were familiar with the basic equipment of a travel trailer, and strong sales in the 1950s reflected its steady appeal to middle-class vacationers. As trailer use increased, trailer bodies became longer and more substantially equipped; many had large picture windows, better insulation, circulating forced-air furnaces, and bottled gas for cooking. The concept of adding an engine and chassis to a travel trailer occurred to several trailer manufacturers.

In the early 1950s John Korleski, a trailer-production engineer in Indiana, supervised the construction of eighteen long, trailerlike Victour "motor coaches." A graduate of Parks College of Aeronautical Technology in St. Louis, Korleski was hired as a salesman for Victor travel trailers, and in 1949 or 1950 he became production manager of the Victor Coach Industries factory in Bristol, Indiana.[1] In 1950 he purchased a Dodge truck chassis and built a self-propelled, luxury house on wheels resembling the Victor trailer, which had "a light, strong, airplane-type structure" with aluminum construction and bridged roof bows for strength and rigidity.[2] Production was set at one Victour motor coach per month. The eighteen vehicles, which emerged from the Victor trailer production line under Korleski's supervision, had all of the furnishings of a travel trailer—beds, a kitchen, hot and cold running water, sink, shower, and tub—on top of a Dodge truck chassis. Korleski hoped that the Victour would have "Cadillac appeal" and would be sold to a small, discriminating market. The market turned out to be too small; Victours were sold through trailer dealers at prices of more than $20,000, and production ceased because too few vacationers could afford them.[3]

A specially designed house car was built in substantial quantities by Howard Industries, a trailer manufacturer in Saginaw, Michigan. In 1952 Herb Shriner, a nationally known humorist, automobile enthusiast, and owner of a streamlined house car named the Graf Zipalong, met Howard J. Doss, president of Howard Industries, at a trailer show and urged him to install an engine and transmission in a travel trailer

In the 1950s several trailer manufacturers installed engines and transmissions in travel trailers. John Korleski displayed a Victour at the 1950 Michigan State Fair and built eighteen units in a trailer factory in Indiana. (Courtesy Murdale Korleski)

and sell it at a moderate price.[4] Howard Industries built a prototype called the Safari, and Doss displayed it in the International Motor Sports Show, which Shriner organized and presented in the Grand Central Palace in New York City in April 1953. The 22-foot Safari prototype had an extended GMC truck chassis with Hydra-Matic drive. The GMC cab was retained, and from the front the vehicle resembled a stand-up delivery truck, but the body resembled a small travel trailer. In place of the brass rail and rear platform found on some house cars of the wealthy, the Safari had a back porch or "terrace" and a ladder to the rooftop "sun deck." Inside were beds for five people, a kitchen, bathroom with shower, closet, and other conveniences. Doss purchased a separate factory and soon began production. The Safari was priced at $7,050 for the standard model; the purchaser could specify a custom interior layout and wall finishes at additional cost. The standard production model had a steel and aluminum exterior, birch panel interior, two

In 1953 humorist and house-car enthusiast Herb Shriner persuaded Howard Industries to manufacture a modified travel trailer with an engine and transmission. The result was the Howard Safari, which Shriner cheerfully demonstrated for the media. (Courtesy Wil Shriner)

dinette seats that converted into beds, and two to four bunks. A double bed could be substituted for the two lower bunks, and storage cabinets could be substituted for the two upper bunks. The kitchen featured a sink, stove, electric refrigerator, and hot water heater, and the bathroom had a shower, toilet, and lavatory. A Presto-Porch could be lowered from the rear. Like the prototype, the 24-foot production model was built on a GMC truck chassis with Hydra-Matic transmission, but Albrecht Goertz, a young industrial designer, restyled the body in a design strangely similar to the Winnebago, which appeared thirteen years later. The Howard Safari was publicized in magazines, on NBC's *The Today Show*, and in the 1954 motion picture *Ring of Fear* starring circus legend and Safari owner Clyde Beatty.[5] According to the Doss family, several hundred Safaris were built before Doss's untimely death in 1956 ended production.

In Michigan's thumb region Thomas Stewart Backus, president of the Backus Oil Company and owner of the Sanigas propane service in Carsonville, decided to build a personal recreation vehicle that he could use while hunting and fishing in Alaska. In the mid-1950s he asked the Marlette Coach Company in Marlette, Michigan, to build a self-propelled version of its travel trailer to his specifications. Marlette declined this request, but Elwyn McNaughton, a Marlette production supervisor working in his off-hours, and McNaughton's nephews, Robert Bader and Dale Bader, built the vehicle in Backus's garage. The 26-foot vehicle had aluminum siding, wrought-iron railing in the rear, a coral-and-white paint scheme, and a modified automobile chassis that Backus had obtained. The prototype also carried a small boat on top. Backus, his wife, Sophia, and their two children traveled through the West in the modern house car, attracting a great deal of interest along the way.

Backus placed an advertisement for house cars in *Alaska* magazine. In 1959 or 1960 he and McNaughton decided to build house cars and chose the name Sani-Cruiser; this name, like Sanigas, was derived from Sanilac County, where Carsonville is located. Backus provided financial support, and McNaughton was the factory manager. Backus purchased the assets of the Rainbow Trailer Company in nearby Yale and moved Rainbow's facilities, including a Quonset hut, machinery, and tools, to Carsonville. Backus and McNaughton built between twelve and fifteen Sani-Cruisers. In about 1966 Backus closed the shop to pursue other interests.

Built on a Ford truck chassis, Sani-Cruiser house cars were made upon request in lengths of 21 or 26 feet. For the smaller model McNaughton extended the chassis behind the rear axle; for the larger model he hired the Scientific Brake and Equipment Company of Saginaw to extend the chassis in the middle. Ceiling height was an ample 6 feet 4 inches. The interior, which was paneled with oak, was equipped with bunks for two people in the shorter model or four in the longer model, a dinette that converted into a small bed, a kitchen with gas oven and range, a gas refrigerator, sink with hot and cold running water, propane gas heater, bathroom with toilet, lavatory, shower, and a wardrobe. The vehicle had external connections for electricity, water, and sewerage for use at trailer parks. An optional air conditioner was available. The exterior was pink and white prepainted aluminum with safety-glass windows and fiberglass insulation. The 1963 models were priced at $6,995 and $7,895.[6]

In the mid-1950s a specialized truck-body manufacturer developed a house car similar to the Safari. Theodore B. Case of Hamburg, New York, founded Custom Bilt Body in 1946 to make custom truck bodies. His product line included dump bodies, vertical lift loaders for cargo aircraft, and many other types of special bodies. An avid archer and hunter, Case designed a house car based on a Ford delivery truck chassis in 1956. The custom body had bunks, a dining table that converted into a double bed, a kitchen with gas stove, oven, refrigerator, sink with running water, hot water heater, gas furnace in the floor, and 110-volt circuit for appliances. It was placed on the market in 1957 as the Case Liv-N-Roam Cruiser and was priced at $5,975 to $6,900 depending on optional equipment. Case traveled around the United States demonstrating the new vehicle. In 1961 he developed a larger house car with almost twice the interior space as the original model.[7]

The growing number of self-propelled vacation vehicles on the market encouraged entrepreneurs who were not vehicle specialists. One such pioneer was Flournoy E. Corey, a mechanical engineer, patent attorney, and president of the Pickwick Company of Cedar Rapids, Iowa. In the early 1950s Corey purchased an unfinished transit-bus camper and completed its interior. The camper did not meet his expectations during a trip from Cedar Rapids to Seattle. When he returned, Corey made and sold several more house cars by cutting and extending Cadillac sedans. The Pickwick Company had manufactured poultry processing machinery since 1939 (the name is based on "pick them quick"), but a decline in sales in the 1950s, a result of tighter federal standards for poultry processing, prompted Corey to diversify into house-car production.

By 1958 Pickwick had developed the Traveliner, a 23-foot house car with fluted aluminum siding, a large windshield and side windows, and a Cadillac engine. By the next year orders were being placed for Traveliners, and Pickwick began to advertise the house car in magazines. Susan Corey, the wife of Flournoy's brother, Fred, managed advertising, and Pauline Corey, Flournoy's wife, wrote promotional literature and test-drove Traveliners. The 1961 models came in lengths of 20 feet or 22 feet and were priced at $5,500 and $6,400 respectively. By 1963 suggested retail prices had risen to $7,922 for the 20-foot model and $8,492 for a new 26-foot model. The longer model had four bunks and a convertible dinette-bed, while the shorter model had a gaucho bed and a convertible dinette-bed. Both models had a kitchen with gas oven and stove and a bathroom with lavatory, toilet, shower, and holding tank. The 1964 models were priced at $8,750 and $9,550 and had four bunks and six bunks respectively. Both models had a gaucho bed and convertible dinette-bed. Pickwick built approximately one hundred house cars and several hundred pickup campers between 1959 and 1974, when the Arab oil embargo and soaring gasoline prices forced the company to end production of recreation vehicles.[8]

MAINSTREAM MOTOR HOMES

Despite these efforts to build and sell house cars, and their appeal to some affluent vacationers, recreation vehicle manufacturers did not embrace house cars with the same enthusiasm as travel trailers and pickup campers. Trailer journals seldom mentioned the new vehicles. In contrast to trailers, which numbered in the tens of thousands, house cars were almost as rare as space capsules.

Automobile manufacturers, however, believed that more Americans would become interested in house cars if suitable models were available. Nationwide sales of house cars began in 1961 when Frank Industries, a small manufacturer of house-car bodies in eastern Michigan, joined forces with the Dodge Division of Chrysler Corporation, which supplied the chassis. Raymond C. Frank, a farmer and engineer in Michigan's thumb region, had worked in a Plymouth automobile factory, studied aviation mechanics at the Dallas Aviation School in Texas, and worked as an inspector in a Packard aircraft engine plant before becoming interested in recreation vehicles. In 1958 he and his teenage son, Ronald, designed a house car with a long trailerlike body and a truck chassis and built it in the family barn near Brown City, Michigan. The Frank family took vacation trips to Florida and the Midwest in the

27-foot long vehicle. They called their creation a "motor home"—a name that would reverberate from their rural homestead through the fledgling house-car manufacturing industry and into the nation's vocabulary in the 1960s.

The Franks began building custom motor homes in their Brown City barn for individuals who admired the prototype; seven such vehicles were made between 1958 and 1960. One was sold to Tommy Scott, a traveling medicine-show entertainer who agreed to advertise Frank motor homes by displaying his vehicle at various show locations.[9] The Franks also placed an advertisement in *Trailer Topics* magazine with a photograph of a 27-foot vehicle featuring a two-tone birch interior, gas furnace, kitchen, bathroom, utility hookups, and beds for six people.[10]

The Franks formed Frank Motor Homes, Inc., and built a factory in Brown City in 1961. Raymond and Ronald were partners in the corporation, and Raymond's wife, Ethel, was secretary and office manager. In their first year 160 Frank motor homes were built. The wood-and-aluminum motor-home bodies came in lengths of 20 feet, 23 feet, and 26 feet and were priced at $6,500, $6,900, and $7,300 respectively.[11]

The Franks' choice of Dodge truck chassis for their motor homes led to a most fortuitous business relationship. As chassis supplier, Dodge often was called upon to provide technical advice to the Franks. Dodge's involvement deepened as Frank Motor Homes's volume grew; Dodge lent the Franks money, and soon Dodge was represented on Frank Motor Homes's board of directors. In 1962 the name of the product was changed to Dodge motor home. The Franks built four hundred Dodge motor homes that year in Brown City and sold them through franchised dealers, including numerous Dodge dealers. Dodge advertised the motor homes in brochures, dealer publications, press releases, and trailer magazines. With the affiliation of Frank and Dodge, consumers began to think of a motor home not as a modified bus but as a cross between a Dodge truck and a travel trailer. This perception helped usher in a new era in motor home manufacturing.[12]

With a V-8 engine, automatic transmission, tinted windshield, and directional signals, the 1962 Dodge motor home was almost as easy to drive as the family car. Dual swivel seats in the driver's compartment provided easy interaction with passengers in the rear. The spacious

In 1961 the Chrysler Corporation became the first manufacturer to sell motor homes at retail outlets nationwide. The 1961 Dodge motor home was built by Frank Motor Homes and was available through Dodge dealers. (Courtesy Frank Industries, Inc.)

body, which came in lengths of 23 feet or 26 feet with an interior height of 6 feet 3 inches, was longer than most travel trailers and offered a level of comfort that automobiles, van campers, delivery-truck campers, and pickup campers could not match. The modern, well-equipped interior had the uncluttered appearance and sophistication of a suburban ranch home. Sofa beds, a dinette, a kitchen with sink, cupboards, gas stove, and refrigerator, draperies, clock, tiled floor, bathroom, nylon upholstery, and an optional air conditioner appealed strongly to affluent vacationers. The two-tone, aluminum exterior siding came in white and a choice of blue, green, beige, turquoise, or black.

Late in 1962 the Franks designed and built another prototype with a steel frame and a light, strong fiberglass exterior. For the first production motor home constructed with fiberglass, they created huge molds for left and right body halves and used a special "gun" to spray the molds with streams of fiberglass roving and plastic resin. The two halves then were bonded along a seam. Smaller body parts such as wheelhouses,

The 1963 Dodge motor home, built by Frank Motor Homes, had a streamlined fiberglass body and was available in turquoise, beige, blue, green, or red. Smooth styling and popular colors harmonized with family sedans and attracted image-conscious suburbanites, who were reluctant to park a bus or truck camper in the driveway. (Courtesy Frank Industries, Inc.)

engine cover, kitchen sink, and instrument panel also were sprayed onto molds.[13] With its smooth, streamlined shape and neat styling, the 1963 Dodge fiberglass motor home looked like a large, expensive automobile and was even more at home than the 1962 model in the driveways of affluent Americans. The 4-ton, 26-feet 6-inch vehicle had 6 feet 4 inches of standing room and was equipped with a double bed or gaucho bed, convertible sofa bed, convertible dinette-bed, and optional bunk. The kitchen had a gas oven and stove; the bathroom had a lavatory, toilet, and shower. The Franks built and sold seven hundred motor homes in 1963.

At $9,612 for the bunk model and $9,566 for the double-bed model, the 1963 Dodge motor home cost three times as much as a travel trailer of similar size. But affluent consumers considered many factors other than price when comparing a Dodge motor home and a travel trailer. One part of the equation was the cost of a suitable tow car. Often the family car lacked the power or gearing necessary to pull a trailer, resulting in overheating or inadequate traction. The combined purchase price of a suitable car and a trailer averaged $4,000 to $9,000. Capacity was another important consideration. Many motorists purchased Dodge motor homes because they had large families and wanted to be comfortable during vacation trips. Riding in a trailer was prohibited in many states, requiring family members to squeeze into the tow car; but in a motor home, the family could ride together in comfort. Roland Clermont, a grocer in Chelmsford, Massachusetts, purchased a 26-foot 1962 Dodge so that there would be enough room for his wife and their three children. He ordered the motor home through a local Dodge dealer and picked it up at the factory in Brown City. The Clermonts used their vehicle during pleasure trips to California, Alberta, Vermont, and New Hampshire. Dr. D. Merlan Debolt, a Dallas physician, purchased a 1962 Dodge motor home for his family of six, and they traveled to western states, Mexico, and world's fairs in Seattle and New York. Dr. William B. Hobbins, a surgeon in Madison, Wisconsin, traveled to Brown City to specify interior modifications to his Dodge motor home that would accommodate his family of eight. The Hobbins family used their motor home during month-long vacations in many areas of the United States, Canada, and Mexico.[14]

Because of Dodge's national, consumer-oriented marketing network and the superior styling, handling, and comfort of the Frank body, the Dodge motor home captured the public's attention in ways that no large, self-propelled camper had done before. Dodge dealers across the nation distributed sales literature and rented motor homes to vacationers who were eager to try them. Brand loyalty influenced some long-time Dodge, Plymouth, and Chrysler automobile customers.[15] Now motor homes were a handsome, comfortable alternative that resembled a suburban house and handled like an automobile. By 1964 more than one-third of the six hundred members of the Family Motor Coach Association owned Dodge motor homes.[16]

The success of the Dodge motor home encouraged Ford to introduce a similar vehicle. In 1962 Ford began selling the Condor, a 26-foot motor home, through their more than seven thousand dealers. Similar in size, shape, and appearance to early Dodge motor homes, the Condor had a trailerlike body with a wooden frame and painted aluminum siding. Like the Dodge motor home, the interior furnishings and equipment of the Condor compared favorably with a modern, suburban ranch house. The Condor had wood paneling, swivel chairs, a desk, Motorola AM/FM radio, and a kitchen with double sink, running water, Formica countertop, metal wall tile, window curtains, wooden cabinets, butane gas range, oven, and refrigerator. The bathroom had a toilet, fiberglass lavatory, and ceramic tile shower. A gas-forced air furnace was standard, and an air conditioner was available as an option. An optional 110-volt generator powered small appliances such as a television, toaster, shaver, or hair dryer. In addition to a double bed, the sofa and dinette converted into a bed. The standard model, which had a base price of $9,204, accommodated six people; for $200 more, a bunk bed could be added to accommodate two additional people. The vehicle's bodies were placed on an extended and strengthened Ford truck chassis, and the power train was a Ford V-8 engine with a Cruise-O-Matic automatic transmission. Approximately seventy Condors were sold by the summer of 1963 and approximately twenty to thirty vehicles each year through the 1960s.[17]

Condor bodies were designed and built for Ford by the Kelson Engineering Company in El Monte, California, a suburb of Los Angeles. Kelson was founded in nearby Whittier in the late 1940s by I. Judson Kelly, a naval architect, Perley H. L. Wilson (also called "Doc" or "Cap" Wilson), who had skippered actor John Barrymore's sailing yacht, *Mariner*, in the 1920s, and F. O. Haas, a tax accountant. The name Kelson was a combination of "Kelly" and "Wilson." Kelson originally made fiberglass boats, but in the 1950s Haas gained control of the company and changed its product line from boats to trailers. After Ford contracted with Kelson to produce Condor motor-home bodies, Ford shipped chassis to Kelson, who then shipped completed vehicles to Ford dealers. Regional dealers such as J. R. Leonard's Condor Sales Service in Bellevue, Ohio, showed Condors to Ford dealers and took their orders. Leonard also sold some Condors directly to consumers, and a few Condor purchasers picked up their vehicles at the factory in El Monte. In the late 1960s Haas sold the company to Walter J. Kiefer Jr., a beauty salon equipment executive who had purchased a Condor for his personal use. Production of motor homes continued until 1973, when the Arab oil embargo, the resulting gasoline shortage, and escalating gasoline prices forced an end to the Condor line.[18]

The recreation vehicle market expanded rapidly in the early 1960s due to the spread of high-speed, limited-access interstate highways and turnpikes across the United States and a renewed interest in outdoor recreation. Production of factory-built travel trailers increased from 28,800 units in 1961 to 76,600 units in 1965.[19] After Dodge and Ford successfully established a niche for luxury motor homes, several trailer and pickup-camper manufacturers entered the motor-home field. Manufacturers of pickup campers had an established following of motorists who preferred self-propelled recreation vehicles, and the introduction of motor homes was a logical extension of their product lines. By 1963 Eugene Krager, a former home builder who manufactured Kustom Koach pickup coaches in Osseo, Minnesota, was building the Krager Motor Home, a self-propelled vehicle priced at $8,495. This 20-foot vehicle had a Chevrolet truck chassis with a V-8 engine and an automatic transmission. Inside were bunks and a convertible dinette-bed that could accommodate four to six people, as well as a heater, hot water heater, and full kitchen and bathroom facilities. In 1964 the company added the 16-foot Krager Kustom Koach, which was also fully furnished and priced at $7,400.[20]

Other pickup-coach manufacturers soon followed Krager's lead. In 1964 Cree Coaches of Marcellus, Michigan, a pickup-coach and travel-trailer manufacturer, introduced a motor home with an anodized aluminum body and a Chevrolet bus chassis. Displayed at selected Chevrolet dealers, the Cree motor home had a gaucho and dinette that converted into beds, walnut cabinets, and full kitchen and bathroom facilities.[21] In the same year the Meade Manufacturing Company, a pickup-camper and travel-trailer manufacturer in Meade, Kansas, introduced the Travel-Inn—a motor home priced at $7,950. Like other Meade products, the body had a wooden frame covered with aluminum. Meade was founded by George A. Isaac, a mechanically inclined farmer who designed numerous improvements to farm machinery. In 1946 Isaac began manufacturing combine cabs and riding lawn mowers, and in the mid-1950s he diversified into pickup-camper bodies with wooden frames and aluminum exteriors. Between 1964 and 1970, when he sold the business, Isaac and his employees built about a dozen Travel-Inns per year. Most Travel-Inns had a Ford chassis and could accommodate four to eight people.[22]

Several experimental motor homes were built. David Peterson, a pilot, businessman, aircraft production manager, and aircraft designer, decided to install an engine in his travel trailer so that he could tow a boat trailer on vacation trips.[23] He thought that a scratch-built aluminum "fuselage" and Chevrolet's new Corvair automobile engine and rear-axle assembly offered a better solution, and in the fall of 1960 he built a prototype in a rented garage in Alameda, California. The vehicle that emerged early in 1961 was a streamlined, egg-shaped house car with a monocoque, aluminum body, a Corvair engine and transaxle bolted to the rear, a modified Corvair suspension, and a curved windshield from a Chevrolet Step-Van delivery truck. The monocoque body and rear engine eliminated the need for a body frame to hold a drive train. The result was a camper with a low center of gravity and low weight; the prototype weighed only 1,800 pounds without furnishings and less than 3,000 pounds fully loaded. Peterson rented a warehouse in Oakland and built a second house car to serve as a demonstrator to potential customers. Between 1961 and 1964 he built and sold about a dozen Go-Homes (later renamed Ultra Van) in lengths of 22 feet or 24 feet, and he built a special 27-foot vehicle for a large family.[24]

In 1965 John E. Tillotson II of Kansas City, Missouri, publisher of *Workbench* (a home woodworking magazine) and other hobby magazines, purchased the right to manufacture Ultra Vans. He learned about this vehicle from his parents, who had driven through Texas in their Travco motor home and were impressed by an Ultra Van that they saw during the trip. Tillotson formed Ultra, Inc., and moved the manufacturing operation to the former Hutchinson Naval Air Base near Hutchinson, Kansas.[25] The unusual camper remained in production until 1970, and David Peterson briefly resumed production in California in 1972. More than three hundred Ultra Vans and Go-Homes were built between 1961 and 1973.[26]

The Cortez, another unorthodox motor home, was introduced in 1963 by the industrial truck division of the Clark Equipment Company, a manufacturer of forklifts, industrial tractors, and powered hand trucks.

Designed quite different than other motor homes, this stubby, heavy vehicle, only 18-feet long, had an all-steel body, a specially designed chassis developed by Clark, and a Chrysler six-cylinder engine. Front-wheel drive made possible a low, flat floor and a generous interior height of 6 feet 4 inches. Four people could sleep in two double beds that converted into a dinette and bench for eating. The kitchen included a gas stove and refrigerator, stainless steel sink, cabinets, and counters. The Cortez also had a fully equipped bathroom and a gas furnace. Clark built Cortez units until 1969 and advertised the home on wheels in magazines and brochures.[27]

Kathleen Mudge, a freelance journalist who had written human-interest stories about the central Michigan area for newspapers in Battle Creek, Kalamazoo, Grand Rapids, and Detroit, became intrigued by the thought of writing and traveling at the same time, after reading John Steinbeck's *Travels with Charley*. A friend suggested that she become a publicist for the new Cortez; Mudge arranged an interview with Clark executives, who accepted her offer to serve as a roving demonstrator, journalist, and goodwill ambassador. Clark provided Mudge with a Cortez, reimbursement for travel expenses and repairs, and a salary. A three-month contract stretched into two years; from February 1964 to April 1966, "Lady Cortez," as Mudge named herself, traveled with her French poodle, Duchess Marie Antoinette (affectionately known as Dutch), to fairs, automobile shows, sports shows, and gatherings of recreation vehicle owners in all regions of the United States except the Northwest. At these events she answered questions about the Cortez for reporters from newspapers, magazines, and radio and television stations. She also showed the Cortez to impromptu gatherings of people almost everywhere she stopped.[28]

Along the way, Mudge wrote travelogues and human-interest articles for magazines, and she gathered ideas for a book, "This Road Has No End," which was never published.[29] She wrote a regular column, "Lady Cortez Visits," for *Family Motor Coaching*, the journal of the Family Motor Coach Association; her diverse topics included Great Lakes ferries, a blizzard on the Pennsylvania Turnpike, and comedian and housecar owner Herb Shriner.[30] In the late 1960s Mudge continued to write articles for *Family Motor Coaching* under the heading "Kathy Mudge

From 1964 to 1966 journalist Kathleen Mudge toured the United States in a Cortez motor home with her French poodle, Duchess Marie Antoinette. Mudge, who was widely known as Lady Cortez, added a personal touch to motor-home promotion as she displayed the compact home on wheels on behalf of its manufacturer, Clark Equipment Company. (Courtesy Francis Sattler and Kathleen Mudge Johnson)

Visits," and articles for other recreation-vehicle journals, including *Wheels Afield* and *Mobilehomes Merchandiser*.[31]

Despite efforts by Dodge, Ford, Clark, and others to popularize the motor home, it was still an oversized, elaborately furnished vehicle that only affluent Americans could afford. A typical model by the mid-1960s cost approximately $9,000, an increase of $2,000 since the early 1960s. The popular Dodge motor home cost $12,291 in 1965, almost $3,000 more than the 1963 model. Manufacturers showed little interest in building scaled-down, affordable motor homes, pointing instead to the costly, labor-intensive nature of their business. Virtually all motor-home manufacturers were content to make luxury models for a small but lucrative market. Even custom bus conversions flourished in the 1960s; in Westchester, Illinois, the Private Coach Company advertised bus conversions ranging from $13,200 to $42,800 and enticed motorists, pleading, "If you have a plan—we'll build it!"[32]

Several new makes of motor homes introduced in the mid-1960s were priced at more than $10,000, an indication that manufacturers were targeting upper-middle-class vacationers. Bus manufacturers discovered this market and began building opulent motor homes that rivalled those produced in bus-conversion shops. Looking for new markets to enter in the early 1960s, the Blue Bird Body Company of Fort Valley, Georgia, a leading manufacturer of school buses, began building several types of special-purpose commercial vehicles. After receiving numerous requests for motor-home conversions of its buses, the company collaborated with the Custom Coach Company of Columbus, Ohio, and the American Coach Company of Milledgeville, Georgia, on a prototype, the Transit Home, which Blue Bird displayed at trailer shows in 1963. With a retail price of $16,000, it did not attract buyers until it was publicized in a 1964 article about motor homes in *House Beautiful*.[33] Blue Bird also consulted several yacht builders who suggested improvements to the interior arrangement, and Blue Bird's marketing firm changed the name of the vehicle to Wanderlodge. Production of the Wanderlodge began in 1965, and it was priced at $15,952. Early Wanderlodge dealers were an eclectic group of pleasure-travel specialists who also sold Rolls-Royce automobiles, travel trailers, Volkswagens, and even yachts. Although the price of a Wanderlodge rose steadily over the years, it was a success and a symbol of high-priced, luxury motor homes.[34]

Another bus manufacturer, the Coachette Company of Dallas, also built luxury motor homes. Established in 1954 by Carl H. Graham and his son, William R. Graham, Coachette built transit buses for cities. In the late 1950s they adapted their standard bus to serve as a motor home, and they built about a dozen motor homes a year through the 1960s. Built on a GMC chassis, the 6-ton, 27-foot Coachette Cruiser was a rugged motor home with steel walls, body frame, and floor decking, and plywood interior paneling. Fully furnished with divans that converted into berths, a dinette that converted into a small bed, a kitchen, bathroom with shower, and storage closets, the 1964 Cruiser was priced at $13,200. For a smaller sum, Coachette sold a bus shell that the owner could furnish.[35]

Some luxury motor homes were not modified buses but had their own distinctive designs. In 1964 a group of investors formed the Roaminghome Company to manufacture motor homes that were as large as a bus but more sleek in appearance. Later that year Paul B. Lowry, a retired army colonel in Tucson, Arizona, purchased the company. Built on a Chevrolet truck chassis, the 25-foot Roaminghome had a fiberglass body with double walls and a honeycomb structure between the walls. Two floor plans were available: the Zuni, which had a double bed, and the Hopi, which had a dinette that converted into a bed. Four persons could be accommodated in either model, and custom furnishings could be installed to accommodate up to nine people. At a base price of $11,975, the Roaminghome was more expensive than most motor homes but less expensive than a converted bus. Fewer than fifty Roaminghomes were built before production ended in about 1966.[36]

In 1964 the Streamline Trailer Company of South El Monte, California, a luxury travel-trailer manufacturer, authorized its franchise in Thorntown, Indiana, to build a massive, gleaming motor home named the Streamline Travel Car. Like Streamline trailers, the Travel Car had an aircraft-type body made of aluminum sheeting riveted onto aluminum ribs. Initially, the Travel Car could be built to fit any chassis, but by 1965 it came in standard lengths of 30 feet, priced at $17,950, and 27 feet, priced at less than $17,000.[37] The glamorous Travel Car seemed to attract celebrities. Art Rouse, the longtime publisher of *Trailer Life* magazine, recalled, "One of my own early assignments was to borrow a Streamline Travel Car from a dealer in the San Fernando Valley. I never got my hands on that unit, because Bing Crosby and Bob

Hope spotted the motor home, borrowed it, and drove off before I arrived."[38] Another Travel Car user was jockey Johnny Longden, winner of the 1943 Triple Crown, who came out of retirement in the 1960s to train jockey Frank McMahon. His motor home, named the Pumper after Longden's nickname, was a familiar sight at racetracks at Hollywood Park and elsewhere.[39]

MOBILITY ON A BUDGET

By 1965 the selection of manufactured, self-propelled camping vehicles had become large and diverse but somewhat stratified according to price and size. At the upper end of the scale there were large, luxury motor homes and custom buses priced at more than $10,000. In the middle range were mid-sized motor homes priced at $7,000 to $10,000, still unaffordable to most motorists but steadily gaining popularity among upper-middle-class Americans. At the low end of the price scale were pickup campers, which cost only a few hundred dollars (plus the price of a pickup truck), and van campers, which could be purchased for as little as $3,000. Some recreation-vehicle enthusiasts, especially those who owned inexpensive, converted trucks, vans, buses, or one-off models, saw the need for a small, simple, well-furnished motor home that could be manufactured and sold at a modest price. In an article in *Family Motor Coaching*, George C. Hardin, the owner of a converted bus, lamented,

> If [pickup] camper builders can build good, solid, good-looking piggybacks, completely equipped with cooking, sleeping, and sanitary facilities, put them on a new three-quarter-ton pickup truck, and sell them at a commercial profit for a price of $4,100 to $4,500, *then why in the world can't they produce a housecar,* using a standard van chassis and the same standard fixtures, with maybe two more windows, and sell it happily for $5,000 or less? . . . What we all need is *one good Henry Ford for housecars.*[40]

At least two manufacturers introduced delivery-truck campers at affordable prices. Despite its homeliness, a camper based on a stand-up delivery truck offered an appealing compromise in terms of both size and price; it was larger than a van camper but smaller and less expensive than a full-sized motor home. The expanding market for motor homes encouraged two manufacturers to introduce delivery-truck campers that competed with the Boyertown Tour Wagon and Chevrolet Traville. In 1965 Heckaman Manufacturing, which built travel trailers and pickup campers in Nappanee, Indiana, introduced the Phoenix Motor Home, a 20-foot conversion of a Chevrolet stand-up delivery truck priced at only $5,995.[41] In the same year the Scandia Iron Works, which manufactured pickup campers near Minneapolis, began selling its own camper conversion of a Chevrolet stand-up delivery truck. Priced at $6,600, the 19-foot Scandia Compact Motorhome had complete sleeping, cooking, and dining facilities and accommodated six adults.[42]

The challenge of building a small, low-priced motor home with the same general appearance and features as luxury models attracted James G. M. Baker, a California businessman who had made a small fortune selling and renting travel trailers. In the 1930s the Baker family sometimes lived in their car while Frank Baker, James's father, picked crops in southern and central California. This was James's first taste of autocamping, as he perceived the experience, and he remained an avid camper and outdoor recreation enthusiast the rest of his life. He turned his passion into a career; in about 1956 James and his wife, Bettye, opened Siesta Vacation Trailer Rentals in San Jose. The Bakers devoted all of their working time to the rapidly expanding business, and by the early 1960s Baker's Trailer Sales was a major dealer offering trailer rentals, sales (new and used), service, parts, and storage. The cornerstone of the Bakers' business was low-cost, short-term trailer rental, which enticed many central California residents to discover recreation vehicles. The Bakers estimated that half of their rental customers later purchased trailers.[43]

By 1964 the Bakers had turned over day-to-day management of their thriving trailer business to employees and spent much of their free time traveling and enjoying outdoor recreation. Missing the hands-on involvement, James and Bettye decided to manufacture motor homes. They designed and built a prototype at their San Jose facility and displayed it at the Annual National Mobile Home and Travel Trailer Show in Louisville, Kentucky, in January 1965. John K. Hanson, an Iowa manufacturer who was displaying Winnebago travel trailers and pickup campers at the show, met the Bakers and saw their prototype. Hanson agreed to manufacture an affordably priced model similar to the prototype and sell finished vehicles only to the Bakers, who would sell them to retail dealers.[44]

James and Bettye Baker formed Life-Time Industries to advertise and sell motor homes (James chose the name after seeing a Life Time metal comb in a barber shop).[45] James Baker and John Hanson signed a contract in November 1965, and 19-foot Life-Time Premier motor homes with Ford chassis began rolling out of the Winnebago factory in Forest City, Iowa. An advertisement in *Family Motor Coaching* described the Life-Time Premier as "only inches longer than a large sedan or station wagon, yet . . . so spacious it contains a complete kitchen, a bathroom with toilet and shower, and sleeping accommodations for four to six people."[46] The suggested retail price of $5,995, approximately half the price of a Dodge motor home, was achieved through the compact design, low unit production cost within Winnebago's large, efficient plant, and the use of Thermo-Panel, a preformed wall material made of bonded layers of aluminum, polystyrene, and plywood. Winnebago had introduced Thermo-Panel in its travel trailers in 1964 to reduce manufacturing costs and increase the thermal efficiency of trailer bodies.[47]

In only fifteen years motor homes had progressed from experimental hybrids of travel trailers and buses to a distinct industry, and by 1965 they were on the verge of becoming affordable to a wide range of consumers. The entrance of James G. M. Baker and John K. Hanson into the motor-home industry marked a new beginning, and later these ambitious, hard-driving men would revolutionize it. Hanson would apply cost-reducing automobile manufacturing techniques, while Baker would drive motor-home prices down to unheard-of levels. Never again would motor homes be regarded simply as expensive toys; by the late 1960s they were family vehicles with all of the mechanical comforts and modern furnishings of a suburban home—a house that one could drive. And thousands of Americans would pick up the keys.

7 MOTOR HOMES IN THE AGE OF AQUARIUS

n the late 1960s the popularity of self-propelled homes on
wheels soared as thousands of Americans discovered their convenience, intimacy, and ease of handling. Motor homes built
by industry leader Winnebago and its competitors multiplied
like mushrooms. Van campers and converted buses remained
popular among many vacationers and also appealed to the new
counterculture. In an era of generational conflicts, clashing
values, and political outspokenness, a motor home often
defined not only the owner's leisure interests but his or her
place in the social and political spectrum. To affluent suburbanites, a manufactured motor home was a symbol of their purchasing power and material success, contentment with modern, well-furnished homes, increased leisure time, and
unprecedented mobility. To rebellious hippies, a homemade
bus camper was exactly the opposite: a means of expressing
their disdain for middle-class culture and the work-earn-spend
ethic by detaching themselves from society. For young Americans who admired hippie values, a van with surrealistic murals
painted on the exterior and a psychedelic interior set them
apart from their parents' generation and turned the plain van
camper into a combined hot rod, bedroom, and ersatz LSD
trip on wheels.

Van campers and homemade cabins on wheels continued
to flourish in the 1970s, but economic, environmental, and so-

cial concerns challenged the meteoric rise of motor-home sales. Conflicts with environmentalists and limits on energy resources tempered the vision of unlimited mobility and easy access to scenic areas that was part of the motor home's appeal. As motor homes grew larger and more numerous, calls for limits on their use in national parks and forests grew louder. The severe gasoline shortages and accompanying price increases of 1973–1974 and 1979 further changed the motor home's image and its place in American culture, making it seem less practical and casting it as a scapegoat of both energy crises because of its high fuel consumption and discretionary purpose. Motor-home production in the late 1970s fell far short of the peak year of 1973, when 65,300 motor homes were built. But the advantages of motor homes still appealed strongly to many vacationers, and an undercurrent of acceptance among consumers, as well as a plentiful fuel supply, eventually restored the motor home to a prominent place in recreation vehicle sales.

A MOTOR HOME IN EVERY DRIVEWAY

In early 1966 Life-Time Industries of San Jose, California, sold hundreds of motor homes built under contract by Winnebago Industries in Forest City, Iowa. The 19-foot Life-Time Premier represented a major change for the motor-home industry because of its relatively low price ($5,995) and its resemblance to more expensive makes. No company before Life-Time had offered an attractive, designed-from-scratch motor home at such a reasonable price. The Life-Time, like other motor homes, was essentially a motorized travel trailer. Its success stemmed from the determination of James G. M. Baker and John K. Hanson to build and sell an affordable motor home with trailerlike amenities.

In 1966 Winnebago began selling similar motor homes with its own nameplate through dealers of its choosing.[1] The Winnebago motor home, like the Life-Time, was an instant hit with consumers because of its handsome, trailerlike body, well-planned interior, driveability, and good mechanical performance. Consumer acceptance of the Winnebago motor home, Winnebago's reputation for economy and quality, the unparalleled production capacity of its plant, and the entrepreneurial ability of its chairman, John K. Hanson, soon placed the company at the forefront of the motor-home industry. Winnebago's extensive dealer network and assembly-line production kept sales high and prices moderate, securing Winnebago's place in history as America's first mass-producer of motor homes.

John K. Hanson had guided Winnebago Industries from its inception as a local business to national prominence. A successful businessman, Hanson owned a furniture and appliance store and a funeral home in Forest City, Iowa. In 1957 he persuaded the town's citizens to supplement the area's shrinking agricultural employment base by becoming part owners of a new branch factory of Modernistic Industries, a California firm that manufactured Aljo travel trailers. The factory closed during the recession of 1958, but Hanson and several partners purchased Modernistic's interest in the Forest City operation and reopened the plant. They named the enterprise Winnebago Industries after the Winnebago Indian tribe, the river that flows through Forest City, and the county that includes the town. In the early 1960s, as demand for recreation vehicles grew, Hanson built a national dealer network, expanded output of Winnebago trailers, and added pickup campers to the product line.[2]

In the late 1960s Hanson established motor home retail outlets at hundreds of trailer and camper dealerships. Unlike its competitors, Winnebago used the classic marketing strategies developed by General Motors and Ford in the 1920s. Like GM, Winnebago offered a wide range of sizes, styles, and prices, from a simple, 16-foot motor home to a luxurious, 27-foot mansion on wheels; but like the Ford Model T, the 22-foot Winnebago D-22, introduced late in 1966, became the company's mainstay and accounted for more than half of Winnebago's motor-home sales by 1968. The company's 1967–1968 annual report noted, "One [assembly] line manufactures Model D-22 continuously. Because this line will not be hampered with model changes, production efficiency will gain additional advantages."[3] Unlike the cut-rate Model T, however, the D-22 was expensive. In 1969 it was priced at $9,185, only $300 to $800 less than competitors' motor homes of similar size, while the 17-foot Winnebago was priced at $6,500, about $1,000 to $2,000 less than comparable models made by other manu-

Introduced in 1966, the D-22 became Winnebago's most popular model and ushered in the era of mass-produced motor homes. In 1968, when this example was built, most of the 4,000 new Winnebago motor homes were produced on the D-22 assembly line. (Courtesy Winnebago Industries, Inc.)

facturers. More customers were attracted by the size, quality, and features of the Winnebago D-22 than by its slightly discounted price.

More than any other single factor, Winnebago's huge, integrated manufacturing plant, which produced all components except chassis, appliances, and bathroom fixtures, was the company's competitive edge. The Forest City location allowed for low labor costs, a central distribution point, and proximity to Michigan chassis suppliers. Hanson's motto was, "The cheapest way to get things done is to do them yourself." By 1965 Winnebago was making its own upholstery and Thermo-Panel and operating four assembly lines in two modern factory buildings. In 1968 Winnebago opened a third factory nicknamed Big Bertha, and that year the company built 4,000 of the 18,000 motor homes sold in the United States.[4] By 1970 Hanson had pushed integration almost to its limits, manufacturing his own upholstered furniture, draperies, windows, doors, screens, grilles, molding, preformed wooden cabinets, Thermo-Panel walls, and molded fiberglass and plastic parts. Applying automobile manufacturing techniques to motor-home production, he built preassembled components on separate subassembly lines and operated three moving assembly lines for finished vehicles.[5]

Several companies, including Krager, Meade, Islander, and others, built motor homes in the $8,000 to $10,000 price range, but the only manufacturers other than Winnebago with moderate prices and a wide spectrum of models were Beechwood Industries of Hemet, California, and James G. M. Baker's company, now called Life-Time Manufacturing, in Mason City, Iowa. By 1968 Beechwood offered seven motor homes ranging from 18 feet to 24 feet and priced at $5,995 to $9,145. Life-Time built motor homes in sizes ranging from the 17-foot Town and Country to the 25-foot Continental. In 1967 the Town and Country was priced at only $4,595, possibly the all-time lowest price for a motor home. The 1968 Life-Time Premier, which was the same size as the Winnebago D-22, was priced at $6,995, about $2,000 less than the D-22. The output of Life-Time and Beechwood factories did not equal the output of Winnebago's plant, but these companies helped to popularize motor homes by offering quality vehicles at affordable prices.

Winnebago's dominant position in the marketplace made the company a national institution and their products the most conspicuous symbol of vacationers' growing love affair with motor homes. Winnebago was so closely identified with the emerging motor-home culture that its name became a synonym for "motor home." By 1969 motor homes accounted for 80 percent of Winnebago's sales, and the company's net income had risen from $185,552 in 1965 to $3,206,142, largely on the strength of its motor-home sales.[6] Winnebago's upwardly spiraling stock was one of the surest bets on Wall Street. Investing in Winnebago became a second form of income for hundreds of Forest City residents; many watched stock indexes as closely as they watched their corn, soybeans, and cattle, and some became millionaires.[7] As Forest City transformed itself into a little Detroit, the prairie town itself became a symbol of America's romance with motor homes. The number of employees at Winnebago rose from seventeen in 1959 to 415 in 1967 and 1,252 in 1969, and the town's population rose from 2,900 to 4,000 during the same period. Winnebago, the "Miracle on the Prairie," was the clearest reminder that thousands of vacationers now preferred motor homes over tent campers, travel trailers, pickup campers, or motels.

In addition to Winnebago's high public profile, network television programs brought motor homes to the attention of the American people. Lucille Ball, who had entertained moviegoers in 1954 with the hit film *The Long, Long Trailer,* devoted the first eight episodes of the 1969–1970 season of her CBS situation comedy, *Here's Lucy,* to a vacation trip in a 27-foot Dodge motor home. The episodes were filmed in the summer of 1969, during a trip by Ball and her family from Los Angeles to Colorado Springs.[8]

Perhaps the nation's best known motor-home user was CBS News correspondent Charles Kuralt. Kuralt did not intend to be a spokesman for recreation vehicles; he just wanted his supervisors to transfer him from "hard" news to feature stories about ordinary but interesting people he would encounter on a random motor tour of America's villages and rural areas. In the fall of 1967 CBS leased a Travco motor home from the National Geographic Society, and Kuralt and a camera and sound crew were off on a journey into the heartland—a journalistic experiment that cast Kuralt as a wandering Edward R. Murrow, Mark Twain, and Norman Rockwell rolled into one. The experiment itself made news because of its novel, low-key approach. Kuralt's "On the Road" segments were peaceful interludes on *CBS Evening News,* and they offered viewers slices of life that were not necessarily newsworthy but worthy of attention. Kuralt looked at traditions and lifestyles that had not changed in generations and hardy nonconformists who seemed oblivious to modern institutions. In Kuralt's offbeat, conservative way, these stories were a soothing counterpoint to the daily news.

Kuralt did not actually sleep or cook in the motor home. After it became obvious that several grown men could not keep house in such a small place, the reporter and his staff decided to spend the nights in motels and eat in restaurants, keeping only lunch meats in their tiny refrigerator. But Kuralt traveled and wrote television and radio scripts in "the Bus," as the motor home was called. Over the years, CBS purchased a series of motor homes for him, including another Travco, two Cortez motor homes, a Revcon, and an FMC with an expansive desk. Unlike John Steinbeck, Kuralt was not inconspicuous when he came to town—the Bus was emblazoned with the CBS logo and ON THE ROAD. Like Steinbeck, Kuralt welcomed visitors who wanted to see the interior

From 1967 to 1983 CBS News correspondent Charles Kuralt toured the United States in a motor home and studied traditional people, places, and activities. His televised reports helped to popularize motor homes by showing their unparalleled access to remote places. (Courtesy CBS Photo Archive)

of the office and studio on wheels. Kuralt's probing, omnipresent motor home became a familiar image to television viewers across the nation and a symbol of recreation vehicle travel. His journey taught many television viewers that motor homes were an easy way to escape fast-paced, modern living and see the "real" America—a land of rugged individualists who never worried, watched the clock, or tried to please the boss.[9]

The interstate highway system, which was growing by leaps and bounds in the 1960s, was another incentive to enjoy motor homes, but it also presented a compromise and a contradiction. Unlike the serenity and sightseeing opportunities along rural roads, high-speed highways simply fast-forwarded travelers to vacation destinations. For the first time, interstate highways made vehicular travel as fast and effortless as train travel; skimming across the country at 70 miles per hour, motor-home users enjoyed all of the comforts and conveniences of a private railroad car. Superhighways saved time and fuel, and their broad, dual lanes and almost-level grading eliminated many inconveniences and hazards. But superhighways were as devoid of cultural experiences as a trip in an airplane; they skirted towns and cities, roadside access was banned, and standard signage homogenized the landscape. As Charles Kuralt wrote, "Thanks to the Interstate Highway System, it is now possible to travel across the country from coast to coast without seeing anything. From the Interstate, America is all steel guardrails and plastic signs, and every place looks and feels and sounds and smells like every other place."[10]

In 1961 David G. Drum and three other businessmen in Billings, Montana, opened an autocamp to attract tent campers and RV owners en route to the Rocky Mountains and the Century 21 Exposition in Seattle. After this venture proved successful, they decided to establish a chain of autocamps that would be located near major highways and population centers. In 1963 they formed Kampgrounds of America (KOA) to create RV and tent campsites with a uniform appearance and predictably high standards of service and cleanliness. KOA camps were individually owned and operated, but the home office in Billings provided national advertising and promotion, a reservation system and directory, regular inspections, and standard design plans for a camp office and store, laundry, showers, picnic tables, fireplace grills, utility hookups, and other facilities. Like autocamps in the 1920s, the roadside camp concept proved to be very popular; by 1965 there were thirty-three KOA autocamps in operation and by 1967 the number had risen to 120. At least six other franchise autocamp chains were in operation by the late 1960s, but KOA remained the largest, and by 1970 they offered more campsites than the National Park Service. For RV owners, KOA and other campground chains combined the conveniences of park autocamps with the speed and efficiency of the nation's highway system and the predictability of nationally advertised motel chains.[11]

As vacationers discovered the pleasures and conveniences of motor homes, production rose sharply to 7,050 vehicles in 1967, 18,220 vehicles in 1968, and 23,100 in 1969. In contrast with homemade house cars of the 1920s, a manufactured motor home was a tangible reward for a lifetime of work and earning. A motor home seemed to represent several values that affluent Americans cherished: mobility, increased leisure time, family intimacy, and sophisticated domestic surroundings. Longer paid vacations, more three-day weekends, and rising median income enticed thousands of working Americans to purchase motor homes and other recreation vehicles for vacation trips. The mating of the suburban house and the motor home was one of the most conspicuous symbols of affluent family life and leisure.

HIPPIE BUSES: A REAL TRIP

Converted buses, vans, and cabins on wheels, not manufactured motor homes, became symbols of the emerging counterculture in the late 1960s and early 1970s. A generation of young Americans were attracted to a movement that preached nonconformity, the importance of individuals, simple, sincere relationships, and rebellion against societal relationships, values, and institutions that to them seemed restrictive, unfulfilling, and self-defeating. Counterculture values combined the "hip" message of disaffected minorities, the spontaneity and informality of "beat" writers, respect for nature and preindustrial lifestyles, introspective eastern religions, use of hallucinogenic drugs, and sexual freedom to create a new ethic that emphasized self-gratification, immediate pleasure, and enhanced spiritual awareness of one's place in the "cosmos." Hippies of the 1960s rejected middle-class values such as wage earning, career goals, material abundance, and saving for the future, and they refused to define personal success in those terms. Unlike beatniks of the 1950s and 1960s, hippies took their message to the public in a wide range of extrovertive, highly theatrical, and attention-getting events and art forms, including mass gatherings and caravans of exotic homes on wheels.

Hippies specifically reacted to the crescendo of materialism, industrial progress, war, nuclear armament, and environmental degradation during the prosperous 1950s and 1960s. For many members of the counterculture, a low-cost bus or van became a symbol of individuality and detachment from society, a testament in favor of primitivism over industrialization, and a celebration of mental and spiritual self-containment. Somehow it was possible for hippies to reject the work ethic that produces motor vehicles and the pollution that vehicles produce and still think of a bus home or van home as an expression of antiestablishment sentiment—the antithesis of the ostentatious, middle-class suburban home. Hippies' bus homes became vivid symbols of their revolutionary lifestyle and an important part of their expressive facade. But instead of escaping temporarily from home and work as their parents had done in station wagons and their grandparents in house cars, hippies escaped permanently from society and, at times, from reality.

The hippie bus burst upon the American scene in 1964 when Ken Kesey, author of the novel *One Flew over the Cuckoo's Nest* and a proponent of the emerging drug culture, crossed the United States in a converted 1939 International Harvester school bus "painted to look like a moving Jackson Pollock painting."[12] A former ward attendant in a mental hospital, Kesey had volunteered for experiments involving the ingestion of hallucinogenic drugs, including LSD, and he became one the most vocal advocates of mental and spiritual revelations through LSD. Like Timothy Leary, a Harvard psychology professor who endorsed mind-altering drugs on the college-campus lecture circuit, Kesey brought LSD to the attention of mainstream America. Kesey also helped to popularize psychedelic art, a wild, gaudy, Technicolor vision that mirrored an LSD trip. The psychedelic style eventually pervaded a wide range of homemade and mass-market art, advertisements, clothing, and even rock-music stars' custom automobiles.

Kesey's psychedelic bus, which was given the poetic name Furthur, became a stained-glass billboard advertising the LSD "religion" and Kesey's belief in spontaneous behavior as a basis for healthy nonconformity. Along with bunks and dining equipment, Kesey and the Merry Band of Pranksters installed a gold-trimmed barber's chair on the rear platform of the bus, a rooftop observation deck, and a sound system that amplified sounds coming from inside or outside the vehicle. They also carried a motion picture camera and planned to make a film of the journey titled *The Merry Pranksters Search for the Cool Place*. Leaving San Francisco in June 1964 to attend the New York World's Fair and celebrate the publication of Kesey's novel *Sometimes a Great Notion*, Kesey and the Pranksters drove through the Southwest and deep South, dropping "acid," playing musical instruments, and "rapping" lines from new novels and plays. It was a kinetic adventure in inner space and outer awareness; Ken Babbs, a Prankster nicknamed the Intrepid Traveller, later recalled, "We were using America as the set, and the people of America as part of the experience and drama that would happen." Like Charles Kuralt and John Steinbeck, Kesey and the Pranksters set out to see America in a new way, but the vision that they sought was not one that could be seen solely through a camera lens or a writer's discerning eye but through the hippie viewpoint and mind-altering drugs. After the 1964 trip Kesey used the bus to travel to a series of "acid tests," his term for parties that featured rock music and LSD, as well as the 1969 Woodstock Music and Art Fair. Then the bus was retired to Kesey's farm in Oregon.[13]

As the counterculture movement spread in the late 1960s, other hippies were attracted to converted bus homes. The concept of "family" was too ingrained for them to shed, and living in buses was a way to have communal families in places of their choosing. Many became disenchanted with urban life and decided that rural places were more compatible with their antiestablishment, antimodern ideology. Bus homes provided the perfect means for a mass exodus and formation of communes. Wavy Gravy (Hugh Romney) lived with his wife, Jahanara Romney (Bonnie Jean), in Ken Kesey's bus Furthur for a while; then Hugh, Bonnie, and several others took up residence on a working hog farm in the Verdugo Hills near Burbank, California, that they acquired rent-free in exchange for feeding and tending some sixty hogs. (They later ran one of the hogs for president of the United States.) Wavy and other Hog Farmers (as they were called) used a bus caravan called the Hog Farm Caravan to spread the celebration of counterculture values. Their peaceful crusade became national and then global, traveling to New York, Vermont, Sweden, Nepal, and many other places. Wavy recalled,

> The Road Hog and other buses in the Hog Farm Caravan served as traveling theaters to expand the consciousness on campuses and cities in the fields of pacifism and the interconnectiveness of all living things. They did this through celebration of diversity where each audience member became an integral part of the event. The buses were owned collectively and registered in Invisible, Inc., a corporation jointly held in California.[14]

In the late 1960s and early 1970s personalized bus homes brought the counterculture message of peace and togetherness to audiences throughout the world with a variety of theatrical, participatory events. In 1968 Wavy Gravy's Road Hog and other buses in the Hog Farm Caravan brightened the Fourth of July with a parade in El Rito, New Mexico. (Photograph by Lisa Law © 1968)

The Hog Farm Caravan started with one bus, the Road Hog, which was a Christmas surprise from the mechanics who lived on the Hog Farm. The Hog Farmers remodeled it with money earned by portraying "flower children" in Otto Preminger's motion picture *Skidoo* (1968). In Wavy's book about the Hog Farm's early days, which he dedicated to Furthur, he explained that the Hog Farmers bought lumber, nails, and other materials and drove the Road Hog to Ken Kesey's farm, where they built and installed bunks that doubled as benches and storage lockers.[15] They also covered the bus body, including the ceiling, with hand-painted murals. Then the Hog Farmers acquired and remodeled several other buses: Chance's Van, Big Pig, Band Bus, Bread Van, Tom Law's Juke Savage Machine (built with cast-off parts from the atomic test facility at Los Alamos, New Mexico), and Peter Whiterabbit's Queens Midtown Tunnel of Love. They drove around the country staging shows, parades, races, and other diverse, impromptu events. They dropped in on a meeting of the Students for a Democratic Society in Boulder, Colorado, served a huge birthday cake for Mouse Babbs, daughter of Kesey Prankster Ken Babbs, inside one of the buses, and attended President Richard Nixon's first inauguration, where they passed out kazoos. The college campus shows were the purest expression of the joy that they felt at being liberated from time, space, and societal norms that seemed irrelevant and harmful—"transforming the world . . . to make it loving and creative and wonderful and fun" as Jahanara Romney recalled.[16] They set up domes with light shows, rock music, and murals and invited local bands and entertainers to join in the spontaneous partying.

In the late 1960s the Hog Farmers purchased land near Llano, New Mexico, for a stationary commune. At first the buses were parked while other forms of housing were assembled, but the buses remained an integral part of the Hog Farm experience. Wavy recalled,

> At least a half dozen buses and Volkswagen vans roamed the New Mexico landscape, and during the 1969 summer solstice celebration, they participated in The Great Bus Race at Aspen Meadows near Santa Fe where the Great bus Road Hog triumphed over the Great bus Furthur, winning its silver bell. The two buses then journeyed on to Woodstock and the Aquarian Festival.[17]

Stephen Gaskin, a former teaching assistant at San Francisco State College, also started a bus commune. Gaskin began an experimental course about the counterculture and then left academia in 1966 to start a hippie ministry. He blended elements of eastern and western religions to create his own message about the transcendancy of spiritualism over materialism and the liberation of the self. With his messianic delivery, long, flowing hair, and full beard, Gaskin attracted growing numbers of followers to his lectures, which were held in a church, a theater, and then a rock-music hall in the San Francisco area. Gaskin lived in a red, white, and blue school bus, and when he decided to tour the United States in the bus and share his message with others, approximately 250 followers joined him in thirty converted buses. The Caravan, as the group named their entourage, left the West Coast in the fall of 1970 and spent several months touring the northern states, New England, mid-Atlantic states, Southeast, Midwest, and Southwest, holding public lectures and attracting more followers and buses.

In 1971, after the tour ended, Gaskin and his group drove their buses from San Francisco to Tennessee and established an agrarian commune named the Farm. Setting their own rules (first names only, four-person marriages allowed, vegetarian diet, shared resources), the commune took root and tripled in size within a few years. Eventually the Farm occupied a 1,700-acre site with its own school, laundry, grist mill, communal bank, telephone system, and publishing company. Gradually, the buses were replaced by tents, huts, and houses.[18]

Vans appealed to young, middle-class Americans who did not join the hippie movement but nevertheless adopted its ways and values. Like rock music, marijuana use, and sexual promiscuity, van culture was an aspect of the hippie culture that became acceptable among young people who wanted to liberalize their personal lives and publicly break away from their parents' generation. Vans combined the freedom of hippie buses with the hands-on appeal of hot rods and the versatility and privacy of the family station wagon. In the early 1970s many young people purchased used vans made in the 1960s, customized their interiors with beds and stereo equipment, and took overnight trips to beaches, campgrounds, rock concerts, and other destinations. A typical van-camper interior had lurid colors and plush fabrics that disoriented the senses, mirrored the psychedelic style, and created an intimate "passion pit." Exteriors were covered with surrealistic nature scenes and geometric patterns that mimicked the hippie style and proclaimed the owner's individuality and nonconformity.[19]

Although the hippie movement was short-lived, the hippie bus became a lasting part of the American landscape as more people withdrew from society, abandoned their conventional housing arrangements, and made a fresh start by adopting a mobile lifestyle. Robert McGraw, who lived in a converted 1960 GMC school bus named the Blunder Bus, rented a vacant lot in Berkeley, California, and started Bus People's Park, an enclave for people who chose to live in buses, vans, or trucks. McGraw summed up the appeal of homes on wheels to people he called truckees:

In the 1970s craftspeople, members of the counterculture, and others who disliked conventional housing and employment situations lived in homemade quarters mounted on trucks. These artistic, personalized vehicles served as remote cabins without the encumbrances of real property. (Photograph © Jane Lidz)

Truckees build houses on these trucks and move into them because they want to own their homes. They are tired of apartments where rents are high, leases binding and you can be evicted at the whim of a landlord. They all talk to me about their plans for buying land somewhere, sometime—a farm maybe, and building a geodesic dome, foam house, tepee, log cabin or some other extension of their creative vision of which their trucks are an example. I have never met a truckee who would live in cities at any time if he had financial choice about it. When I think about truckees I get the kind of vision that you would probably get of a mellow, pioneer type such as once peopled the wilderness. I have visions of sharing meals with them at a table made of logs, set up in the middle of a circle of buses deep in the woods at night. Everyone in my vision is smiling and the tensions that I have felt in apartments and houses in the city are not there.[20]

A new type of escapist vehicle, the cabin truck, appeared on the West Coast in the 1970s. Built on a truck or bus chassis, these homemade vehicles literally were cabins on wheels and had house-type wooden siding or shingles, Victorian-style doors and windows, dormers, skylights, bay windows, and ornate brass hardware. Their interiors had naturally finished wood panels, houseplants, wood stoves, and other quaint or natural furnishings. Like buses, cabin trucks appealed to people who wanted to drop out of nine-to-five society and live in a portable cabin with few of the encumbrances of real property. Cabin trucks added the reactionary appeal of turn-of-the-century houses at a time when neo-Victorian suburban houses were not yet popular. Cabin-truck owners lived between hippie culture and mainstream America, respecting the earth and the individual's place in it and disdaining the encroachments of industrialization. Many worked with their hands; artists, silversmiths, jewelry makers, leather workers, gem cutters, and other craftspeople were among the many occupants of cabin trucks.[21]

BOOM, BUST, AND BEYOND

By the early 1970s manufactured motor homes were a ubiquitous feature of the American landscape and a major segment of the recreation vehicle industry. Motor homes became more attainable if not more affordable. Production reached 64,600 motor homes in 1972 and 65,300 in 1973, a record that would stand for decades.[22] Beginning in 1971, the Winnebago Acceptance Corporation offered credit to retail purchasers of motor homes through participating financial institutions. Motor home rentals, pioneered by Dodge in the early 1960s, became an increasingly popular way to enjoy motor homes at the lowest possible cost; in 1972 even Hertz and Avis added motor homes to their rental fleets. In 1973 General Motors began a broad initiative to manufacture, rent, sell, and service motor homes; GM set up special dealerships and offered retail financing through General Motors Acceptance Corporation. Across the nation motor homes became a familiar sight on highways and at vacation destinations. The Stardust Hotel in Las Vegas opened a parking lot with 150 spaces reserved for motor homes. In South Dakota Republican gubernatorial candidate Carveth Thompson campaigned through the state in his motor home. Celebrity entertainers Bob Hope, Bing Crosby, and John Wayne owned motor homes,

When motor homes became popular in the late 1960s, specialized sales and service centers catered to the needs of motor-home owners. The Meco Motor Home Servicenter in Brick, New Jersey, was a dealer for Beechwood, Condor, and other makes and offered parts and repair service for all motor homes. (Courtesy Meco Distributors, Inc.)

singer-actor Robert Goulet traveled in a Dodge that doubled as a dressing room, and Graham Kerr, television's Galloping Gourmet, rode about in a Life-Time.

The growth of national RV clubs provided more evidence of the expanding, maturing motor-home market. Thousands of RV owners formed social clubs, often with a particular make of vehicle as the common bond. In the 1950s Airstream's Wally Byam popularized brand-affiliated trailer clubs with the formation of the Wally Byam Caravan Club. Similar clubs were formed in the late 1960s and 1970s: Dodge Motorcade Club, Winnebago International Travelers, Cortez Clubs, Condor Travel Club, Lazy Daze Caravan Club, Ultra Van Motor Coach Clubs, and others.[23] Club members enjoyed newsletters, group rallies, group trips led by "wagonmasters," and other benefits. Like social gatherings of Model T owners in the 1910s and the Tin Can Tourists of America, an association of autocampers, in the 1920s, these RV clubs provided a way to share the excitement and pride of owning a camping rig, exchange information about roads and vehicles, and build a network of "neighbors."

The Good Sam Club, the nation's largest RV-owners' organization, is affiliated not with a vehicle but with a publication. It was established in 1966 by the Griffin Publishing Company, publisher of *Griffin's Trailer News* and *Camper Coachman*, as a promotional activity for subscribers. The club's name, which is based on the New Testament parable of the good Samaritan, was chosen in response to a reader's description of his trailer club's efforts to assist other RV owners on the road. In 1968 Art Rouse's Trailer Life Publishing Company, which published *Trailer Life* and *MotorHome Life*, purchased the Griffin Publishing Company and acquired the Good Sam Club. Between 1968 and the mid-1980s, when Rouse retired, he expanded the club from a 10,000-member organization subsidized by the parent company to a 400,000-member, dues-paying organization that hosted social activities (including a national Samboree), lobbied for legislation favorable to RV users, and provided member benefits such as mail forwarding and discounts on gasoline, campground fees, RV supplies and services, and RV and health insurance. The Good Sam Pledge, which new members were required to read and sign, obliged them to give aid to fellow members, keep their RVs in safe condition, obey traffic laws, avoid slowing traffic, obey rules at outdoor recreational facilities, and leave their campsites in better condition than they found them. The Scout-like activities and moral tone of the Good Sam Club reinforced the RV's image as a family vehicle and helped form its reputation for safe, healthy fun.[24]

As the number of motor homes grew, they drew criticism from some campers and environmentalists who challenged the appropriateness of RVs in parks and other natural preserves. As early as the 1950s critics of the National Park Service's plans to add modern roads and service buildings had objected to "civilizing" parks with suburban-style parkways, laundromats, cafeterias, trailer parks, and parking lots, all designed to attract more motorists and RVs.[25] By the 1970s some park roads had become congested with motor-vehicle traffic; as a result, the

National Park Service banned automobiles in high-use areas of some parks, notably Yosemite, and substituted buses and trams.[26] On park roads where automobiles and RVs were still permitted, wide, tall motor homes and pickup campers irritated some park users by obscuring the view, breaking tree branches, and flattening roadside vegetation. Fueling the conflict between RV owners and other park users was the growing number of 25-foot to 30-foot motor homes with widths up to 8 feet. Often a boat or canoe rested on top, bicycles clung to the rear, and a small car for side trips trailed merrily behind like a dinghy, adding to the motor home's already generous proportions.

Clearly, RV living was a form of portable housing, not camping. "Separated from the natural world by glass and metal, one cannot be in touch with wind, water, woods and stars," wrote a *New York Times* journalist.[27] Motor-home owners made no apologies for reproducing their suburban homes in parks and forests; one owner said, "I came here to relax, not to be uncomfortable."[28] Tent campers and RV owners often shared park campgrounds, and the serenity of these enclaves was increasingly disturbed by motor-home engines, auxiliary generators, and on-board air conditioners, radios, televisions, stereos, and appliances. Frances Greiff, an avid camper and prolific travel writer, praised RVs until the early 1970s, when she abruptly reversed her position, calling for the exclusion of RVs from parks to preserve their ecosystems and their quiet beauty. In an article in *National Parks and Conservation Magazine*, she explained her conversion and her pessimistic view of RVs in parks:

> I will write no more articles in support of recreation vehicle camping in state and national parks. . . . If you continue to campaign for more and bigger drive-through pads—unencumbered by overhanging branches—or for universal water, electric, and sewer hookups, or for around-the- corner dumping stations in every fragile national and state park, I will contest your rights. And I will do my best to push you to the outermost perimeter of the parks, where you can less easily destroy the unique environment your machinery now pervades.
>
> I have seen instant tenements created by the mounting influx of bigger and bigger vehicles. Once inside the crush of vehicles, I feel bombarded by noise and air pollution and sometimes begin to grow claustrophobic. . . . By afternoon in summer the campground resembles a gigantic parking lot; and when

we return from daytime activities, we become separated from the natural features of the park. The granite cliffs, a volcanic skyline, the brilliant red soil, the twisted cypress—whatever distinguishes the place—must be viewed from the perspective of the parking lot.[29]

Many large families still regarded a do-it-yourself converted bus as a superior type of motor home because of its capacity and low initial cost. J. Raymond Hogan and his wife of New Branford, Connecticut, purchased a used, 40-foot bus that had carried passengers around their state; they removed all but twelve seats, which they left in place for their twelve children ranging in age from infant to teens. In the remaining space they installed beds, a kitchen, a chemical toilet, and a storage compartment. The Hogans made a complete set of window curtains and seat covers for the bus.[30] Dr. Harold George, who operated a clinic in Mount Vernon, Missouri, purchased a used, 32-foot school bus for $500, and for another $800 his family of six converted it into a vacation home on wheels.[31] And in 1971 Dawson and Mary Gillaspy of Pennsylvania converted a 1958 Superior school bus into a motor home for their family of six. They removed all but two seats and installed plywood and aluminum partitions, mattresses, a kitchen, water tank, window screens, and other conveniences. Mary Gillaspy decorated the interior of the bus in an orange and white color scheme with floral prints.[32]

Among the most elaborate and expensive bus conversions were custom models owned by country and western entertainers. Since the 1920s a number of country music stars had achieved celebrity status equal to that of motion picture and television actors. By the 1960s buses for road tours had evolved from simple transportation for personnel and equipment to rolling homes that were both status symbol and refuge from the grinding regimen of one-night performances, constantly changing surroundings, and aggressive fans. Margaret Jones, one of Patsy Cline's biographers, summarized the significance of bus homes to country and western performers: "Nowadays musicians tour in customized buses made to accommodate life on the road, but in the fifties everyone traveled in Cadillacs or Chryslers, often in caravans. . . . The road was punishing, or as Barbara Mandrell, whose career dated back to Patsy's era, put it, 'The road is tough, but the road is a piece of cake now compared to what it was before we had buses.'"[33] Waylon Jennings seldom left his bus during tours except to perform. After traveling in "a succession of limousines and station wagons, beat-up motor homes and pickup trucks," he purchased a Blue Bird bus conversion and then traded up to a Silver Eagle, a Golden Eagle, and finally a 45-foot Prevost.[34] A typical country and western singer's bus had private quarters for the star, including a bedroom, sofa, dressing room, and closet, bunks for his or her accompanists, and a common dining area. Storage bays under the body held the group's instruments and equipment. Loretta Lynn paid $147,000 for a 38-foot bus, and she personally designed its interior decor of purple velvet, gold trim, and white leatherette.[35] Jeannie C. Riley purchased a converted bus and named it the Harper Valley Express after her hit song "Harper Valley PTA"; the interior was decorated in gold and black with gold carpet and tufted, gold vinyl walls. Later she purchased a converted Silver Eagle bus as a way of "keeping up with the country-music Joneses."[36]

Van campers also became more popular in the late 1960s and early 1970s because they offered the intimacy and driveability of a motor home, if not its spaciousness, at prices that people could afford. Van campers and van conversions with pop-up tops or raised, rigid tops were manufactured and sold in large numbers at prices ranging from $4,000 to $8,000. Some vans, such as the 1969 Ford Econoline, were longer and had more interior space than earlier models, which appealed to more vacationers. In 1969 Ford began selling the $4,800 MiniHome, an Econoline van camper with an extended fiberglass top that provided extra headroom.[37]

A new type of camper with a body that was wider, longer, and taller than previous van campers revolutionized this sector of the industry. The chopped van or mini motor home, a van with the cargo section cut away and replaced with a cab-over body similar to a pickup camper, was introduced in 1966 by Newham Industries of Pomona, California, manufacturer of Lazy Daze slide-in and chassis-mounted pickup campers. The 1966 Lazy Daze Sportsman Housecar had a Dodge van chassis and driver's compartment, but the body was designed and built to resemble a chassis-mounted pickup camper. Newham sold its products directly from the factory to consumers, and the low price of $5,295 made the Sportsman Housecar especially attractive to budget-conscious vacationers.[38] Within a few years the chopped-van concept caught on; in 1973 more than eighty manufacturers built 36,700 mini motor homes. The mini motor home was the final solution to the problem of cramped quarters inside a van camper. In terms of price and size it offered an appealing compromise between a van camper and a motor home. To accommodate the growing number of mini motor home conversions, automakers lengthened the wheelbase of van chassis, introduced dual rear wheels and front disc brakes, and began to offer van chassis that were already chopped (cab but no body).[39]

The motor-home industry experienced a retrenchment in 1973 and 1974. In the spring of 1973 consumers' anxieties over inflation, a sluggish stock market, and rumors of spot gasoline shortages were blamed for slower sales of motor homes. In the fall of that year the Arab oil embargo, widespread retail gasoline shortages, and escalating gasoline prices led to a sharp decline in motor-home sales. Suddenly, the boom was over, and it now seemed to many Americans impractical and even unpatriotic to drive a vehicle that averaged only 7 or 8 miles per gallon. Thousands of motor homes sat idle in driveways, yards, and RV dealers' lots.

During the energy crisis, the motor home was targeted as a symbol of excess and an object lesson in the need to limit discretionary use of energy. The RV establishment defended the viability of motor homes and trailers. An editorial writer for *MotorHome Life* minimized the effects of gasoline price hikes, pointing out that gasoline expenditures were only a fraction of the total budget of a typical RV owner.[40] In the fall of 1973 the Recreational Vehicle Institute (RVI), an industry trade association, launched a counteroffensive to disprove assertions that motor-home travel was wasteful and nonessential. The RVI advertising campaign focused on energy savings gained when a vacationing family closed their house, parked their cars in the driveway, and lived in a motor home, which (according to RVI figures) used one-fourth as much energy as a house.[41] Although gasoline retailers openly discriminated against recreation-vehicle owners and federally mandated closure of gasoline stations on Sundays put a crimp in leisure travel, motor-home advocates continued to defend their pastime and its recreational benefits. Nevertheless, changes in motor-home design and usage were inevitable. In 1974 Winnebago, which had introduced its Minnie Winnie chopped van in 1971, brought out the smaller, slimmer Winnie Wagon, a motor home that was only slightly larger than a station wagon. RV journalists advised all motor-home owners to conserve gasoline, urging them to cut speed, avoid headwinds and jackrabbit starts, adjust brakes so they would not drag, and keep tires inflated.[42]

Despite efforts to rationalize the gasoline shortage or adjust to it, the crisis had a profound effect on the motor-home industry. Production fell from 65,300 vehicles in 1973 to 26,700 vehicles in 1974, and many manufacturers went out of business. Even Winnebago, which was strong enough to survive the crisis, suffered sharp earnings losses, laid off most of its employees, and diversified into other products, including transit buses, cargo vans, and agricultural trailers. Although gasoline became plentiful again by 1975 and motor-home sales rebounded, the effects of a second gasoline shortage in 1979 were deeper and lasted longer. Winnebago shut down its motor-home production facility for six weeks in the spring and summer of 1979. Total U.S. production fell to only 9,800 motor homes in 1980, and consumer interest did not become strong again until the mid-1980s. Once the motor home's weaknesses were exposed, many Americans became interested in more fuel-efficient RVs. Between 1974 and 1986 combined production of economical van campers and chopped vans exceeded motor-home production in every year except one.[43]

The motor home boom of 1966–1973 took Americans on a ride that they would never forget. During this period, the dream of ultimate mobility—a seamless, limitless marriage of car, home, highway, and scenic places—became a reality for tens of thousands of Americans. Unfortunately, the very real limits of a finite, unstable fuel supply and overcrowded facilities brought a sudden, sobering reassessment of the motor home's place in recreational travel. Despite its drawbacks and its mechanical inefficiency, the motor home had lasting, fundamental appeal because of its ease of handling and its efficient living space. In the 1980s and 1990s a new generation of vacationers would discover the pleasures of homes that they could drive, and as suddenly as the boom had ended, the motor home found a new and more secure place in Americans' leisure activities.

EPILOGUE

Motor-home sales were strong in the 1980s and 1990s as more consumers became familiar with the advantages that full-sized models offered. Although the gasoline shortage of 1979 was a painful setback, production rebounded from 9,800 units in 1980 to an average of 34,250 units per year between 1983 and 1996, well below the peak year of 1973 but still a respectable 15 percent of annual recreation vehicle output. Expansion of the interstate highway system, a strong economy, Americans' healthy appetite for outdoor recreation, and liberal, five- to seven-year payment plans stimulated the buying spree. Young Americans—the "baby boom" generation who grew up in the 1950s and 1960s—became interested in recreation vehicles, and many purchased new or used motor homes or took advantage of rental opportunities.

During this period, motor-home manufacturers made some radical design changes that improved efficiency and marketability. Diesel engines and weight reduction through the use of lightweight materials boosted fuel economy from 7 or 8 miles per gallon to 15 or 20 miles per gallon. Alternative fuels (e.g. gasohol and liquid propane) and dual-fuel engines further eased motorists' and dealers' apprehensions about coping with another gasoline shortage. Other borrowed technologies—fuel injection, catalytic converters, on-board computers for engines and environmental controls, global positioning devices, and

This well-furnished Blue Bird Wanderlodge motor home resembles a page in House Beautiful. *(Courtesy Blue Bird)*

closed-circuit television for better visibility—improved performance, reliability, safety, and utility. Manufacturing technologies borrowed from the automobile industry, like computer-aided design and robot welding, improved stress and weight distribution and increased uniformity of assembled parts. The motor home of the 1980s and 1990s was a lean, clean machine compared with the lumbering, fuel-guzzling houses on wheels that preceded it.

Motor-home bodies followed well-established patterns, but many took on sleek, aerodynamic shapes and styles. Motor homes of the 1980s and 1990s still came in three basic sizes: vans, motorized travel trailers, and buses. Traditional trailer-sized ("Type A") motor homes built by Winnebago, Coachmen, Fleetwood, and many other companies once again dominated sales. Van conversions ("Type B" motor homes) remained popular because they cost less to own and operate than full-sized motor homes and doubled as station wagons, but fewer van campers were manufactured than in the 1970s; motorists preferred custom conversions of existing vans. Van-sized motor homes such as Winnebago's Winnie Wagon II and EuroVan (codeveloped by Volkswagen) with chiseled front ends and a streamlined, futuristic appearance attracted some buyers. Mini motor homes or chopped vans ("Type C" motor homes) built by Winnebago, Shasta, Fleetwood, and others still accounted for a large percentage of motor-home sales, and the micro mini motor home, a new breed of chopped van based on small, imported pickup trucks, was a popular seller.

A healthy market for bus-sized, luxury motor homes led to the introduction of Winnebago's Vectra, Elante, Luxor, and Chieftain models, Fleetwood's American Dream and American Eagle, and several others. "Basement"-style models such as the Winnebago Superchief featured underbody storage compartments similar to those on long-distance buses. Although Winnebago and other mass-market companies helped to popularize bus-sized motor homes, smaller manufacturers such as Blue Bird, Prevost, Eagle, and Newell were still the Rolls-Royces of the industry. Celebrities, actors, and entertainers were among the purchasers of these mansions on wheels. Actor Ernest Borgnine visited small towns and met admiring fans in the Sunbum, a modified Prevost. Well-known musicians Bruce Springsteen and Harry Connick Jr. and singing groups Alabama and the Doobie Brothers traveled in buses custom-furnished by Hemphill Brothers of Nashville, Tennessee, coach builder to the stars.

After a century of development, the motor home has come to symbolize and reaffirm the unity of home, family, travel, and outdoor lifestyles more than any other possession or institution. From RV resorts to houses with specially designed RV garages to motor-home villages at world's fairs, motor homes have become part of the fabric of everyday life. In 1992 Winnebago rolled out its 250,000th motor home, and in 1998 the Family Motor Coach Association registered its 250,000th family, with more than 100,000 families still active members. No longer an experiment or fad, the comfortable, well-equipped home on the road is here to stay.

NOTES

INTRODUCTION

1. John Muir, *Our National Parks* (Boston: Houghton Mifflin, 1901), 1.
2. Seymour Dunbar, *A History of Travel in America*, vol. 1 (Indianapolis: Bobbs-Merrill, 1915), 223.
3. Burton Willis Potter, *The Road and the Roadside* (Boston: Little, Brown, 1893), 89.
4. Michael L. Berger, *The Devil Wagon in God's Country: The Automobile and Social Change in Rural America, 1893–1929* (Hamden, Conn.: Archon Books, 1979), 23.
5. W. W. Culver, "A Typical Gypsy Camp of the Better Class," *Inter-State Journal* (June–July 1903), front cover.
6. "'Camping Wagon' for Outing Trips," *Philadelphia Record*, 7 October 1901.
7. Unpublished notes by Ralph Renner, n.d., Recreation Vehicle file, Transportation Collections, National Museum of American History, Smithsonian Institution (hereafter cited as NMAH).

1. EARLY HOMES ON WHEELS

1. "First across Continent," *New York Herald*, 26 July 1903.
2. Letter from Hugh L. Willoughby to the editor, *Automobile* (26 September 1903): 313.
3. "Across the Continent in Big Touring Car," *New York Times*, 30 December 1906.
4. Harriet White Fisher, *A Woman's World Tour in a Motor* (Philadelphia: J. B. Lippincott, 1911).
5. Alice Huyler Ramsey, *Veil, Duster, and Tire Iron* (Pasadena, Calif.: Castle Press, 1961), 44.

6. Percy F. Megargel, "Good Weather Favors Tourists," *Automobile* (7 September 1905): 272. See also Percy F. Megargel, "Crossing the Plains," *Automobile* (21 September 1905): 331.
7. "Rambler in the Rockies," *Motor Age* (18 June 1908): 29.
8. Claude H. Miller, "Camping with an Automobile in Maine," *Country Life in America* (June 1908), 177, 198, 200.
9. Ira H. Morse, "My Hunting Trip in the Maine Woods," *Cycle and Automobile Trade Journal* (1 June 1909): 79.
10. Ezra H. Fitch, "Hunting by Motor Car," *New England Magazine* (March 1909), 61–69.
11. "Automobiles Especially for Camping," *Automobile* (12 October 1905): 401; George Lorando Lawson, "An Automobile Prairie Schooner," *Country Life in America* (June 1908), 176–77.
12. Hrolf Wisby, "Camping Out with an Automobile," *Outing* (March 1905), 739–45.
13. Hrolf Wisby, "The Automobile Camper," *Country Life in America* (April 1905), 696, 698, 700, 702.
14. Warren James Belasco, *Americans on the Road: From Autocamp to Motel, 1910–1945* (Cambridge, Mass.: MIT Press), 1979.
15. H. H. Dunn, "Touring Automobile Rivals Limited Train," *Motor Car* (December 1909): 13, 45.
16. "A Luxurious Touring and Camping-Out Car," *Carriage Monthly* (April 1911): 96; *Six Weeks in a Motor Car: Camping and Sleeping Out* (Syracuse, N. Y.: Franklin Automobile Company, n.d.), Walter E. Gosden personal collection, Floral Park, New York.
17. Blanche McManus, "The Woman Who Drives Her Own Car," *Harper's Bazar* (July 1912), 354.
18. H. H. Brown, "Novelties in Bodies at the Auto Shows," *Horseless Age* (12 January 1910): 58–60; "Pierce-Arrow Touring Landau," *Horseless Age* (16 February 1910): 265.
19. *Arrow* (Fourth Quarter 1968): 11–13.
20. Bernard J. Weis, *Pierce-Arrow Scrapbook, 1910–1911* (Rochester, N.Y.: published by the author, 1990), 18–19.
21. Nettie Leitch Major, *C. W. Post: The Hour and the Man* (Washington, D.C.: Judd and Detweiler, 1963), 134–35.
22. Weis, *Pierce-Arrow Scrapbook*, 30, 31, 33, 37.
23. "Has Horse Car Body," *Motor World* (1 August 1901): 347.
24. "An Automobile Sleeping Car," *Motor World* (4 September 1902): 664.
25. "A Motor 'Caravan,'" *Automobile* (29 August 1903): 217; "A House on Wheels," *Automobile* (7 January 1905): 16–17; "Automobile House Car the Latest," *Popular Mechanics* (October 1903), 135–36. The name of this ve-

hicle, Le Bourlinguette, translates as "one that goes from place to place without an itinerary."

26. "Freak Road Locomotive," *Automobile* (5 March 1904): 283; "Largest Automobile in the World," *Popular Mechanics* (July 1904), 701; Richard Wager, *Golden Wheels: The Story of the Automobiles Made in Cleveland and Northeastern Ohio, 1892–1932* (Cleveland: John T. Zubal, Inc., 1986), 49–50. Shoenberg later changed his name to Louis D. Beaumont, the French translation.

27. "The Advent of the Camping Car," *Horseless Age* (13 September 1911): 376–77; "Scenes and Incidents in Sussex County," *Wilmington (Delaware) Morning News*, 20 September 1911; "Complete Motor Camping Outfit," *Motor* (October 1911): 26; Coleman du Pont, "The Coleman du Pont Highway through the State of Delaware," *Scientific American* (March 1912): 244–45, 255–56; John B. Rae, "Coleman du Pont and His Road," *Delaware History* (Spring–Summer 1975): 171–83.

28. "The Advent of the Camping Car," 377.

29. Ibid.

30. Charles K. Hyde, "Henry Bourne Joy," in George S. May, ed., *The Automobile Industry, 1896–1920* (New York: Facts on File, 1990), 274–80.

31. *Horseless Age* (11 June 1913): 1063; "Along the Proposed Lincoln Highway," *Motor Age* (10 July 1913): 20–23; Richard M. Langworth, "Sea to Shining Sea: Packard and the Lincoln Highway," *Packard Cormorant* (Spring 1989): 2–17.

32. "Joy on the Line of Action," *Packard* (June 1916): 4. In 1937 Helen Joy donated the 1916 Packard camping car to the Henry Ford Museum in Dearborn, Michigan.

33. "Woonsocket Company's New Camping Body," *Carriage Monthly* (September 1914): 61.

34. Charles Alma Byers, "Equipping the Automobile for Travel," *Scientific American* (27 February 1915): 200.

35. "The Advent of the Camping Car," 377.

36. "The Land Yacht 'Wanderer': The Story of a Horse-Drawn Mobile Home and Its Designer," *Carriage Journal* (Winter 1982): 124–26; William Gordon Stables, *Cruise of the Land Yacht 'Wanderer' or Thirteen Hundred Miles in My Caravan* (London: Hodder and Stoughton, 1886); C. H. Ward-Jackson and Denis E. Harvey, *The English Gypsy Caravan* (New York: Drake Publishers, 1973); W. M. Whiteman, *The History of the Caravan* (London: Blandford Press, 1973); Nerissa Wilson, *Gypsies and Gentlemen: The Life and Times of the Leisure Caravan* (London: Columbus Books, 1986).

37. Unpublished biographical notes by Albert E. Meier, Recreation Vehicle file, Transportation Collections, NMAH. Meier based much of his research on the papers of Powell C. Groner, Conklin's attorney.

38. "Roland Ray Conklin," in *National Cyclopaedia of American Biography*, vol. 15 (New York: James T. White and Company, 1916), 108–9; Roland R. Conklin's obituary, *New York Times*, 3 January 1938.

39. Mary Conklin, *The Trail of the Gypsy* (Huntington, N.Y.: published in a limited edition by Roland and Mary Conklin, 1916), 1. Huntington (N.Y.) Historical Society Collection.

40. "Rosemary Farm, the Residence of Roland R. Conklin, Esq.," *Architectural Record* (October 1910): 236–53; Roland R. Conklin, "Rosemary: An Estate to Withstand a Siege," *Country Life* (May 1918): 49–52; Edward Teitelman and Betsy Fahlma, "Roland R. Conklin Residence, 'Rosemary Farm,'" in Robert B. Mackay, Anthony K. Baker, and Carol A. Traynor, eds., *Long Island Country Houses and Their Architects, 1860–1940* (New York: W. W. Norton and Company, 1997), 159–62.

41. "Gypsying De Luxe across Continent," *New York Times*, 21 August 1915; "Conklin Builds Wonderful Motor Land Yacht," *New York American*, 22 August 1915; Mary Conklin, *The Trail of the Gypsy*.

42. "Conklin Road Yacht Hits a Shoal of Mud," *New York Times*, 23 August 1915.

43. "Big Motor Land Yacht Has Reached Chicago Safely," *New York Times*, 26 September 1915; Mary Conklin, *The Trail of the Gypsy*.

44. "Land Yacht Here; Hunts Up Big Garage," *San Francisco Examiner*, 13 October 1915.

45. "Big Motor Land Yacht Has Reached Chicago Safely," *New York Times*, 26 September 1915.

46. "This Auto Is a Flat on Tires," *New York Times Magazine*, 22 August 1915, 8–9; "Luxurious Road-Yacht on Bus Chassis," *Commercial Vehicle* (1 September 1915): 21–22; "The Motor 'House-car,'" *Scientific American* (11 September 1915): 228; "A Yacht on Wheels," *Literary Digest* (25 September 1915): 661–62; "A Motor Land Yacht," *Independent* (18 October 1915): 103.

2. HOUSE CARS AND THE AUTOCAMPING CRAZE

1. Autocamping equipment catalogs in the Trade Literature Collection, National Park Service Library, Harpers Ferry Center, Harpers Ferry, West Virginia.

2. *Motor Age* (1 July 1915): 38.

3. Letter from Thomas Crotty to the editor, *Old Cars Weekly*, 3 March 1988.

4. "Camping Cars as Advertisements," *Horseless Age* (1 November 1916): 299.

5. "Living in the Car," *Outing* (April 1923): 18–19, 46–47.

6. *Automobile* (13 November 1913): 926–27; advertisement for the Spaulding Sleeper, *Grinnell (Iowa) Herald*, 30 March 1915; Curt McConnell, *Great Cars of the Great Plains* (Lincoln: University of Nebraska Press, 1995), 133ff.

7. "Jackson Builds Standard Touring Car Sleeping Body," *Automobile* (27 May 1915): 941.

8. Entry for the Pan in G. N. Georgano, ed., *The New Encyclopedia of Automobiles: 1885 to the Present* (New York: Crescent Books, 1986), 473.

9. Entry for the Flapper in Beverly Rae Kimes and Henry Austin Clark Jr., *Standard Catalog of American Cars, 1805–1942* (Iola, Wis.: Krause Publications, 1989), 543.

10. *Facts and Figures of the Automobile Industry* (New York: National Automobile Chamber of Commerce, 1930), 8.

11. Folke T. Kihlstedt, "The Automobile and the Transformation of the American House, 1910–1935," in David L. Lewis and Laurence Goldstein, eds., *The Automobile and American Culture* (Ann Arbor: University of Michigan Press, 1983), 160–75.

12. "Studebaker Sedan Equipped with Berths for Touring," *Motor Age* (16 September 1915): 25.

13. Modell's Camp Outfitters catalog, 1927, National Park Service Library, Harpers Ferry, West Virginia.

14. Advertisement, *Motor World* (3 October 1923): 66–67; "Detachable Seats Are Chief Feature of New Overland Sedan," *Automotive Industries* (4 October 1923): 694–95; *Willys-Overland Starter* (20 September 1924): 11; *Motor Camper and Tourist* (September 1925): 247; "Overland Champion Renamed," *Automotive Industries* (26 June 1924): 1401; Keith Marvin, "The Rise and Fall of the Overland Champion," *Knight-Overland Starter* (Winter 1983–1984): 6; Overland Champion sales literature in the collection of the Willys-Overland-Knight Registry, Batavia, Illinois.

15. "A Seven-Passenger Landau-Type Sedan Arranged by Judkins as an Emergency Sleeping Car," *Autobody* (December 1924): 218.

16. George Reid Clapp, "A Pierce-Arrow Camper," *Arrow* (First Quarter 1991): 22–23.

17. Clifford Edward Clark Jr., *The American Family Home, 1800–1960* (Chapel Hill: University of North Carolina Press, 1986).

18. Ibid.

19. Edgar C. Mechen, "The Motor Gypsy at Home," *Motor* (September 1916): 82–83, 147.

20. Captioned postcard of the Adventurer, 1916, John Baeder personal collection, Nashville, Tennessee.

21. "Low-rent Relic," *Old Cars Weekly*, 6 October 1988.

22. "Remarkable Touring Ford," *Fordowner* (February 1916): 16–17.

23. G. E. Morris, "A Caravan Touring Car," *Fordowner* (July 1919): 73–74; R. D. Count, "A Practical Camping Car," *Ford Owner and Dealer* (June 1920): 53–55; "The Gypsy Ford Truck," *Ford Owner and Dealer* (June 1922): 68–69.

24. "Three Designs of Automobile Camping Bodies," *Motor Vehicle Monthly* (March 1924): 24–25, 54.

25. Ray F. Kuns, "Building a Camp Car," pt. 1, *Popular Mechanics* (July 1923):

147–53; Ray F. Kuns, "Building a Camp Car: Part 2," *Popular Mechanics* (August 1923): 310–14.

26. Ray F. Kuns, "Camp Cars—Wanderlust—and Some Other Things," *Industrial-Arts Magazine* (May 1924): 186–90.

27. Albert G. Bauersfeld, "A Camp Car and the Open Road Used as a Means for Avocational Education," *Industrial-Arts Magazine* (June 1924): 230–34.

28. *Motor Camper and Tourist* (April 1925): 661.

29. *Trailer Topics* (December 1940): 15.

30. *Motor Camper and Tourist* (May 1925): 749.

31. *Butte (Montana) Daily Post*, 26 July 1922. In 1978 the Motor Palace was purchased by Pioneer Auto and Antique Town in Murdo, South Dakota.

32. Edgar C. Mechen, "The Motor Gypsy at Home," *Motor* (September 1916): 82–83, 147.

33. William H. Hunt, "Auto-Bungalow Touring within Reach of All," *Popular Mechanics* (March 1921): 336–39.

34. Rector R. Seal, "Early Motor Home," *Antique Automobile* (September–October 1987): 13.

35. *Wyoming County (New York) Herald*, 15 October 1926; ibid.,17 June 1927; ibid., 22 July 1927.

36. Pamphlet, "The Motor Chapel 'St. Peter,'" souvenir of the Annual Exposition of Motor Trucks, Chicago, 10–15 February, 1913, Recreation Vehicle file, Transportation Collections, NMAH; "A Chapel on a Motor Truck," *Scientific American* (19 April 1913): 352; Edith O'Malley, "Something New in Churches—A Motor Chapel," *Extension* (April 1913): 9, 28; Rev. E. B. Ledvina, "The Motor Chapel Car at Work in the Field," *Extension* (August 1913): 9–10; Rev. Y. Tymen, "A Week on the Motor Chapel in Texas," *Extension* (December 1913): 13–14, 30; Rev. Y. Tymen, "The Motor Chapel in Texas," *Extension* (February 1914): 13; Rev. W. W. Hume, "The Motor Chapel St. Peter in Texas," *Extension* (December 1914): 16, 23; S. A. Baldus, "The Chapel Car Service—A Layman's View," *Extension* (March 1915): 15, 28; Rev. P. A. Heckman, "Work in the Motor Chapel 'St. Peter,'" *Extension* (March 1917): 14, 34–35.

37. Waldemar Kaempffert, ed., *The 1918 Motor Annual of the Popular Science Monthly* (New York: Popular Science Monthly, 1917), 57.

38. "Camping Cars on Tour," *Motor Camper and Tourist* (September 1924): 218.

39. "Novel Motor Bungalows," *Motor Camper and Tourist* (June 1924): 32.

40. Belasco, *Americans on the Road*, 96.

41. Brochure, n.d., Wilber F. Persons Papers, Yorkshire Historical Society Collection, Delevan, New York.

42. *One Hundred Years of Power: Cooper-Bessemer* (Cooper-Bessemer Corporation, 1933); John G. White, *Twentieth Century History of Mercer County, Pennsylvania* (Chicago: Lewis Publishing Company, 1909), 372–73.

43. Fithian's legacy continued in the Cooper-Bessemer Corporation, which was formed in 1929 through a merger of the Bessemer Gas Engine Company and the C & G Cooper Company. Fithian was chairman of Cooper-Bessemer from 1929 to 1940.

44. In 1954 James Melton, a well-known tenor, star of opera, radio, and motion pictures, and an avid collector of antique automobiles, purchased the house car from Fithian's estate. In 1960 Melton traveled in the house car while performing in a summer theater production of *The Student Prince*. The Fithian house car later became part of Harrah's Automobile Collection in Reno, Nevada. In 1985 it was sold to the Imperial Palace Auto Collection in Las Vegas, Nevada.

45. "More Comforts than Pullman Affords Are Found in this Vacation Wagon," *National Petroleum News* (15 July 1921): 49.

46. *Marion (Indiana) Chronicle*, 1 July 1919; ibid., 18 August 1919; ibid., 19 September 1919; ibid., 17 November 1919; *Marion (Indiana) Leader-Tribune*, 10 August 1919; ibid., 13 August 1919; ibid., 20 August 1919; ibid., 24 August 1919; ibid., 20 September 1919; ibid., 7 December 1919.

47. "The Three Weeks of Four Weaks," log of the business trip in July 1925, Donald M. Bekins personal collection, Belvedere, California.

48. "Luxurious Motor Bus," *Kohler of Kohler News* (April 1927): 14; "H. H. Linn Tours Country in Bus," *Motor Truck* (February 1928): 9; Rene Elliott, "Those Creepy, Crawly, Wonderful Linns," *Wheels of Time* (September–October 1985): 10–11. A later owner of the Linn Haven, Purcey Kingsley of Cohoes, New York, added a loudspeaker system and permitted the local Democratic organization to use the vehicle to promote the presidential candidacy of Franklin D. Roosevelt. The Linn Haven carried a group of Cohoes Democrats to the 1936 presidential nominating convention in Philadelphia. Its loudspeakers broadcast campaign songs and proceedings from within the Municipal Auditorium, where the convention was held. Plastered with campaign posters, the Linn Haven made other appearances on behalf of the Democratic ticket. Kingsley also used the vehicle to promote Hudson River steamships and theaters in New York City. The Linn Haven still exists and is privately owned.

49. "Sumptuous Residence on Wheels Installed with Kohler Electric Plant," *Kohler of Kohler News* (December 1927): 11, 13; "De Luxe Traveling Home Has Ideal Arrangements," *Motor Vehicle Monthly* (October 1927): 28, 37; J. Arthur Kieffer, "Whittiers' 1927 Trailer [*sic*]," *Chemung Historical Journal* (September 1991): 4077–80.

50. *Motor Coach Age* (September–October 1990): 28.

51. "Inside Information," W. K. Kellogg's leaflet about the Ark, n.d., Recreation Vehicle file, Transportation Collections, NMAH.

52. "Rolling Palace Has the Comforts of Home," *Scientific American* (November

1923): 343; Horace B. Powell, *The Original Has This Signature—W. K. Kellogg* (Englewood Cliffs, N.J.: Prentice-Hall, 1956), 220.

53. Edith Rohrbough Slate and Geri Ellen Howard (ed.), "Our Automobile Trip to the West, 1921," *Oregon Historical Quarterly* (Fall 1984): 253–77. Thomas Slate remained a prolific inventor of automotive and aircraft devices and later developed an automatic tire pump, an internal-combustion water pump, and a method of dispelling smog.

54. Letter from George T. Mason to Peter Koltnow, 11 January 1993, in Recreation Vehicle file, Transportation Collections, NMAH; George T. Mason, interview by Peter Koltnow, 26 January 1993, notes in Recreation Vehicle file, Transportation Collections, NMAH; George T. Mason, interview by author, 3 March 1993, notes in Recreation Vehicle file, Transportation Collections, NMAH.

55. *Motor Age* (3 January 1924): 25.

56. "Rolling Homes that Gather No Rent," *Literary Digest* (4 December 1920): 64.

57. *Motor Chat* (March 1926): 16.

58. "Away Back When!" *Trailer Topics* (May 1937): 22; Charles G. Phillips's obituary, *Warren (Ohio) Tribune Chronicle*, 16 November 1931; Thomas J. Kachur, *Historical Collections of Bazetta Township, Cortland, Ohio* ([Apollo, Pa.:] published by the author, 1983), 55–57.

59. Dorothy B. Hughes, *Erle Stanley Gardner: The Case of the Real Perry Mason* (New York: William Morrow and Company, 1978), 104–6.

60. Maristan Chapman, "The Nomad," *Motor Camper and Tourist* (July 1925): 130, 131, 155, 159; Maristan Chapman Collection, Division of Special Collections, University of Oregon. In 1970 the Chapmans sold the Nomad to a Tucson family, and it passed through several other owners. Robert D. Miller, the last individual owner of the Nomad, donated it to the Henry Ford Museum in Dearborn, Michigan, in 1981.

61. Slate and Howard, "Our Automobile Trip to the West"; interviews with George T. Mason; account of trip by Martin and Laura Trester, *Butte (Montana) Daily Post*, 26 July 1922; "The Three Weeks of Four Weaks"; Angie Holloway, interview by Jean Holloway-Burkhart, 1984, transcript in Recreation Vehicle file, Transportation Collections, NMAH; recollections of Ralph Renner in *Family Motor Coaching* (November 1993): 18, 20.

62. Victor Appleton, *Tom Swift and His House on Wheels* (New York: Grosset and Dunlap, 1929); John T. Dizer, *Tom Swift and Company: "Boys' Books" by Stratemeyer and Others* (Jefferson, N.C.: McFarland and Company, 1982).

63. "Home Comforts in Motor-Car Camping Outfit," *Popular Mechanics* (May 1916): 642–44; "Automobile Telescope Apartment," *Horseless Age* (15 May

1916): 405; "Fitting Makes Motor Car Just Like a Pullman," *San Francisco Examiner*, 13 February 1916; "An Apartment that Travels on Wheels," *Scientific American* (29 April 1916): 446; promotional literature in the personal collection of David Woodworth, Tehachapi, California.

64. "Demountable Body Turns Any Automobile into Traveling Camp for the Whole Family," *Popular Mechanics* (May 1921): 680–81; "Tourist Camp Bodies to Fit Standard Chassis," *Motor Age* (14 July 1921): 17.

65. Norrington Auto-Home sales brochure, n.d., National Automobile Museum Collection, Reno, Nevada; "An Auto Home," *Sunset* (December 1921): 62; *San Francisco Chronicle*, 2 November 1970.

66. Correspondence in the personal collection of George P. Dorris III, St. Louis, Missouri.

67. "New Camping Car Will Be Built in St. Louis," *St. Louis Daily Globe-Democrat*, 13 March 1921.

68. Lamsteed Kampkar sales brochure, 1921, National Automobile Museum Collection, Reno, Nevada.

69. Lamsteed Kampkar advertisement, *Field and Stream* (July 1923): 419; Lamsteed Kampkar brochure, n. d., Anheuser-Busch Archives, St. Louis, Missouri. A Lamsteed Kampkar was purchased in 1962 by Harrah's Automobile Collection, now the National Automobile Museum in Reno, Nevada. The Road Cruiser Wampus has been preserved by George P. Dorris III of St. Louis, Missouri.

70. Letter from John W. Clements, president, Wayne Works, to prospective Touring Home dealers, in brochure, "The Wayne Touring Home," n.d., n.p., Wayne Works file, Wayne County Historical Museum Collection, Richmond, Indiana.

71. "Motor Touring Home," *Scientific American* (September 1923): 193; Wayne Touring Home brochures, n.d., and price list, 1 June 1923, Wayne County Historical Museum Collection, Richmond, Indiana; Wayne Touring Home brochure, n.d., reprinted in *Model T Times* (July–August 1975): 3–11. The Wayne Works published letters from several satisfied owners of Touring Homes. M. E. Shea of New York City traveled 15,000 miles in twenty-four states in his Touring Home and J. Arthur Benham, an ice cream manufacturer in Fresno, California, traveled 5,300 miles in his vehicle.

72. Brochure, "The Wayne Touring Home: A Lifetime through Ticket to Health and Happiness," 1923, p. 11, Wayne Works file, Wayne County Historical Museum Collection, Richmond, Indiana.

73. Wiedman brochure, Recreation Vehicle file, Transportation Collections, NMAH; "Wiedman Camping Body," *Motor Vehicle Monthly* (March 1925): 22.

74. *Motor Camper and Tourist* (October 1925): 371; Zagelmeyer catalog, 1928,

John Margolies personal collection, New York City; Zagelmeyer catalog, 1928, David Woodworth personal collection, Tehachapi, California; *National Geographic* (May 1928); *National Geographic* (June 1928).

75. Pierce-Arrow Caravan brochure, 1925, Recreation Vehicle file, Transportation Collections, NMAH.
76. "A Texas-style Motor Home," *Arrow* (Fourth Quarter 1996): 18–21.
77. F. E. Brimmer, *Motor Campcraft* (New York: Macmillan, 1923), 47–52.
78. Elon Jessup, *The Motor Camping Book* (New York: G. P. Putnam's Sons, 1921), 145.

3. HOUSE CARS BECOME STREAMLINED

1. David A. Thornburg, *Galloping Bungalows: The Rise and Demise of the American Travel Trailer* (Hamden, Conn.: Archon Books, 1991), 103–5, 185–86.
2. See Farm Security Administration/Office of War Information Photograph Collection, Prints and Photographs Division, Library of Congress, Washington, D.C.
3. Recollections of Jack V. Loos, Anita Johnson's son (by her first marriage), in a letter from his wife, Maralyn Loos, to author, 28 March 1995, Recreation Vehicle file, Transportation Collections, NMAH. Loos accompanied his mother on one trip in the Californian.
4. Buster Keaton, *My Wonderful World of Slapstick* (Garden City, N. Y.: Doubleday and Company, 1960), 231; Rudi Blesh, *Keaton* (New York: Macmillan, [1966]), 329–30; Tom Dardis, *Keaton: The Man Who Wouldn't Lie Down* (New York: Charles Scribner's Sons, 1979), 185–86; Marion Meade, *Buster Keaton: Cut to the Chase* (New York: Harper Collins, 1995), 211–12; Bill Kennedy, "The Memory Room," *Los Angeles Evening Herald-Examiner*, 7 June 1962. Keaton's published recollection that he purchased the Californian from the widow of a railroad president was refuted by Jack V. Loos, who met Keaton when he came to purchase it from Loos's mother, Anita Johnson. At that time, Johnson was divorced from Los Angeles physician H. Clifford Loos.
5. Title and catalog records for the Adolphus, Museum of Transportation, St. Louis, Missouri.
6. Ibid.; Peter Hernon and Terry Ganey, *Under the Influence: The Unauthorized Story of the Anheuser-Busch Dynasty* (New York: Simon and Schuster, 1991), 175. In the 1950s and 1960s the original Adolphus passed through several more individual owners. In 1969 it was donated to the National Museum of Transport (now the Museum of Transportation) near St. Louis, Missouri.
7. "Pribil Housecar," *Special-Interest Autos* (May–June 1971): 29; Frederick C. Russell, "Revolutionary Self-Driven Trailer Home," *Modern Mechanix* (September 1937): 36–40, 122.

8. John F. Katz, "Mr. Hunt's Home-Grown House Cars," *Special-Interest Autos* (November–December 1993): 18–23.

9. "Comforts of Home in a Steam-Powered House Car," *Popular Science* (September 1941): 131.

10. "Bungalow Bus," *Trailer Topics* (November 1940): 33; W. Harold Schelm, interview by Peter Koltnow, 26 April 1994, notes in Recreation Vehicle file, Transportation Collections, NMAH.

11. Samuel C. Johnson, *The Essence of a Family Enterprise: Doing Business the Johnson Way* (Racine, Wis.: S. C. Johnson and Son, 1988); Frances E. Norton, "Johnson's Wax," in Janice Jorgensen, ed., *Encyclopedia of Consumer Brands*, vol. 2 (Detroit: St. James Press, 1994), 300–3.

12. "Brooks Stevens: The Seer Who Made Milwaukee Famous," in Michael Lamm and Dave Holls, *A Century of Automotive Style: 100 Years of American Car Design* (Stockton, Calif.: Lamm-Morada Publishing Company, 1996), 248–49; biographical files, Brooks Stevens Museum, Mequon, Wisconsin.

13. "New Tow Car for Plankinton," *Milwaukee Journal*, 18 October 1936; Walter W. Belson, "Mercury-Motored Tractor Propels America's Finest Travel Trailer," *Ford Field* (April 1940): 10–12, 34; Jack Stone, "Bill Plankinton: Bachelor in a Trailer," *American Weekly* (21 December 1947): 6–7.

14. "Johnson Research Car Is 1940 Covered Wagon," *Milwaukee Journal*, 25 February 1940; "Covered Wagon, 1940," *Manufacturers News* (March 1940): 13–14; Verne Hoffman, "S. C. Johnson's 'Land Yacht' Complete Home and Laboratory," *Racine (Wisconsin) Journal-Times*, 11 August 1940; "Johnson Research Car Contains Office, Home," *Milwaukee Journal*, 11 August 1940; "Linn Single Unit Car Bought by Nationally Known Manufacturer," *Oneonta (New York) News*, 20 September 1940; Brooks Stevens, "Your Victory Car," *Popular Mechanics* (December 1942): 82–85, 162; Brooks Stevens, interview by Peter Koltnow, 4 October 1994, notes in Recreation Vehicle file, Transportation Collections, NMAH.

15. Paramount publicity kit for *Sullivan's Travels*, 1941, copyright deposit number LP 11049, Motion Picture, Broadcasting, and Recorded Sound Division, Library of Congress, Washington, D.C.

4. AUTOCAMPING IN THE POSTWAR ERA

1. Albert R. Krause's notes about his house car, n.d., Recreation Vehicle file, Transportation Collections, NMAH.

2. Ibid.; written recollections of Eric L. Krause, son of Albert and Esther Krause, 1995, Recreation Vehicle file, Transportation Collections, NMAH. The house car still exists, though modified. It is privately owned.

3. Jon G. Robinson, "Nomad III from USC: Seven Tons of Cutting-Edge Motorhome," *Old Cars Weekly* (27 January 1994); James Hinckley, "Too

Much Too Soon: The Unique Nomad III," *Special Interest Autos* (November–December 1994): 62–64. The shell of the Nomad III still exists in Chloride, Arizona.

4. "He Drives His House to the Country," *Popular Science* (June 1952): 118–20; Jim Earp, "Unique Cars for Sportsmen," *Motor Trend* (October 1952): 13–16; Pete Brower, "Ruffinit," *Trailer Life* (July 1976): 97, 160–62.

5. "Guest House Becomes a Gala 'Rambling Rancho,'" *Compton-Lynwood (California) Herald American Home and Garden Magazine* (19 October 1952).

6. Ibid.

7. Ibid.; Dorothy Powell, interview by Peter Koltnow, 17 November 1994, notes in Recreation Vehicle file, Transportation Collections, NMAH. In the early 1950s the Powells also built two house cars similar to their prototype and sold them to individuals. The prototype house car is still owned by a member of the Powell family.

8. Letters from Robert G. Crise Sr. to author, 27 March 1985 and 3 July 1996, Recreation Vehicle file, Transportation Collections, NMAH. The Landyacht still exists and is privately owned.

9. "Home Is Where They Park It," *Popular Mechanics* (January 1950): 115.

10. Nash sales literature, James Dworschack personal collection, Richfield, Wisconsin, and Recreation Vehicle file, Transportation Collections, NMAH; Duncan F. Holmes, "The Perfect Outdoorsman's Car," *Old Cars Weekly* (5 December 1991).

11. Jim Robinson, "'Sleeper' for Your Car," *Popular Mechanics* (August 1946): 186–87.

12. Matthew Howard, "Your Car a Motel," *Popular Mechanics* (May 1951): 185.

13. Kavvy Barish, "Camping on Wheels," *Trailer Travel* (July 1947): 33.

14. Franklin M. Reck and William Moss, *Ford Treasury of Station Wagon Living* (New York: Simon and Schuster, 1957).

15. Ibid., 114.

16. Ibid., 114–29.

17. "A Car that Has Everything," *Life* (10 March 1952): 127; Bob Loeffelbein, "Everything AND the Kitchen Sink," *Special Interest Autos* (October 1979): 44–51; Louie Mattar, interviews by Peter Koltnow, 18 April 1995, 9 May 1995, and 13 June 1995, notes in Recreation Vehicle file, Transportation Collections, NMAH; letter from Valerie Mitchell to author, 11 March 1999, Recreation Vehicle file, Transportation Collections, NMAH.

18. Sven-Ake Nielsen, "Gadgeteer's Dream Car," *Cavalier* (January 1954): 30–32.

19. "The Fabulous Car of Louis [*sic*] Mattar," *Car Life* (May 1955): 60–63; Bob Loeffelbein, "The Wheels Never Stopped Turning," *Old Cars Weekly* (7 October 1982). After its glory days, the Fabulous Car was displayed in parades, automobile shows, and at orphanages and hospitals. One tour raised funds for

St. Jude's Hospital in Memphis, Tennessee, one of entertainer Danny Thomas's favorite charities; Thomas, like Mattar, was a Lebanese-American, and the two men knew each other. Mattar lovingly preserved the Fabulous Car, but for family camping trips he purchased a motor home.

20. Bruce Briggs, *The Station Wagon: Its Saga and Development* (New York: Vantage Press, 1975); Donald J. Narus, *Great American Woodies and Wagons* (Glen Ellyn, Ill.: Crestline Publishing, 1977).

21. Russell Rosene, "Honeymoon Wagon," *Ford Times* (August 1947): 41–44.

22. Joe Ott, "Car-Top Sleeper," *Popular Mechanics* (May 1953): 182–85; Eric De-Groat, "How to Build a Makeshift Car-Topper," *Camping Guide* (April–May 1961): 36; Herbert R. Miller, "Station Wagon Penthouse Sleeps Two," *Popular Science* (May 1961): 126–28.

23. William D. Kennedy (director of publications, Ford Motor Company), in Reck and Moss, *Ford Treasury of Station Wagon Living*, 10–11.

24. Reck and Moss, *Ford Treasury of Station Wagon Living*.

25. Ibid.

26. Ibid.; Franklin M. Reck and William Moss, *Ford Treasury of Station Wagon Living*, vol. 2 (New York: Simon and Schuster, 1958); Burgess H. Scott and Franklin M. Reck, *The Ford Guide to Outdoor Living on Wheels* (Garden City, N. Y.: Doubleday and Company, 1964).

27. Ibid.

28. Reck and Moss, *Ford Treasury of Station Wagon Living*, vol. 2, 180–81, 186, 188–89.

29. Camp'otel sales literature, 1963–1971, Recreation Vehicle file, Transportation Collections, NMAH; Virginia Guerrant (wife of Edmonds L. Guerrant), interview by Peter Koltnow, 20 June 1995, notes in Recreation Vehicle file, Transportation Collections, NMAH; Jean Woodbury, "History of Penthouse Campers Association," unpublished monograph, 1994, Recreation Vehicle file, Transportation Collections, NMAH.

30. Reck and Moss, *Ford Treasury of Station Wagon Living*, vol 2., 22–25; "The Show Is on the American Road," *Ford Times* (July 1959): 48–49; "American Road Shows on the Move," *Ford Times* (May 1960): 54–55.

31. Reck and Moss, *Ford Treasury of Station Wagon Living*, vol. 2; George and Iris Wells, *The Handbook of Auto Camping and Motorist's Guide to Public Campgrounds* (New York: Harper and Brothers, 1954); George and Iris Wells, *The Handbook of Auto Camping and Motorist's Guide to Public Campgrounds*, revised and enlarged edition (New York: Harper and Brothers, 1958); George S. Wells, *American Vacation Book* (Boston: R. C. Dresser and Company, 1959).

32. George and Iris Wells, *The Handbook of Auto Camping and Motorist's Guide to Public Campgrounds* (New York: Harper and Brothers, 1958), 246.

33. Ibid.

34. Ibid., 247; Richard West Sellars, *Preserving Nature in the National Parks: A History* (New Haven, Conn.: Yale University Press, 1997), 180–91.
35. Private bus roster, Anheuser-Busch Archives, St. Louis, Missouri; Anheuser-Busch file, Museum of Transportation, St. Louis, Missouri.
36. "Spaeth Ship," *New Yorker* (7 January 1950): 18–19; "Otto Spaeth's 'Yacht' Unusual," *Dayton (Ohio) Herald*, 2 January 1948; Otto L. Spaeth Jr., interviews by Peter Koltnow, 27 August 1996 and 15 October 1996, notes in Recreation Vehicle file, Transportation Collections, NMAH.
37. Associated Press bulletin, n.d., Recreation Vehicle file, Transportation Collections, NMAH.
38. Land Cruiser sales literature, Kenneth Utterback personal collection, Loudonville, Ohio; Lee Cavin, *They Rose from the Valley* (Loudonville, Ohio: Truax Printing, 1990), 110–11.
39. James Dudte, interview by Peter Koltnow, 11 July 1995, notes in Recreation Vehicle file, Transportation Collections, NMAH.
40. "Cruiser on Wheels," *Popular Mechanics* (January 1949): 110–12; "Luxurious Highway Yacht Has Living Quarters for Seven Inside," *Business Week* (30 April 1949): 33.
41. "Traveler Purchases 'Land Yacht' Here," *Atlanta Journal*, 9 April 1948; "Land Cruiser Will Make Charleston Good Will Tour," *Anderson (South Carolina) Daily Mail*, 30 April 1952; "Charleston Ambassadors of Good Will," *Charleston (South Carolina) News and Courier*, 14 May 1952; Joyce Long Darby, interview by Peter Koltnow, 18 July 1995, notes in Recreation Vehicle file, Transportation Collections, NMAH; Eunice Kearney, interview by Peter Koltnow, 18 July 1995, notes in Recreation Vehicle file, Transportation Collections, NMAH.
42. Kirwan Elmers, interview by Peter Koltnow, 27 June 1995, notes in Recreation Vehicle file, Transportation Collections, NMAH; "Miles Martin Elmers" in *National Cyclopedia of American Biography*, vol. L (Clifton, N.J.: James T. White and Company, 1972), 599–600.
43. Custom Coach advertisement, *Family Motor Coaching* (June 1964): 41.
44. "Highway 'Pullman' Sleeps Eight," *Popular Mechanics* (July 1954): 113; Ernest Scrivener Jr., interview by Peter Koltnow, 10 January 1995, notes in Recreation Vehicle file, Transportation Collections, NMAH.
45. Vehicle roster, private bus file, Anheuser-Busch Archives, St. Louis, Missouri.
46. Tommy Dorsey III, interview by Peter Koltnow, 5 December 1995, notes in Recreation Vehicle file, Transportation Collections, NMAH; Ed Gildea, "Yes, Tommy Dorsey Really Did Own a Home on Wheels," *Valley Gazette* (Lansford, Pennsylvania), May 1993. The Sentimentalist still exists and is privately owned.
47. George Barris and Jack Scagnetti, *Cars of the Stars* (Middle Village, N.Y.: Jonathan David Publishers, 1974), 58–60.

48. Audrey Stone, "Rolling with the Rolling Stones," *Family Motor Coaching* (Fall 1964): 16–17, 27.

49. "They Bought a Bus to See the World," *American Magazine* (April 1953): 58.

50. "Bus Serves as Home for Family of Nine," *Popular Mechanics* (April 1954): 114; Dennis Mason, "Family of Nine University Namesakes Has Vacation Home in School Bus," *Florida Times-Union* (Jacksonville, Florida), 29 August 1954; Loyola Bardwell, "The One and Only Collegiate Caravan," *Parade* (24 April 1955): 2; Stanford Bardwell Jr., interview by Peter Koltnow, 13 December 1994, notes in Recreation Vehicle file, Transportation Collections, NMAH.

51. Letter from Harold Putzke to author, September 1995, Recreation Vehicle file, Transportation Collections, NMAH.

52. Lew Dietz, "Deer Camp on Wheels," *Field and Stream* (December 1963): 37–39, 64.

53. "A History of Family Motor Coach Association," *Family Motor Coaching* (15 February 1964): 9–10; Thomas Duck, interview by Peter Koltnow, 7 November 1995, notes in Recreation Vehicle file, Transportation Collections, NMAH.

54. *Commenter*, newsletter of the Courtesy Coach Club, June 1963; Genny Luckey, interview by Peter Koltnow, 7 November 1995, notes in Recreation Vehicle file, Transportation Collections, NMAH.

55. "A History of Family Motor Coach Association," 9–10; Jean Richter, interview by Peter Koltnow, 28 March 1995, notes in Recreation Vehicle file, Transportation Collections, NMAH.

56. For profiles of early FMCA officers and directors, see *Family Motor Coaching* (15 February 1964): 8; Ken T. Scott, "The Homes of FMCA," *Family Motor Coaching* (January 1988): 46, 48, 52; Ken T. Scott, "FMCA's Past Presidents," *Family Motor Coaching* (February 1988): 68–70, 242.

57. FMCA membership list compiled by Robert Richter, 1964, Jean Richter personal collection, Hanson, Massachusetts.

58. Dick and Bess Pierce, "A Luxury Motorhome for Only $2,000," *Mechanix Illustrated* (July 1974): 58–60, 120–21; Bess Pierce, interview by Peter Koltnow, 23 May 1995, notes in Recreation Vehicle file, Transportation Collections, NMAH.

59. Horace Sutton, "At Home in a Bus," *Saturday Review* (5 December 1964): 45–47.

60. Letter from Dorothea Baker to author, n.d., Recreation Vehicle file, Transportation Collections, NMAH.

61. Thomas F. Moroney, interview by Peter Koltnow, 6 August 1996, notes in Recreation Vehicle file, Transportation Collections, NMAH.

5. HOUSE CARS REVISITED

1. Among the widely used motor vehicles with cargo beds were the Sears, Overland, and Reo Power Wagon.

2. Letter from Barbara Pugh Neel to author, 29 May 1995, Recreation Vehicle file, Transportation Collections, NMAH.

3. Dorotha Cree Bent, interview by Peter Koltnow, 1 August 1996, notes in Recreation Vehicle file, Transportation Collections, NMAH; obituaries for Howard L. Cree, February 1970, Recreation Vehicle file, Transportation Collections, NMAH.

4. Cree sales literature, Dorotha Cree Bent personal collection, Marcellus, Michigan; Henry Cole, "Howard Cree's Pipe Dream," *Trailer Travel* (October 1968): 64, 96. In 1965 Cree sold his business to the Sterling-Salem Corporation, a division of the Elgin Corporation, but he was involved with the product line until 1969, when he retired. His daughter, Dorotha Cree Bent, worked for the new owner until 1987. The company changed hands several times and continued to build travel trailers, mobile homes, and motor homes until the early 1990s.

5. Henry Cole, "Howard Cree's Pipe Dream"; brochure, "Bwana M'bogo," Dorotha Cree Bent personal collection, Marcellus, Michigan; letter from Pablo Bush Romero to Howard L. Cree, 24 August 1957, Dorotha Cree Bent personal collection.

6. Sandra King, interview by Peter Koltnow, 30 July 1996, notes in Recreation Vehicle file, Transportation Collections, NMAH; Max D. Todd, "Father of the Pickup Camper," *Wheels Afield* (October 1974): 54–55.

7. Shirle Duggan, "Turtlebacks: The Newest Thing in Camping!" *Camping Guide* (March 1960): 6–9, 58.

8. Mabel Maidl Privateer, interview by Peter Koltnow, 12 August 1997, notes in Recreation Vehicle file, Transportation Collections, NMAH.

9. Powell sales literature, Recreation Vehicle file, Transportation Collections, NMAH.

10. Ibid.

11. Merle D. McNamee and Ronald McNamee, interview by Peter Koltnow, 2 April 1996, notes in Recreation Vehicle file, Transportation Collections, NMAH; Art Rouse, "Pickup Camper or Housecar," *Trailer Life* (April 1963): 70.

12. Bill Beebe, "Camper—Hunter—Sportsman—DON HALL," *Western Outdoors* (July 1974): 20–21, 76; Alaskan Camper sales literature, Recreation Vehicle file, Transportation Collections, NMAH. The telescoping body was not a new idea. In the late 1920s and early 1930s Arthur Thompson of Ontario, California, built several house cars with telescoping bodies that raised and lowered electrically. At least one of Thompson's "Raise the Roof" house cars still exists and is privately owned.

13. Irene Hall, interview by Peter Koltnow, 2 April 1996, notes in Recreation Ve-

hicle file, Transportation Collections, NMAH; obituaries for Robert Donald Hall, January 1991, Recreation Vehicle file, Transportation Collections, NMAH.

14. Jane Rhyne, "How We Built Our Tour-Car," *Travel* (June 1954): 21–23.

15. Kenn Hore, "Mobile Vacation Home," *Mechanix Illustrated* (April 1954): 148–51, 200–1.

16. *Motor Truck Facts* (Detroit: Automobile Manufacturers Association, 1961), 13.

17. Recreation Vehicle Industry Association statistics, quoted in *Motor Vehicle Facts and Figures* (Detroit: Motor Vehicle Manufacturers Association, 1976), 27.

18. Letter from John Steinbeck to Frank and Fatima Loesser, 25 May 1960, in Elaine Steinbeck and Robert Wallsten, eds., *Steinbeck: A Life in Letters* (New York: Viking Press, 1975), 666–67.

19. John Steinbeck, "In Quest of America," pts. 1–3, *Holiday* (July 1961): 26–33, 79–85, (December 1961): 60–65, 116–18, 120–21, 124, 126–28, 130–31, 134–36, (February 1962): 58–63, 122–23; John Steinbeck, *Travels with Charley: In Search of America* (New York: Viking Press, 1962); John Steinbeck, "I Rediscover America," *Family Weekly* (21 April 1963): 2.

20. Letter from John Steinbeck to Elizabeth Otis, June 1960, in Steinbeck and Wallsten, *Steinbeck: A Life in Letters*, 668–70.

21. Steinbeck, *Travels with Charley*, 5.

22. Jackson J. Benson, *The True Adventures of John Steinbeck, Writer: A Biography* (New York: Viking Press, 1984), 883.

23. Letter from John Steinbeck to James Pope, 16 June 1960, in Steinbeck and Wallsten, *Steinbeck: A Life in Letters*, 671.

24. Ibid., 686.

25. Letter from John Steinbeck to Elaine Steinbeck, 24 September 1960, ibid., 677–78.

26. Letter from John Steinbeck to Elizabeth Otis, June 1960, ibid., 668–70.

27. Letter from John Steinbeck to Elaine Steinbeck, 1 October 1960, ibid., 683–84.

28. Steinbeck, *Travels with Charley*, 243–44.

29. Lacking a use for Rocinante, Steinbeck sold it in 1961 to William B. Plate, a New York banker. Plate kept the vehicle in its original condition and used it for light duty at his rural retreat, Maiden Point Farm, near St. Michaels, Maryland, as well as family trips to the Atlantic Ocean. In 1990 Plate donated Rocinante to the city of Salinas, California. See Dickson Preston, "O Fair Rocinante Who Hast Seen the World: Welcome," *Sun Magazine (Baltimore Sun)*, 20 February 1972, 14, 16; Frances Spence Plate, "Maiden Point Farm," *Woman's National Farm and Garden Magazine* (June 1975): 4–5.

30. James K. Wagner, *Ford Trucks since 1905* (Sarasota, Fla.: Crestline Publishing, 1978); George H. Dammann, *Seventy-Five Years of Chevrolet* (Sarasota, Fla.:

Crestline Publishing, 1986); Thomas A. McPherson, *The Dodge Story* (Glen Ellyn, Ill.: Crestline Publishing, 1975).

31. Elaine Boren Dodge, interview by Peter Koltnow, 24 January 1995, notes in Recreation Vehicle file, Transportation Collections, NMAH; Jeanne Boren Caldwell, interview by Peter Koltnow, 24 January 1995, notes in Recreation Vehicle file, Transportation Collections, NMAH; Paul Hafer, retired president of the Boyertown Auto Body Works, interview by Peter Koltnow, 18 October 1994, notes in Recreation Vehicle file, Transportation Collections, NMAH.

32. Paul Hafer, interview; Boyertown Tour Wagon sales literature, Paul Hafer personal collection, Boyertown, Pennsylvania; "Road Cruiser Made from Light Truck," *Popular Science* (October 1949): 122–25; "Tour Wagon," *Ford Times* (October 1949): 50–51; Erminie Shaeffer Hafer, *A Century of Vehicle Craftsmanship* (Boyertown, Pa.: The Hafer Foundation, 1972), 166–67.

33. Boyertown Tour Wagon sales literature, Recreation Vehicle file, Transportation Collections, NMAH.

34. Letter from Eugene Lewis to author, 20 November 1984, Recreation Vehicle file, Transportation Collections, NMAH; letter from Eugene Lewis to author, 4 June 1985, Recreation Vehicle file, Transportation Collections, NMAH.

35. R. D. Hatfield, interview by author, 3 April 1995.

36. William L. Searle, "Beach Buggies on Cape Cod," *Ford Times* (August 1954): 22–24; Judith F. Leonard, "Beach Buggy Camping," *Camping Guide* (July 1961): 24–27, 51–53; Reck and Moss, *Ford Treasury of Station Wagon Living*, vol. 2, 56–59.

37. John Du Barry, "Houses on Four Wheels," in *True's Automobile Yearbook* (Greenwich, Conn.: Fawcett Publications, 1957), 77; Walter Glascoff III, interview by Peter Koltnow, 8 August 1995, notes in Recreation Vehicle file, Transportation Collections, NMAH.

38. Traville sales literature, Recreation Vehicle file, Transportation Collections, NMAH.

39. Walter Zeichner, *Volkswagen Transporter/Bus, 1949–67* (West Chester, Pa.: Schiffer Publishing, 1989); Laurence Meredith, *VW Bus Custom Handbook* (Bideford, England: Bay View Books, 1994).

40. *125 Jahre Fahrzeugbau* (Wiedenbrück, West Germany: Westfalia-Werke Franz Knöbel and Söhne, n.d.).

41. "Camping in a Volkswagen," *Popular Mechanics* (July 1955): 84–85.

42. Ibid.

43. Meredith, *VW Bus Custom Handbook*, 111.

44. Company files, Volkswagen of America, Auburn Hills, Michigan.

45. "Now You Can Live on Wheels," *Mechanix Illustrated* (August 1961): 77.

46. Charles Borskey, interview by Peter Koltnow, 5 August 1997, notes in Recreation Vehicle file, Transportation Collections, NMAH.

47. "GMC Introduces L'Universelle," *Florida Truck News* (February 1955): 3–7; Wesley S. Griswold, "New Trend in Trucks," *Popular Science* (March 1955): 140–43; Harley J. Earl, Charles M. Jordan, and William F. Lange, "Development of a New Concept in Panel Delivery Truck Design," *General Motors Engineering Journal* (May–June 1956): 85–91; Dave Newell, "L'Universelle: Front Wheel Drive in '55," *Special Interest Autos* (August 1982): 18–23. In 1955 Harley Earl, acting on behalf of General Motors, applied for a patent for a "front wheel drive vehicle with cab-over-engine" and received patent number 2,820,523 in 1958.

48. "GMC Truck and Coach to Produce L'Universelle," *GM Folks* (July 1955): 12–13.

49. Ibid.

50. Corvair sales literature, Larry Claypool personal collection, Frankfort, Illinois.

51. Ibid.

52. Marcus J. Simon, interview by Peter Koltnow, 29 October 1996, notes in Recreation Vehicle file, Transportation Collections, NMAH.

53. Van camper sales literature, Recreation Vehicle file, Transportation Collections, NMAH.

54. "Sports Conversions for Ford Econoline," *Ford Times* (June 1961): 38–39.

55. Ford van sales literature, Recreation Vehicle file, Transportation Collections, NMAH.

56. Charles Borskey, interview by Peter Koltnow, 5 August 1997, Recreation Vehicle file, Transportation Collections, NMAH.

57. Robert Lee Behme, "Dodge: Camper Home Test Report," *Mobile Home Journal* (December 1964): 48, 68–70.

58. Van camper sales literature, Recreation Vehicle file, Transportation Collections, NMAH.

59. *Better Camping* (November–December 1965): 28.

60. Lola Mae Bryant, "Comfort in a Kombi," *Better Camping* (November–December 1965): 51–54.

61. Phil Geraci, "Coast to Coast in a VW Camper," pts. 1–3, *Camping Guide* (June 1963): 23–25, 50–55, (July 1963): 28–31, 55, 58–59, 64–65, (August–September 1963): 32–33, 49–53; Philip Geraci, interview by Peter Koltnow, 27 August 1996, notes in Recreation Vehicle file, Transportation Collections, NMAH.

6. EARLY MANUFACTURED MOTOR HOMES

1. Letter from Murdale Korleski (John Korleski's wife) to the RV/MH Heritage Foundation, Elkhart, Indiana, 17 October 1995. In addition to domestic comforts, some Victours had space for retail displays of products such as golf clubs, golf clothing, and children's clothing. Victor Coach Industries was

founded by Victor Judson, who also owned Judson Wholesale Nurseries, a large wholesale supplier of strawberries and flowering plants. See Jean Ann Young, ed., *Tales of a Hoosier Village: A History of Bristol, Indiana* (Bristol, Ind.: Wyndham Hall Press, 1988), 37–42.

2. *Trailer Travel* (January 1950): 57.

3. John and Murdale Korleski, interviews by Peter Koltnow, 6 August 1996, 27 August 1996, 15 April 1997, and 1 July 1997, notes in Recreation Vehicle file, Transportation Collections, NMAH.

4. "Land Yacht," *Holiday* (August 1953): 24. The Graf Zipalong was built before World War II as the Wanderlust. Of monocoque construction, it had a tubular steel frame and aluminum sheeting. Herb Shriner drove it across the United States in 1947.

5. *Automotive Industries* (1 August 1953): 59; "Saginaw Firm Produces Self-Powered Land Yacht," *Trailer Topics* (September 1953): 36; "No Car Needed to Pull Howard Industries' New 'Trailer,'" *Saginaw (Michigan) News*, 29 March 1953; Jack D. Parker, "Saginaw's Howard 'Safari' America's Pioneer in Production Motorhomes," *Saginaw News*, 4 March 1973.

6. Sani-Cruiser sales literature, Recreation Vehicle file, Transportation Collections, NMAH; Sophia Backus (Thomas Stewart Backus's wife), interview by Peter Koltnow, 28 March 1995, notes in Recreation Vehicle file, Transportation Collections, NMAH; Elwyn McNaughton, interview by Peter Koltnow, 18 April 1995, notes in Recreation Vehicle file, Transportation Collections, NMAH.

7. Case Liv-N-Roam Cruiser sales literature, Recreation Vehicle file, Transportation Collections, NMAH; "House-Car Provides Traveling Home," *Motor Trend* (August 1957): 70; "Self- Propelled Liv-N-Roam Cruiser," *Trailer Travel* (May 1961): 32; Jean Case (Theodore Case's wife), interview by Peter Koltnow, 25 February 1997, notes in Recreation Vehicle file, Transportation Collections, NMAH.

8. John Reynolds, "Pickwick Company Building Plush Camper Coaches," *Cedar Rapids (Iowa) Gazette*, 27 December 1959; Mrs. Fred Corey [Susan Corey], "Pickwick Traveliner Makes Traveling Easy," *Camper Coachman* (December 1963): 18–21, 35; Pickwick sales literature, Arthur Cieslak personal collection, Brecksville, Ohio; Walter Corey, interviews by Peter Koltnow, 8 November 1994 and 25 July 1995, notes in Recreation Vehicle file, Transportation Collections, NMAH. There is no connection between the Pickwick Traveliner and Pickwick sleeper buses, which ran on long-distance routes in the West.

9. Letter from Tommy Scott to author, 5 February 1985, Recreation Vehicle file, Transportation Collections, NMAH; Robbin Maue, "A Star among Us," *Family Motor Coaching* (August 1990): 142–43. In the late 1930s Scott took

over a medicine show founded by M. F. Chamberlain in 1890. Scott was still touring and entertaining audiences in the 1990s.

10. *Trailer Topics* (March 1959): 196.

11. Production statistic courtesy of Raymond Frank; prices from *Trailer Travel* (June 1961): 65.

12. Letter from Raymond Frank to author, November 1996, Recreation Vehicle file, Transportation Collections, NMAH; Ronald Frank, interviews by Peter Koltnow, 10 December 1996 and 15 July 1997, notes in Recreation Vehicle file, Transportation Collections, NMAH; "Xplorer Celebrates 30th Anniversary," *Camping and RV Magazine* (August 1988): 40–41. The Dodge motor home with fiberglass body by Frank continued with minor modifications into the 1964 model year. In October 1964 the Franks sold the business to Peter Fink and Kenneth Robertson, whose company, Travco Corporation, continued to build motor homes with the Dodge nameplate. Raymond Frank introduced the Xplorer van camper in 1967.

13. "Huge Fiberglass Components Used in Dodge Motor Homes," *Automotive Industries* (15 February 1963): 58–59.

14. Roland Clermont, interview by Peter Koltnow, 26 November 1996, notes in Recreation Vehicle file, Transportation Collections, NMAH; D. Merlan Debolt, interview by Peter Koltnow, 7 January 1997, notes in Recreation Vehicle file, Transportation Collections, NMAH; William B. Hobbins, interview by Peter Koltnow, 19 November 1996, notes in Recreation Vehicle file, Transportation Collections, NMAH.

15. Mrs. Lloyd Lawson, interview by Peter Koltnow, 24 December 1996, notes in Recreation Vehicle file, Transportation Collections, NMAH; Dr. and Mrs. Donald Norquist, interview by Peter Koltnow, 28 January 1997, notes in Recreation Vehicle file, Transportation Collections, NMAH.

16. Roster of Family Motor Coach Association members and their vehicles prepared by Robert Richter in 1964, Jean Richter personal collection, Hanson, Massachusetts.

17. Condor sales literature, Recreation Vehicle file, Transportation Collections, NMAH; "Homes-on-Wheels by Ford," *Ford Times* (August 1962): 56–59; Robert Lee Behme, "Condor," *Mobile Home Journal* (July 1963): 46–47, 61, 63–64.

18. F. O. Haas, interview by Peter Koltnow, 21 February 1995, notes in Recreation Vehicle file, Transportation Collections, NMAH; Ruth Haas (F. O. Haas's wife), interviews by Peter Koltnow, 29 October 1996 and 16 September 1997, notes in Recreation Vehicle file, Transportation Collections, NMAH; J. R. Leonard, interview by author, 1 August 1997, notes in Recreation Vehicle file, Transportation Collections, NMAH. The sailing career of Perley H. L. Wilson is documented in John Kobler, *Damned in Paradise: The Life of John Barry-*

more (New York: Atheneum, 1977), 236–37, and Margot Peters, *The House of Barrymore* (New York: Alfred A. Knopf, 1990), 293.

19. Recreation Vehicle Industry Association statistics, quoted in *Motor Vehicle Facts and Figures* (Detroit: Motor Vehicle Manufacturers Association, 1976), 27.

20. *Minneapolis Morning Tribune*, 14 January 1963; Krager sales literature, Eugene Krager personal collection, Baxter, Minnesota; Eugene Krager, interviews by Peter Koltnow, 17 November 1994 and 28 January 1997, notes in Recreation Vehicle file, Transportation Collections, NMAH.

21. "Lightweight Motor Home Will Carry Heavy Loads," *Trailer Travel* (June 1964): 39. The motor home became company founder Howard Cree's favorite mode of travel. He died in a Cree motor home in 1970 while on vacation in the Florida Keys.

22. *Camping Guide* (April 1964): 65; Meade Travel-Inn sales literature, Recreation Vehicle file, Transportation Collections, NMAH; George A. Isaac, interview by Peter Koltnow, 15 October 1996, notes in Recreation Vehicle file, Transportation Collections, NMAH.

23. David Peterson's early years were spent in the design and production departments at Spartan Aircraft and the Stearman Airplane Company. In the late 1930s he started a charter-airplane business, and during World War II he worked for Boeing Aircraft in Wichita, Kansas, as final-assembly supervisor for the B-29 bomber. From about 1945 to 1957 he was chief pilot for the Sinclair Oil Company. In the late 1950s he designed a modified twin-engine, aluminum Beechcraft Bonanza airplane named the Super-V.

24. W. Christy Barden, "The Ultra Van Story," *CORSA Communique* (April 1980): 5–9; Chuck Palmer, "The History of a Dream," *CORSA Communique* (February 1993): 8–14; James Hinckley, "Corvair with a Lived-in Look: The Unusual Ultra Van," *Special Interest Autos* (January–February 1996): 40–41.

25. John E. Tillotson II, interview by Peter Koltnow, 28 January 1997, notes in Recreation Vehicle file, Transportation Collections, NMAH.

26. Ultra Van Motor Coach Club membership directory and roster of Ultra Vans, 1988, Recreation Vehicle file, Transportation Collections, NMAH.

27. Cortez sales literature, Recreation Vehicle file, Transportation Collections, NMAH; "A Cortez History," brochure courtesy of Cortez National, an owners' association.

28. Kathleen Mudge Johnson, interviews by Peter Koltnow, 29 February 1996 and 7 January 1997, notes in Recreation Vehicle file, Transportation Collections, NMAH; Cortez publicity file, Kathleen Mudge Johnson personal collection, Delton, Michigan.

29. Kathleen Mudge, "This Road Has No End," Kathleen Mudge Johnson personal collection, Delton, Michigan.

30. Kathleen Mudge, "Lady Cortez Visits [the Pennsylvania Turnpike]," *Family*

Motor Coaching (Spring 1965): 21; Kathleen Mudge, "Lady Cortez Visits [Herb Shriner]," *Family Motor Coaching* (Summer 1965): 21; Kathleen Mudge, "Lady Cortez Visits [a Lake Michigan Ferry]," *Family Motor Coaching* (Fall 1965): 27, 39.

31. [Kathleen Mudge,] "You May Be Wrong about Women!" *Mobilehomes Merchandiser* (November 1967): 34–35; Kathleen Mudge, "For Women on the Road Alone," *Wheels Afield* (December 1967): 52–53, 67.

32. Advertisement for the Private Coach Company, *Family Motor Coaching* (Fall 1964): 2.

33. "The Land Yacht—A New Breed of Rolling Home," *House Beautiful* (April 1964): 135–47, 191–99.

34. William W. Purser, interview by Peter Koltnow, 17 December 1996, notes in Recreation Vehicle file, Transportation Collections, NMAH.

35. Coachette sales literature, Recreation Vehicle file, Transportation Collections, NMAH; William R. Graham, interview by Peter Koltnow, 27 May 1997, notes in Recreation Vehicle file, Transportation Collections, NMAH.

36. Paul B. Lowry, interview by Peter Koltnow, 21 February 1995, notes in Recreation Vehicle file, Transportation Collections, NMAH; Roaminghome sales literature, Paul B. Lowry personal collection, Tucson, Arizona.

37. *Trailer Travel* (April 1965): 67; Streamline advertisement, *Trailer Topics* (July 1966): back cover.

38. Art Rouse, *My Life on Wheels* (Malibu, Calif.: Rouse RV Enterprises, 1992), 70.

39. "Famous Jockey Tours Tracks in Streamline Travel Home," *Trailer Topics* (September 1966): 36B.

40. George C. Hardin, "Motor Homes Cost Too Much!" *Family Motor Coaching* (June 1964): 15–16.

41. Advertisement for Phoenix recreation vehicles, *Trailer Travel* (February 1966): 99.

42. "Motor Home from Scandia," *Trailer Travel* (May 1965): 55–56.

43. Bettye Baker, interview by Peter Koltnow, 2 September 1997, notes in Recreation Vehicle file, Transportation Collections, NMAH; Patty Baker Perreira, interviews by Peter Koltnow, 23 September 1997 and 17 February 1998, notes in Recreation Vehicle file, Transportation Collections, NMAH; unpublished autobiographical notes by James G. M. Baker, Bettye Baker personal collection, Laguna Beach, California; "Jim Baker's Secret of Traveltrailer Sales Success . . . Rentals at a Profit," *Mobilehomes Merchandiser* (March 1965): 32, 34.

44. Bettye Baker and Patty Baker Perreira, interviews.

45. Bettye Baker, interview.

46. *Family Motor Coaching* (May 1966): 11.

47. Between 1957 and 1963 Merle D. McNamee developed a material similar to Thermo-Panel. McNamee's "sandwich foam construction" had bonded layers

of aluminum sheeting, exterior plywood, styrofoam, and interior ash. McNamee found that this type of construction made his Kamp King pickup campers stronger and better insulated than other campers with ordinary wood frames and metal sheeting.

7. MOTOR HOMES IN THE AGE OF AQUARIUS

1. In 1966 Winnebago stopped building motor homes for Life-Time without the latter's consent, and in 1970 James G. M. Baker and Life-Time Manufacturing sued John K. Hanson and Winnebago Industries for breach of contract. The court ruled in favor of the complainants, and in 1973 Winnebago and its executives paid Life-Time and Baker $5.8 million.
2. [Winnebago Industries,] *The Winnebago Story: Our First Quarter Century, 1958–1983* (Forest City, Iowa: Winnebago Industries, 1983); Maura Troester, "Winnebago," in Janice Jorgensen, ed., *Encyclopedia of Consumer Brands*, vol. 3 (Detroit: St. James Press, 1994), 625–27.
3. Winnebago Industries, *Corporate Report, 1967–1968* (Forest City, Iowa: Winnebago Industries, 1968), 6.
4. "Saving a Small Town," *Time* (19 September 1969): 90.
5. "Manufacturing Recreational Vehicles Like Automobiles," in Winnebago Industries, *Annual Report, Year Ending February 28, 1970* (Forest City, Iowa: Winnebago Industries, 1970), 9–20.
6. "John Hanson Speaks Out," *MotorHome Life* (Summer 1969): 46–49; Winnebago Industries, *Annual Report, Year Ending February 28, 1970,* 27.
7. "Striking It Rich in Forest City," *Forbes* (1 June 1972): 37–39; Betsy Keiffer, "And Then They Were Millionaires," *Good Housekeeping* (February 1973): 40–48.
8. Alice Robison, "See the USA the Lucy Way," *MotorHome Life* (Fall 1969): 32–33, 53.
9. "Into the Heartland," *Newsweek* (1 January 1968): 54; "Travels with Charley," *Time* (19 January 1968): 44; Alice Robison, "Charles Kuralt . . . On the Road with Motorhome," *MotorHome Life* (Spring 1969): 48–49, 68–69; Charles Kuralt, *On the Road with Charles Kuralt* (New York: G. P. Putnam's Sons, 1985), 13–14; Charles Kuralt, *A Life on the Road* (New York: G. P. Putnam's Sons, 1990), 122–30.
10. Kuralt, *On the Road with Charles Kuralt,* 53.
11. Bill McKeown, "The KOA Story," *Camping Trade Journal* (Fall 1968): 20–21, 47–48.
12. *Publishers' Weekly* (20 July 1964): 66.
13. Ibid., 66–67; Paul Perry, *On the Bus: The Complete Guide to the Legendary Trip of Ken Kesey and the Merry Pranksters and the Birth of the Counterculture* (New York: Thunder's Mouth Press, 1990).

14. Wavy Gravy, quoted in letters from Lisa Law to author, 4 January 1999 and 5 January 1999, Recreation Vehicle file, Transportation Collections, NMAH. See also Lisa Law, *Flashing on the Sixties: Photographs by Lisa Law* (San Francisco: Chronicle Books, 1987; revised edition, 1997). Law's photographs of Hog Farmers, bus homes, and other counterculture activities are in the Photographic History Collection, National Museum of American History, Smithsonian Institution. Many of her photographs were presented in a 1998 Smithsonian exhibition, "A Visual Journey: Photographs by Lisa Law, 1964–1971," curated by Shannon Thomas Perich, William H. Yeingst, and Margo Edwards.

15. Wavy Gravy, *The Hog Farm and Friends* (New York and London: Links Books, 1974). See also Wavy Gravy, *Something Good for a Change: Random Notes on Peace thru Living* (New York: St. Martin's Press, 1992).

16. Jahanara Romney, interview by Lisa Law, 1989, transcript in Recreation Vehicle file, Transportation Collections, NMAH.

17. Wavy Gravy, quoted in letter from Lisa Law to author, 4 January 1999, Recreation Vehicle file, Transportation Collections, NMAH.

18. "A 35-Year-Old Guru Ministers to Hippies in Northern California," *New York Times*, 21 September 1970; "'Family' of 270 Forsakes Coast for Tennessee Hollow," *New York Times*, 5 April 1971; Stephen Gaskin, *The Caravan* (New York: Random House, and Berkeley, Calif.: The Bookworks, 1972); Stephen Gaskin et al., *Hey Beatnik! This Is the Farm Book* (Summertown, Tenn.: The Book Publishing Company, 1974).

19. Steve Green, "West Coast Vans," *Hot Rod* (August 1971): 82–86; Baron Wolman and John Burks, *Vans: A Book of Rolling Rooms* (Garden City, N. Y.: Doubleday, Dolphin Books, 1976); Lucian K. Truscott IV, *The Complete Van Book* (New York: Crown Publishers, Harmony Books, 1976); Keith Sessions, *Fixin' Up Your Van on a Budget* (Blue Ridge Summit, Pa.: TAB Books, 1977); Editors of *Van World*, *Super Vans* (Blue Ridge Summit, Pa.: TAB Books, 1978). Specialized magazines in this field include *Van World* and *Travelin' Vans*.

20. Rob McGraw, "My Old Truckee Home," *Globe Magazine* (Boston Globe), 15 July 1973, 8–10, 22–25.

21. Jane Lidz, *Rolling Homes: Handmade Houses on Wheels* (New York: A&W Visual Library, 1979).

22. Recreation Vehicle Industry Association statistics quoted in *AAMA Motor Vehicle Facts and Figures* (Detroit: American Automobile Manufacturers Association, 1993), 11.

23. Dorothy Gray Smith, "Join Up . . . Just for Fun," *MotorHome Life* (Summer 1969): 42–43, 78–79.

24. Art Rouse, *My Life on Wheels* (Malibu, Calif.: Rouse RV Enterprises, 1992), 82–91.

25. Richard West Sellars, *Preserving Nature in the National Parks: A History* (New Haven, Conn.: Yale University Press, 1997), 180–95.
26. George B. Hartzog Jr., "Clearing the Roads—and the Air—in Yosemite Valley," *National Parks and Conservation Magazine* (August 1972): 14–17.
27. Nelson Bryant, "Wood, Field, and Stream," *New York Times*, 13 March 1973.
28. Vernon Herum, quoted in B. Drummond Ayres Jr., "Today's Campers Bring the Comforts of Home," *New York Times*, 13 August 1972.
29. Frances Greiff, "The Motorized Assault," *National Parks and Conservation Magazine* (July 1973): 17–19.
30. H. L. Miller, "Motorhome with the Dozen," *MotorHome Life* (October 1973): 61.
31. Larry Moore, "School Bus on Vacation," *MotorHome Life* (Fall 1969): 55, 70–71.
32. Dawson Gillaspy, "We Bronzed Our Bus," *MotorHome Life* (December 1973): 78–79, 90.
33. Margaret Jones, *Patsy: The Life and Times of Patsy Cline* (New York: Harper Collins Publishers, 1994), 178.
34. Waylon Jennings, with Lenny Kaye, *Waylon: An Autobiography* (New York: Warner Books, 1996), 320–31.
35. Loretta Lynn, with George Vecsey, *Loretta Lynn: Coal Miner's Daughter* (Chicago: Henry Regnery Company, 1976), 178–81.
36. Jeannie C. Riley, with Jamie Buckingham, *Jeannie C. Riley: From Harper Valley to the Mountain Top* (Lincoln, Va.: Chosen Books, 1981), 107, 146.
37. Ken Fermoyle, "Ford's Revolutionary New Vans," *Wheels Afield* (May 1968): 28–29; Alex Markovich, "Ford's New $4,800 Motor Home," *Popular Mechanics* (June 1969): 116–19, 202.
38. Max Todd, "Testing the Lazy Daze," *Trailer Life* (October 1966): 98–99, 108; advertisement for the Lazy Daze Sportsman Housecar, ibid., 104.
39. Oren Bates, "Mini-Motor Homes," *Wheels Afield* (April 1973): 82–89.
40. Richard Bastle, "Gas: Is the Sky Really Falling?" *MotorHome Life* (August 1973): 22, 36.
41. Denis Rouse, "The Roadside Rest," *MotorHome Life* (October 1973): 19.
42. Ken Fermoyle, "Beat the Gas Squeeze," *Wheels Afield* (November 1973): 32–33, 78; V. Lee Oertle, "Fifty Fuel-Saving Tips," *MotorHome Life* (May 1974): 34–35, 93–96.
43. Recreation Vehicle Industry Association statistics quoted in *AAMA Motor Vehicle Facts and Figures*, 11.

FURTHER READING

Belasco, Warren James. *Americans on the Road: From Autocamp to Motel, 1910–1945*. Cambridge, Massachusetts: MIT Press, 1979.

Edwards, Carlton M. *Homes for Travel and Living: The History and Development of the Recreation Vehicle and Mobile Home Industries*. East Lansing, Michigan: Carl Edwards and Associates, 1977.

Groene, Janet. *RVs, The Drive for Independence: The Illustrated Story of RV Travel and Camping in America*. Louisville, Kentucky: Crescent Hill Books, 1997.

Lidz, Jane. *Rolling Homes: Handmade Houses on Wheels*. New York: A&W Visual Library, 1979.

Mergen, Bernard. *Recreation Vehicles and Travel: A Resource Guide*. Westport, Connecticut: Greenwood Press, 1985.

Perry, Paul, and Ken Babbs. *On the Bus: The Complete Guide to the Legendary Trip of Ken Kesey and the Merry Pranksters and the Birth of the Counterculture*. New York: Thunder's Mouth Press, 1990.

Rockland, Michael Aaron. *Homes on Wheels*. New Brunswick, New Jersey: Rutgers University Press, 1980.

Rouse, Art. *My Life on Wheels*. Malibu, California: Rouse RV Enterprises, 1992.

Winnebago Industries, *The Winnebago Story*. Forest City, Iowa: Winnebago Industries, 1983; revised edition, 1988.

INDEX